The 10
Habits *of*
Happy
Mothers

||||||||||||||||||||||||

The 10 Habits *of* Happy Mothers

|||||||||||||||||||||||||||||||||||||||||||||||||||||||||||||||||||||||||

Reclaiming Our Passion, Purpose, and Sanity

MEG MEEKER, M.D.

BALLANTINE BOOKS | New York

While the stories presented in this book did in fact happen, some of the names and personal characteristics of the individuals involved have been changed in order to disguise their identities. Any resulting resemblance to persons living or dead is entirely coincidental and unintentional.

Published in the United States by Ballantine Books, an imprint of The Random House Publishing Group, a division of Random House, Inc., New York.

BALLANTINE and colophon are registered trademarks of The Random House Publishing Group.

Library of Congress Cataloging-in-Publication Data

Meeker, Margaret J.
The 10 habits of happy mothers : reclaiming our passion, purpose, and sanity / Meg Meeker.— 1st ed.
p. cm.
ISBN 978-0-345-51806-4 (hbk. : alk. paper)
ISBN 978-0-345-51808-8 (ebook)
1. Mothers—Psychology. 2. Motherhood—Psychological aspects. 3. Self-esteem.
I. Title. II. Title: Ten habits of happy mothers.
HQ759.M438 2010
646.70085'2—dc22   2010037887

Printed in the United States of America on acid-free paper

www.ballantinebooks.com

9 8 7 6 5 4 3 2 1

First Edition

Book design by Jo Anne Metsch

To my beloved mother, Mary:
You have given me more than I deserve.

To my second mother, Marty:
Thank you for always being there for me.

Contents

||||||||||||||||||||||||||||||||||||||||||||||||||||||||||||||||||||||||||||||||||||||||||||||||||||||||

Introduction

|||||||||||||||||||||||||||||||||||||||||||||||||||||||||||||||||||||||||||||||||||||||||||||||||||||||||||||||||||||

AS A PEDIATRICIAN of twenty-five years and a mother for twenty-six, I have listened to a whole lot of mothers. And I think that I have come to understand some fundamental truths about us. At least, some things that I think are true. First, we are a group that wants desperately to be good at what we do. We want to be good to our friends and husbands and we want to be great to our kids. We love intensely and we work hard. But we have a problem. In the past fifty years, we have been given an overwhelming number of opportunities. We can be whoever we want to be and our hard work will (usually) be rewarded. This is good. But in the midst of the onslaught of opportunity in our lives, we have become confused, and some of us have become a bit obsessed.

We stress over how well we are parenting and if we are taking full advantage of other opportunities. We wonder if we should work outside the home (of course, some of us don't wonder, because we have to). Others wonder whether we are working too much or too little. And there is so much more. We worry about whether our kids are given enough opportunities, whether their friends like them, or whether they are being bullied at school or at day care. But mostly, we worry about what we can do for our kids in order to make their lives better. We do this because we really want to be good at mothering. We want to get it right, just as we want to get our jobs right.

This need—to get parenting right—has become an obsession for many of us. It consumes our thinking, our energy, and our time. Let me be clear: Striving to be a great mom is a noble goal, and as a pediatrician, I applaud those who choose it. But that's not what I'm referring to. I am talking about a full-blown obsession with getting mothering right. And it is taking many of us down.

Over twenty-five years I have seen us move from worrying about which school to send a daughter to, to which band to hire for her high school graduation party. I see mothers work two jobs in order to afford piano lessons for Susie and guitar lessons for Mike. I have watched mothers scream at teachers who gave their kids a C on a paper when just a short time ago, we would have let that child rewrite his paper to get a better grade or told him to work harder on the next paper. We are tired. We never feel that we're doing a good enough job at almost anything we do; not because we're not good at things, but because we are trying to do too much, too well. We have become competitors. We have learned over the past twenty-five years to compete with other mothers and compete with ourselves. The problem is, none of us feels as though we're winning.

In short, we've gone off the deep end. Don't take this personally; we're all in the same boat. Employed, at-home, adoptive, biologic, wealthy, poor, young, and older mothers—we're all in this together. We have arrived at a similar place. So, we have a lot of company in one another. That's the good news.

Here's the rest of the good news. We can make some simple changes that will bring us back from the edge (or pull us back on top of the cliff if we've fallen off completely) and bring some fun and sanity into our lives. We can love being moms again. We can sit. We can laugh with our kids. We can stop running around, acting like crazy people. We can love life and enjoy our wonderful kids. In the following pages, you will find real mothers whose lives illustrate our collective plight, and you will find many mothers who have moved over to the positive side. They are getting this mothering thing right. No, they aren't better mothers, but they are *enjoying* being mothers more. This is not a book about being a better mother, because there are plenty of books on that. This is a book for you, and only you, to help you become a happier mother.

Freeing ourselves from some of the craziness that we have adopted means changing some habits. This is hard, but we can do it because we are mothers and doing hard things is what we're really good at. If we can endure pushing an eight-pound watermelon through an eight-inch opening we can do just about anything that we put our minds to. Anything.

In the following pages, you'll learn about ten new habits that work to bring joy, order, and calm back into our lives. Listed briefly, they are understanding your value as a mother, maintaining key friendships, valuing and practicing faith, saying no to competition, creating a healthier relationship with money, making time for solitude, giving and getting love in healthier ways, finding ways to live simply, letting go of fear, and making the decision to have hope. Some may seem peculiar at first— letting go of fear, for instance. Others may seem too simple, but keep reading because usually the simplest changes are the most profound. Some of the habits you will be able to adopt right away, while others may need to wait until your kids are a bit older. But I can guarantee you that they work. I have seen other mothers adopt them and I have seen their facial expressions and their demeanor become calmer. I believe the reason that they work is that integrating these habits into our lives nurtures the core of who we are as mothers. And we have veered way off track when it comes to nurturing our inner selves. We have been lured into focusing on the external parts of our character and spent far too much time, money, and energy on things that don't matter at all in comparison. We need solitude, not another diet. We need to figure out our spiritual lives more than we need another activity to run our kids to. We need hope instead of more stuff to do, which will only make us more anxious. We need to spend less so that we can loosen the grip that money has on us. There is much more we can get out of life.

I wrote this book with a grateful heart because I am thankful for you. I am so appreciative of the hard work that you do and of the love you have for your kids because taking care of kids has been my life's passion for many years. When you succeed, kids get healthy and that makes me very happy. My hope is that the following pages will open doors for you to have greater joy and contentment in your lives. So let's get started!

The 10 Habits *of* Happy Mothers

|||||||||||||||||||||||||||

|||||||||||||||||||||||||||||||||||||||||||||||||||||||||||||||||||||||||||||||||||||||||||||||||||||||||||||||||||||||

Understand Your Value as a Mother

MOTHERS, SELF-CRITICISM, AND OUR VALUE

If every mother in the United States could wrap her mind around her true value as a woman and mother, her life would never be the same. We would wake up every morning excited for the day rather than feeling as though we'd been hit by a truck during the night. We would talk differently to our kids, fret less about our husbands' annoying habits, and speak with greater tenderness and clarity. We would find more contentment in our relationships, let mean remarks roll off our backs, and leave work feeling confident in the job we performed. And best of all—we wouldn't obsess about our weight (can you imagine?), physical fitness, or what kind of home we live in. We would live a life free from superficial needs because we would know deep in our hearts what we need and, more importantly, what we don't need. Each of us would live a life of extraordinary freedom.

Here's the great news: Any one of us mothers is a few beliefs away from living a life like this. These beliefs are simple, life altering, and wholly un-American because they counter the enormous "bill of goods" (as one prominent writer told me recently) that we mothers are being sold. What are these beliefs that we must embrace if we want a different life? First, we must have a palpable sense of why we are valuable, and second, we must like who we are. Why? Because our real value as mothers comes from three places: We are loved, we are needed, and we are born for a higher purpose.

These sound good, but from a practical standpoint, if we don't experience them regularly, we lose sight of the fact that they form the foundation of our value. They are difficult to keep at the center of our beings. Every day we are distracted from realizing them because we are lured into believing that our value comes from other things: what we look like, whether our kids are happy with us, or how big our paycheck is. But we must be reminded where our real value lies because we need to have a conscious awareness of it if we are to be genuinely happy. In this chapter, I'll show you examples of how mothers learned to recognize their own value, as well as specific tips about how to put the habit into practice, including making a list of what's most valuable about yourself, living to impress no one at all, and figuring out what's going to be the most important in the end.

A HIGHER CALLING

Do you feel loved? Sometimes, perhaps, but many times you don't. You are a mom, and your days are filled with too much work to finish and complaining kids. Chances are, you are in the camp with the rest of us exhausted women who flop onto the couch at 10 P.M. with a pint of almond fudge ice cream and try to calm ourselves at least enough to get to sleep that night. If you have teenagers you may seriously question your kids' love for you. Conflict between you and your kids can peak during these teen years and conflict hurts. When our teens snarl, we take it personally. By the end of some days we wonder whether they even like us.

Are you needed? If you have small children, you have a palpable sense that you are needed. Kids need us when they're young to drive them, feed them, nurture them, and give them physical and emotional stability. We know that we are needed, but often we get frustrated because we feel that anyone could fill our shoes. Our work feels, well, trite at times. Doing laundry, sweeping peas off the floor, and changing diapers feels anything but glamorous. That's because it isn't. When it comes to our value, the deeper question is, does doing things for our kids when they are young give us value? Absolutely.

But there's more. Babies, toddlers, and teenagers all need Mom for so many reasons. They need us to listen, to discipline, to comfort them. And believe it or not, they need to see us do the menial, boring chores for them because, while these feel trite to us, they communicate to our kids that when it comes to caring for them, no task is unimportant. Our value to our kids is that they need us—to do the big stuff for them and the small stuff, too.

Finally, I believe that every mother is born to fill a higher calling. Every mother is gifted uniquely and she is to use those gifts to make her world better. A mother uses those gifts in parenting. Many mothers use them only there, but others use them outside their parenting. The question for every mother is: Do you feel that you were born for a great purpose? If you're honest, probably not. You may find yourself overcome by worry, wondering whether anything you did that day was valuable. The kids woke up mad and they went to bed angry at you. You carved out a tiny slice of time to go for a walk with a friend but that was cut short. Your husband told you that you never pay attention to him and the truth is, you really don't sometimes. Fatigue controls most of what you do or don't do during the day. Everywhere you turn you feel like you simply aren't giving enough. You aren't a good enough friend, wife, or mom. These feelings take a toll on you and if you are truthful, you wonder if you are worth much of anything at all.

The wonderful truth is, you are worth more than you can imagine. I don't care if you feel like a lousy mom or you are fabulous. Whether you're a workaholic who feels like she never sees her kids or a stay-at-home mom who feels unappreciated, you are woefully misguided in your thinking. Yes, your beliefs about your worth as a woman and mother may be skewed because you live in a world that doesn't like you very much. It tells you to keep up with too many things at once and since you can't, you work faster and longer and still feel like a failure in whole or in part. There's the lie in the whole mess—you are not a failure. But you feel like one. I can confidently say this because, as a pediatrician, my job is to watch you and keep your kids healthy. And when I see them, I see kids who love their mom. I see how your kids look at you, hang on to your knees, and hold your hand. I see you more akin to how they see you—as a woman who is needed, loved, and cherished.

YOU ARE MORE PRECIOUS THAN YOU KNOW

I know this because in my twenty-five years as a pediatrician, I have gotten a peek from behind your kids' eyes. I can see you as they see you. I have heard the excitement in their voices after you have praised them. I have seen your kids define you as their hero when you were in the other room. I have heard them cry over your hurt, laugh at your jokes, and pull their hair out because of your stubbornness (which, by the way, they appreciate). I have literally read the value that you hold in your kids' lives, all over their faces and through their body language. When you walk into a room, your son changes immediately. He relaxes because you are there and life feels safe again. If you recently scolded him, he scours your face to see if you are still mad, because he needs to know how you feel. You matter. Your mood changes his world a bit. If you are in a good mood, he can relax and play with his trucks. If you are upset with him, he wants to make up (he may not show it, but he does) because you are the center of his small world. He needs you to like him again. You. No one else. Because once you are happy with him, he can go about his business and life will feel good again. He can focus at school, get his homework done, and pay attention during his basketball game. That is the power that you have and that power comes from the fact that in this one child's life—your child's life—who you are matters as much as life itself. You are loved.

I want you to feel good about who you are as a mother because you should. That's another thing that I have learned about you as I have watched over the years. You need to feel good about the job that you are doing because, if you are like most American moms, you are far too critical of the job you're doing. I know this because I can see that being a great mom matters to you. You want to get it right and you assess your performance daily. What you need to know is that you assess your performance far more critically than your kids do—they just want *you*. Kids don't care if you're thin or plump, they don't care if you make brownies from scratch, from a box, or if you buy them. They just want to eat the brownies with you. Feeling good about your value to them is important because the better you feel, the better your relationship with them will be and the happier both of you will be. Sounds simple, but understanding our value and then feeling good about the mothers that we are (or maybe even saying it out loud!) is one of the toughest challenges we mothers face.

GET A (GOOD) GRIP ON HUMILITY

Contrary to what many mothers believe, being humble does not mean being self-effacing. In fact, it is quite the opposite! Mothers who have an elevated understanding of their own value are *more* humble.

Humility means appropriating an honest sense of one person's worth relative to another's worth. The truth is, we all have equal value. Once we accept that we share the same value as another, two things will happen: We will appreciate others more and we will appreciate our own worth more. We think of humility as seeing ourselves as lowly or less than others. In fact, humility is just the opposite. It is embracing a realistic look at our frailties as well as our strengths and then believing that we, just as other mothers who have their own frailties and strengths do, share inordinate value. We can love others because we can accept and love ourselves in our less-than-perfect states.

Humility brings extraordinary freedom. When we lower ourselves, refuse to admit our strengths and gifts, or live with false modesty, we lower all mothers. Many of us do this without even realizing that we are doing it. Consider the following exchange I recently heard. Many of us mothers can identify.

While speaking at a large women's conference in Michigan, my friend

Jill, the session's lecturer, was discussing how women frequently perceive themselves. While she wasn't specifically addressing mothers, her point was applicable to us. At one point in her lecture, she asked for two volunteers. Jill selected Ellen and Laura from the sea of hands. Ellen and Laura said they came to the conference together and were longtime friends. Jill brought them to the stage and seated them in chairs facing each other. Then she began to ask simple questions. To Ellen she asked, "Would you describe your friend Laura to the audience, please?"

Ellen was happy to comply and described Laura as kind, a good listener, easy to talk to, fun to be with, and a good mother. Jill continued: "Would you describe Laura as pretty?"

"Absolutely," Ellen replied. "She's lovely, at least to me, though granted I am a bit biased."

"Do you feel that you would like her more if she lost weight, got a nicer home, or went back to school?" Jill continued.

Ellen looked at Jill directly and said decisively, "Of course not. She's fabulous just the way she is."

Pressing her point, Jill asked, "So, is it fair to say that Laura is worth loving just the way she is? Or do you think she needs a bit of improvement?"

Now Ellen was annoyed. "No, I told you. She's great—just the way she is. I mean, we all need to work on certain things, but that has nothing to do with our friendship. I just like her, or love her, just the way she is."

Jill thanked Ellen and then turned to Laura, asking her the same kinds of questions about Ellen, and getting the same kinds of answers. Laura had the benefit of having heard her friend defend and compliment her first, but her answers were no less heartfelt. Laura was clear that there was nothing that Ellen needed to change and nothing that she could change that would make Laura love her more.

Jill paused and looked at the audience. Ellen and Laura stood up to leave but Jill stopped them: "No. Don't go just yet; we're not quite done."

Jill turned to Ellen. "You just heard your friend here talk about you. She said that she doesn't feel that you need to change—lose weight, get a new haircut, buy a new house, or go back to work in order for her to think better about you. She thinks you're perfect just the way you are. Now I want you to describe yourself to me. Can you say those same things about yourself?"

Silence fell over the room. Ellen stared at Jill and stumbled for words. "No, I mean, I don't know," she started.

"So is your friend wrong, do you think?" Jill continued. "If so, tell me where she's wrong."

Again Ellen fumbled for words and looked at her friend Laura, in front of her. They both appeared uncomfortable and Ellen became flushed. Jill turned to Laura and asked her the same questions. "So tell me. You've heard the same thing. You heard your friend Ellen describe you as lovely, fun to be with, and likable. As a matter of fact she even told everyone here that she cherishes you so much as a person that she loves you like family. Are you worth her feeling that way?"

Everyone in the audience stared at Laura, who clearly wanted to blurt out "No!" but didn't. I think the only reason she held her tongue was that she knew she wasn't supposed to say it. Every woman in the audience leaned forward, seemingly groping for words to give to the woman on-stage.

Ellen could see Laura's strengths and as her friend, ascribed great value to Laura. She saw her worth as a friend, beyond what Laura could see herself. As her friend, she had the freedom to like Laura and boast about Laura in ways that Laura couldn't seem to do herself. Some might call Laura modest, but I think that there was more than modesty going on. I believe that Laura, like thousands of women, and mothers especially, honestly failed to see her goodness. Her friends could see it, maybe even her kids could see it, but she couldn't. Or perhaps she could see it, but couldn't accept it because so much of her emotional energy was spent on comparing herself to other mothers that whenever she began to feel good about something she was doing, she felt immediately shot down because some other mother (in her mind) was doing a better job.

Now imagine that you are at the same conference. You are seated across from your best friend and she describes you. She uses words such as *kind, patient, pretty,* and *an outstanding mother*. If the leader asked you to state those very attributes about yourself out loud and mean it, could you?

Most of us would balk. Or at least our heads would drop and we'd mumble something at the tops of our shoes. Saying positive things about ourselves out loud simply isn't easy. Is this just false modesty? I don't think so. I think that quite often, we really don't feel that we have much positive to say about ourselves. Here's the reason I say this. First, we are supercritical of ourselves because we heap unreasonable expectations on ourselves. We tell ourselves that we should be great listeners, caregivers, psychologists, cooks, breadwinners, bedtime storytellers, sports fans, schedulers, and room moms. No matter how well we do in one area, we always feel that we're falling short in another. Second, we continually look to the wrong places to feel valuable. We look at how well we perform at various functions rather than accepting that we are valuable simply because we are our kids' moms and we are loved and needed because of that.

FOCUS ON YOUR DEEPER PURPOSE IN LIFE

Each of us was created to fill a calling. First and foremost, we were born to be really good moms. We weren't born to be mothers who are thin, rich, smart, who drive a lot, buy our kids great clothes, or get them into good colleges. We were born to leave a mark in our world. And usually, that mark is made on our kids and then on others' lives. Sometimes it leaves its mark because of something we have done for another person and other times it happens because we were with that person. We are beings—mother beings. We are human beings but we focus so constantly on the doing of life that we forget how to be. Our deeper purpose in life flows from a sense that our presence is important to another person. We have something to share with another and sometimes this takes work, and sometimes it means simply being who we are in the company of another.

In addition to fulfilling our purpose as good moms, we were born to do more, *in time*. At the risk of sounding overly philosophical I would like to assert that we have lost this sense of being because we are afraid of what lies beneath the superficial in us. If we set aside the energy we put into fitness, dieting, trying to be a better mom than the next mom, what is left? we wonder. What we find below the dieting, working, running around in the car, and exercising is a deepness that has been undiscovered. The tricky part about discovering our giftedness is that it may be in an area that feels unexpected. For instance, one mother I know does humor therapy workshops for abused women and children. This isn't her career (she is a nurse-practitioner) and it falls outside her calling as a mom. She has told me repeatedly that she was "born to bring healing through laughter." And she is great at making people laugh when she is doing her therapy. Women and children come in droves to hear her. The interesting thing about her is that she does not perceive herself as funny. She describes herself as a very serious person. When she happened upon her calling to help others laugh, she was substituting for a friend who ran the same workshops. No, my point isn't to get mothers to squeeze one more thing into their day, to jam "solitude" or "living out" a deeper purpose into an already exhausting schedule—it is to help mothers reprioritize. That's what I want to get across.

Other mothers are born to comfort. Some of the most extraordinary comforters I have met work with hospice. Often their work in comforting falls outside their vocation. Some mothers open their homes to younger mothers who need help; others give free medical care. One mother I know translates for Latino immigrants new to the United States.

Our calling comes through a series of providential occurrences. For instance, about ten years ago, a friend of mine and I were discussing the need for a home for troubled teen girls in our area. I was frustrated by the lack of support services for the teens I saw in my practice and she just liked adolescent girls. She was a mother of a teen daughter and owned a large hair salon. We chatted, then went our separate ways.

Three years later, I called her on a whim. She was soaking in the bathtub and I asked her again what "we" were going to do about this situation. No one seemed to be paying attention to troubled teen girls. Within a year she had raised six hundred thousand dollars to start a home for girls.

Now, nine years later, scores of teen girls and boys have lived at the home and found profound restoration in their lives. Ellie was a businesswoman and hairstylist by trade, a loving mother, but her calling was to help teens. She will tell you that when she is working with the kids, something very satisfying flows outward from deep within her.

We know we have happened on our deeper purpose when we overlook the money we make, the people we impress, or the length of hours it takes when we are fulfilling it. Living from our giftedness stirs a deeper passion and a sense that we are somehow "home." I believe that these gifts are supernatural and stem from the hand of God Himself.

Two very important points must be made. First, realizing our unique gifts and using them outside parenting is not more important than being a mother; it is simply different. As women, we are more than mothers and our value comes from being mothers and being women with other gifts. The two are separate and of equal value.

Second, thinking about those undiscovered things we're good at can feel overwhelming to mothers who are simply trying to get through the day doing what must be done. Why even wonder what we're good at when we don't have time to do what's expected of us already? Isn't this an exercise in frustration? No, because each of our gifts doesn't need to be used at this very moment. The whole point is that often we expend too much time doing too many things that don't need to be done because we get distracted. We lose sight of our deeper purpose in life—to raise good kids and to use our strengths to better the lives of others, over the course of our lifetimes. Once we decide what matters most, what we're really here on earth for, then and only then will we understand our real value as moms and as women. The very best we can do at any moment is to realize that, as moms, we are needed now and if we are meant to use other gifts to help others we will be afforded the opportunity when the time comes.

WHAT JULIANNE TAUGHT ME ABOUT SELF-VALUE

Every time Julianne brought her kids in for their checkups, something in her demeanor intrigued me. She was born in Japan, had married an American, and both of her children were stunning. They had thick licorice hair, soft brown eyes, and perfect skin. But her ability to produce stunningly beautiful children wasn't what made me marvel. It was her demeanor. She had an aura of self-confidence. Not the obnoxious kind, but the genuine sense that she liked herself and she liked her life. Her clothes weren't flashy and she never boasted about the activities that her kids were involved in. When I asked her about her kids' schoolwork and behaviors, she neither boasted nor apologized. Instead, she related to me what she did with them and how much they all enjoyed their time together. This type of report is rare in the histories I take. Usually mothers rattle off a list of sports, reading groups, art or music lessons their kids do, all closed with a groan, asking me to empathize with their exhaustion.

Over the years, I tried to uncover what made Julianne tick. I wanted to know, in the midst of her normally busy life, what operated in her that made her so calm and happy. Was she just one of those lucky mothers who was born with an easygoing, no-nonsense personality that afforded her the ability to simply roll with whatever difficulties came her way? Or was there something else going on?

She held a job as a CPA at a large firm and worked part-time from home. Did she simply love her work and that kept her in a good mood? Maybe it was her marriage, I thought. Perhaps her husband was one of those guys who adore their wife and kids, do more housework than most, and encourage their wives to have time away with friends. Nope. Then I thought that perhaps her kids were unusually enjoyable. Maybe they were born great sleepers, never fought with her or with each other. But I knew them and I knew that this wasn't true. As I dug to find the key to her calmness, to her obvious lack of envy toward other women (she frequently complimented her girlfriends in my presence), I finally gave up. So, one day, I simply asked her how she seemed to be so content.

Julianne's response surprised me. Just as a humble person can't understand how another sees her as humble, Julianne couldn't understand my commenting on her contentment. Being content was so much a part of who she was that it never dawned on her that others would notice. So when I asked, her surprise at my question made her pause.

She began: "Well, I have an extraordinary life, I suppose. I love my kids, my parents are alive and well, and my husband is very supportive." Good for a start, I thought, but many mothers can say that. So I prodded more.

"You seem as though you don't struggle with feeling competitive with others, you appear to genuinely have fun with your kids, and I don't sense that your kids are spoiled. They always act respectful to you and to me, but not stiff. Do you have any secrets that I could share with other mothers?" (What I really wanted to say was "with me?")

"I guess I take after my mother. She loved being a mom. My sisters and I were her whole life and she enjoyed being with us. I never felt pushed to be anything other than who I was and I always knew that she enjoyed our company. I adored my mom. I was so grateful that she cared so much for my sisters and me and I suppose that I learned from her that being a good mom is an extraordinary joy. When I became a mother, I wanted what she had and I think I do. It's simple really—I like myself as a mother. I'm important to Jade and Tommy. I am their life and I like that." She waited to see if she had answered my questions adequately.

"Do you ever wish that you had something else, like a different career, more friends, time for yourself?" I seemed to grab into the air to find the right question so she could quench my desire to hear the specifics of how she liked herself so much.

"No. I'm a good mother. And these two need me. I do feel irreplaceable to them and I guess that comes from my feeling that my mom was irreplaceable to me when I was growing up. And she still is. Right now, I don't need anything else. I know that when they're older I can go back to finance full-time but right now, what I give these two monkeys is more important to me than anything. That's just the way I feel about things."

After my conversation with Julianne percolated through my mind, I understood what gave her such deep contentment and lack of anxiety about her life. She knew her value as a mother to Jade and Tommy. She got it. She felt indispensable and made no apologies. She allowed herself to accept her importance and this is something many of us mothers refuse to do. We don't want to accept that we are valuable and that we are extraordinary to our kids. Julianne's joy came from her ability to embrace her value as a mother and give no excuses to anyone for her belief.

Once I understood her better, I realized what attracted me to Julianne in the first place. When a mother really understands her value, she has more self-confidence. She sets boundaries with her kids, her husband, and herself and this makes life more palatable. She is less anxious and feels less inclined to compete with other women, because beneath everything she likes who she is. Finally, mothers who feel valuable can view the larger picture in life, knowing that, while they will always be moms, someday the intense parenting phase will pass and they will be on to utilizing different gifts. And when we wrap all of these into one package—a mother like Julianne surfaces.

Healthy self-esteem buffers us from the bad stuff in life. When tough times surface, those of us who like who we are allow ourselves to accept that we are the center of our children's lives. We are their anchor and lifeline. We mothers are irreplaceable and the sooner we avail ourselves of this very simple, deep truth, the more content we can be. I challenge every mother to live as Julianne lives.

WHAT ELISE LEARNED FROM HER MOTHER

I first met Elise while we were on a medical mission trip to the Dominican Republic. She accompanied her seventy-five-year-old mother, Carol, on the trip and our introduction came as we were preparing the room that would serve as our bedroom for the next two weeks. As I draped mosquito netting over my top bunk, I introduced myself. I was nervous because I saw her spraying her mattress with some sort of bug spray while I talked. Lucky for her, I thought. The scorpions and poisonous spiders will crawl into my bed in the night and nibble on my flesh. Of course, she offered to share her bug spray just a moment later, and we started talking.

Elise and I, along with her mother, were assigned to the same medical unit, which would travel via a rickety, aging school bus held together with twine and duct tape to remote areas in the inner island hills to dispense medicines to patients. Elise and I grew close quickly because pain does that to women. As we treated babies with bellies swollen from intestinal worms, women with abdominal pain from starvation, we quickly learned that shared anguish is lightened anguish.

I learned that Elise was a mother of three young children, ages seven, nine, and ten. We chatted about our kids and how much we missed them. At least I was fortunate to have one of my daughters with me on the trip, and Elise let me know early on that she would bring her own kids back to the island to work on a similar trip as soon as they were old enough.

Something about Elise intrigued me when I first met her. She was calm, self-confident, and kind. I was eager to uncover what made her so, and I began asking her questions. A bit peculiar of me, I thought, since she was at least six or seven years my junior.

"With small children at home, what made you come on our trip now?" I asked one night at dinner. Without hesitation, she answered.

"Oh, that's easy," she said. "My mom."

"You mean, your mom wanted to come on the trip and she needed you to help her?" I doubted this was true after having watched her mother dealing with the intense heat and long days a bit better than Elise was.

"Oh, no. Are you kidding? She can outdistance me any day when it comes to working here. I came because of who she is," she said. Now I was really intrigued. I waited and she continued. "My mother came on these trips every other year when I was growing up. She left us at home with my dad or a nanny, but when she came back, she told us stories of the people she met. And when she told us stories, she was excited. Sometimes she laughed, sometimes she cried, but she always told us as much as she could about everything she did when she was away."

"So what does this have to do with why you came?" I asked.

"My mother was a great mom. She worked part-time at a health clinic in our hometown but taught my sisters and me how to value the right things. She said that what she did was important—not just her work in the Dominican, or her work at the clinic. She said that her number one job was being a good mom. And because she wanted to be a good mom, she felt that she needed to teach us how to make a difference in someone's life. She taught us by living it out. And that changed me. I saw her trips as a means of teaching us. Sure, she did them because she liked them, but she did them because she knew that they would impact us as kids growing up. She took herself as a mother very seriously and we always knew that."

I was beginning to understand more about Elise and more about her mother. How wonderful it was for me to witness the two in action, side by side, and to see the depth of the impact of Carol's work on her daughter. She was transferring something very great to Elise and as Elise described this very phenomenon to me, I had the privilege of seeing it.

As we neared the end of our trip, I garnered the courage to ask Carol a few important questions. Somehow I knew she wouldn't discount me as simply a nosy person; she would probably get precisely what I was trying to draw out of her.

"Carol," I asked, "you always seem to have so much energy. You make me feel like a wimp. Were you born with all that energy?" I could feel myself wimping out. Of course she wasn't born with it, but I was trying to make the question shallower, perhaps.

"No. I didn't always have it. I make energy. Well, not literally, I suppose, but I operate as though I have a lot, and it seems to come," she said.

Now I felt really stupid. She wasn't quite making sense and she was certainly not giving me answers I could sink my teeth into. Somehow, I think she knew as much.

I foundered. "Well, you just seem to enjoy yourself so much more than the rest of us and . . ." I was stuck. She knew what my next words were going to be and I was afraid I was insulting her already.

"I know—I'm twice everyone else's age." Oh, God, I thought, I want to crawl out of the room. Then she opened her mouth and assuaged my obvious guilt. "It isn't about age. It's not about ability, talent, or even personality. Doing what I do—and I've been doing this for a number of years now—is about attitude. I'm good at helping these folks. I fit here. I was born to help and to love these people. And they need me. I believe that when you love the life you're supposed to be living and you happen on fulfilling the deep meaning of your life, it works. The energy comes, you get bolder, and you live less fearfully. I have friends back home who tell me I'm crazy. I'm too old or I'll have a heart attack. I feel sorry for them because they don't really get what life's all about. Knowing who you are and living what you were born to do, that's the good stuff. This is it, right here, right now, and I'm not going to miss it."

No mother can teach a child his or her own value if she doesn't first understand her own value as a mother. We are their teachers. We are the ones whom they admire and long to emulate. Our kids take the best of who we are (and unfortunately, sometimes the worst as well) and pull what they see inside of themselves. They take on our character qualities. They don't always take on the character qualities of teachers, coaches, nannies, or relatives, but they always take on ours. Therein lies just a part of our great value to them.

How can we assume that we have little value when we give them life, shape their lives, and ultimately change their lives? We mothers are indispensable to our kids because no one can teach them how to love, empathize, nurture, or value others like we can. No one. And when it comes to teaching them how to love and value themselves, we are the ones with the greatest power to impart these profound and necessary truths to them. Just as Carol did for Elise.

THREE WAYS TO MAKE THE HABIT STICK

#1: Make a list

Many of us mothers don't know what we are good at, what we can accomplish, and what brings us real pleasure. We obsess so much about what we don't like in ourselves, our husbands (aren't we good at telling them what we don't want them to do?), and our kids that we completely fail to define ourselves by what we *do* like about ourselves.

So let's stop. Make a list of the things you are really good at and write them down. If you think your thighs are fat, forget about them and write down what looks good about your figure. Write down what you are, what you like, what you dream about, and whenever the negative thoughts come, think on these things.

Then go a step further: *Act* on them. Buy an outfit that shows off the best part of your figure. Schedule an activity that makes you feel good about your life. Make a date with a friend who is upbeat and who likes who you are. Start being the kind of friend you want to be and stop thinking about how you let your friends down. Tremendous amounts of energy leave us daily because we exhaust it in trying what not to be rather than embracing what we want to do.

We can retrain our negative thought processes but it requires work. Beginning the process means identifying the negative stream of thoughts and facing them. Then we must replace them over and over with clearly defined positive ones. This takes time and often feels as though it isn't working. But it is.

As we begin to do this, our feelings begin to soften toward ourselves and we become emotionally lighter. Here is where we can begin to reverse the habit of defining ourselves by what we don't want or what we don't like and begin to embrace what we do want and like. The process can feel like thick molasses dripping from a bottle, but it works. It really works.

#2: Live to impress no one

Women who have a healthy sense of their own value are delightful to be around because they never play games, put on airs, or try to impress anyone. They don't need to because they have a sense that they lack very little. It isn't that they are enamored with themselves—quite the opposite, they are humble. They are so comfortable with who they are that they are free to elevate others. Insecure mothers scour the territory before them to find a way to elevate themselves, primarily through making another mother look just a little smaller, uglier, less informed, or even stupid. Mothers who constantly badmouth others are profoundly insecure but mothers who feel secure speak with an ease and joy that lets the hearer see their confidence.

Whenever we feel twinges to impress our company, we know that we are struggling with poor self-esteem. One of the best ways to feel better about who we are as mothers is to push ourselves to accept who we are. We do this by refusing to pretend with anyone. And we pretend whenever we feel the tiniest nudge inside to impress someone. We all do this but we can change because real joy and real contentment come from believing that we are good just the way we are. We refuse to give in to the urge to impress others, we force ourselves to accept ourselves, and this is real freedom.

I recently witnessed an extraordinary example of this. I was at the wedding of a close friend's daughter. It was a big, formal wedding followed by a gorgeous reception held beneath an enormous tent. The candles were lit on all the tables, which were dressed with hydrangea topiaries, and the meal was being served. Servers in formal attire brought our dinners. I looked up as I was being served and noticed one of the guests standing at the edge of the tent looking lost. It was Edward, a forty-five-year-old man with mental retardation who had been invited to the wedding. He had gone to use the restroom and when he came back, he didn't know where he was to sit. He couldn't read, so finding his name card was no help. I thought that I should jump up and grab him so that he could sit at my table in the back. He talked loudly and demanded a lot of attention.

Then I saw an extraordinary sight. The mother of the bride, dressed in a long periwinkle taffeta gown, got up from her seat and went over to him. She took him by the hand and, weaving him through a sea of lilac tablecloths, brought him to her table and pulled out a chair for him, adjacent to hers. She was sitting next to the bridal table. When she walked over to Edward, I looked at her face and studied her body language. She was smiling and comfortable—as a mother would be bringing her adored child into a party, ready to show him off. She was not embarrassed. Other mothers might have refused to invite the mentally handicapped man. After all, this was their daughter's big day and they wouldn't want anything spoiled by excessive noise. Others might have invited the odd guest but put him at a table in the back, asking a close friend to watch over him. Not this mother. She was concerned with impressing no one. She was ready for loud noise at her table, peculiar dinner manners, and whatever odd facial gestures he might make. She didn't care if the other guests thought she was odd. Every ounce of her behavior in this simple gesture spoke volumes about her self-esteem. She knew who she was and refused to pretend to be otherwise. Clearly she was a woman who embraced a deep sense that she was valuable. And the beauty of her knowledge was that she was free to show one so less fortunate than herself a greater sense of value as well.

#3: Write down what goes in the box (and what doesn't)

There is no secret that I have come to believe that faith and God are intimately interwoven into our lives as mothers. I have seen enough deaths to question the afterlife and the will of God and I have seen enough births to believe in the goodness of God. That is why I cannot discuss our value as mothers without including Him in the conversation.

John Ortberg wrote a lovely book called *When the Game Is Over, It All Goes Back in the Box*. A bit of a downer of a title, but nonetheless poignant. While Ortberg refers to our inability to bring along things that we amass in our lifetimes, I think there is more to the title.

Like putting away the play money and titles to Park Place or Water Works at the end of a game of Monopoly, there is little we take with us at the end of our days. This is important to reconcile with now because doing so changes the way we live before we end up in the box ourselves. I have asked myself what will go in mine, other than a scrawny, wrinkly body? More importantly, what will my kids be thinking about when they throw the dirt on top?

Moving past the dark imagery, let me get to my point. God goes in the box with me, I believe. No, He doesn't die, but He is there with me, or rather, I with Him. There is life before life on earth and there is life after. That's because in addition to our earthly life, we have a spiritual dimension—our soul. And this soul counts. It gives us extraordinary value. It connects us with God. It is the deepest part of who we are, which is adored by the God of the universe. It doesn't die. It doesn't eat or diet and it doesn't wear nice clothes. It is within us and in some way, which I cannot aptly quantify, it gives us worth.

Women in the Jewish tradition understand this. Women in the Muslim tradition understand this. And women in the Christian tradition stake their lives on this fact, for we believe that Christ loved us enough to die for us. Whatever our faith, this is not to be taken lightly. If we believe that we are flesh and spirit, then we must also believe that each has value. And it stands to reason that our spiritual self—our soul—has inestimable value. This truth is astonishing. As mothers who believe in a spiritual self, we have no choice but to embrace our worth and take it very, very seriously. Clearly, God does.

Here's the simplified translation: If we are both flesh and spirit, then God loves both. At the beginning of our lives and at the end, He alone will accompany us. The One who made all things stoops to accompany us in order that we will never be alone and never feel unloved. Now that is something to celebrate when pondering our worth.

||||||||||||||||||||||||||||||||||||||||||||||||||||||||||||||||||||||||||||||||||||||||||||||||||||||

Maintain Key Friendships

WHEN MARIE AND I were twelve, we would saddle our blond ponies on a Saturday morning at the barn where an elderly woman kept our steeds and head to the miles of trails in the woods behind it. Saturdays were our favorite days. Marie's pony was mild-mannered and well behaved, but mine wasn't. More than once I got bucked off and Marie chased after my horse and brought him back to me. I felt humiliated because I felt like a bad rider, but Marie always blamed my horse. Even then, she was my fan. I'm sure that at twelve she knew she was better at riding than I was and that my horse wasn't as poorly behaved as I thought he was. But Marie was my buddy, my confidante, and my best friend. She always made me feel better about myself, and about life, than I would have felt on my own.

Forty years later, she still makes me feel the same way. We don't see each other much and Facebook keeps us connected more than phone calls, but nothing has changed the fondness we have for each other. Since those easy, lovely Saturdays, we have endured failed college exams, the deaths of best friends, the birth of children, and the overnight acceptance of stepchildren. Parents have aged and gone into nursing homes or died. The joys that our children and stepchildren have given one of us have been given to the other. When we have the chance to chat on the phone, we are sometimes twelve, sometimes twenty-one and in college, and sometimes fifty and feeling eighty. We have lived side by side at so many different ages that, in a moment, we can become that age to the other. Marie's voice pulls me into an age of carefree joy or consoles me when I don't feel that I can make it through a day. Maybe it isn't her voice; maybe it's just her. Marie has stayed a part of my life for all these years because women friends can do that. We can follow each other through the years, listening, questioning, or crying for each other. No perfection is needed. Love is required but even that can be woefully broken, because at the end of the day what we really need as mothers is a friend who simply stays. Because when she stays, we know that we are loved. We can go to sleep at night, awaken the next day, and know that we can make it because she is out there—loving us.

But friendship, which seemed so simple when Marie and I were kids, has gotten harder as the years have passed, and not just for me but for all mothers. We labor intensely during the years when our children are young, and we think that we will have time for fun, occasional lunches with women friends, or even trips with friends after the kids leave. The truth is, when something needs to be cut out in the crunch of daily demands, friends are the first to go. Sometimes friendship seems expendable, unnecessary. So we delay friendships and put women off, all the while believing that we will catch up later.

The problem is, most of us don't. There is no catch-up time. Life gets even more demanding as we age. We have parents to care for and bills to pay. Work shifts gears and we move in different directions. Marriages become strained, faces wrinkle, and body parts begin to move southward. Life presents a whole new set of imminent challenges, which need our attention more, we think, than friends do.

Let us not be so fooled. We need other women if we are to work more efficiently, worry less, and stay healthier. Find me a mother who doesn't harbor a silent fear of being all alone one day and there you'll find a woman who doesn't need more friends. But she just isn't out there. Why?

Mothers are by nature relational creatures. We thrive on loving and being loved, talking and listening, seeing and being seen. Some of us have our relational needs met through our families. Others try through work, still others through romantic relationships and marriage. And these are extremely important, but they don't fully satisfy our relational needs because the others in the relationship are too dissimilar from us. Husbands can't be everything to us and certainly our children shouldn't be. Coworkers may be able to double as confidants, but the nature of work adds competition and strain, which can damage good friendships.

Some of us are lonely, especially when our kids are little, because we don't have time for friends. We want them and sometimes physically ache to spend time with friends, but nap times, car pools, or job schedules preclude that. Other times, particularly if loneliness sets in over a long time, lack of friendship prompts us to ponder deeper questions about ourselves.

Loneliness gouges a woman's heart because inherent in loneliness is a subconscious feeling that we deserve to be alone. A mother who feels lonely believes on some level that she is unlikable, even unlovable. She is too inept, stupid, disorganized, or messed up to be with. My purpose in exaggerating here is to verbalize some of the severe thoughts that women silently have but would never dare verbalize. When she feels this way, she retreats from other women and finds herself even lonelier. Stay away from the tennis crowd, because they have money. Don't go to the book club, because you don't have anything worthwhile to add. Avoid the playgroup, because those mothers stay at home with their kids and are better mothers. And on and on the voices go in our heads. Loneliness begets loneliness and pretty soon we sink into a deeper belief that life is probably better lived by ourselves in our own muddy mix of frustration, disorganization, or compulsions. With all of the pain Mother Teresa witnessed during her life, she counted loneliness as the worst. She said, "The most terrible poverty is loneliness and the feeling of being unloved."

So we must fight loneliness fiercely. Friends are a necessity, not a luxury. Like my friend Marie, your true friend will be the one who will cook food for your family when you are sick, drive car pool when your car runs out of radiator fluid, throw baby showers for your kids, still see you as gorgeous when you can't lose the extra sixty pounds after baby number three, join Weight Watchers when she doesn't need to be on a diet but you do, help plan your father's funeral, and maybe, just maybe, plan yours. She is your best friend and will never let you drop into the deep chasm of loneliness. Nothing about her friendship is expendable. In this chapter, I'll talk about some of the wonderful friendships I've seen, and one particular friend who truly changed my life. And at the end of the chapter, I'll show you three ways to make the habit stick—having an inner and an outer circle of friends, balancing the types of friends you choose, and loving a friend better than you know how.

FRIENDS HUMOR US

Friends who bring humor into our lives hammer tiny cracks into the protective shells around our hearts. The cracks turn into craters and we find one day that, miraculously, pieces of the hard stuff have fallen away from our hearts. We become a bit more tender and allow ourselves to feel more vulnerable. And where the pieces of shell have fallen away, joy seeps into those tender parts of our hearts.

It is hard to laugh without feeling pleasure or enjoyment. Believe it or not, many mothers subconsciously refuse to let themselves feel pleasure. This sounds peculiar, but it is true. Mothers who sacrifice, protect, and martyr themselves take themselves and their behaviors extremely seriously. And when life is serious, there is little room for joy, because joy doesn't feel serious. It feels fun and light and brings with it a sense of vulnerability. Think about it for a moment. Have you ever been with a friend who fights laughter? Most of us have. Perhaps you are one of those mothers. These are women who are afraid to let go of serious thoughts and feelings for even a moment because doing so doesn't feel safe. Laughing makes us feel out of control for a moment (even if we don't laugh uncontrollably).

Each of us mothers needs a friend who can bring humor into our lives, so that we can allow ourselves to open just a little—long enough to let our guard down and begin to let joy in. And we need joy. So many women wake up every morning with heaviness in their chests. Perhaps it is unresolved sadness or present anger at a husband who is aloof, cold, or unfaithful. Maybe it is simply a heaviness erupting from a deep sense of dread for the day. If you are one of these women, you know how guarded you feel against enjoyment. It doesn't fit. It is scary and contrary to what life is all about for you at this particular time. And then there are some of us who are almost superstitious about laughter. If life feels dark and worry consumes you, laughter tempts you to leave the darkness for a moment and you are afraid that if you do this, you will lose charge over it. Worry will escape you and then you will have to run after it and retrieve it so that you can chew on it more. Humor is the antithesis of worry. Many of us can't reconcile that the two can sit side by side in one's emotional repertoire. The truth is, however, that they can and they should. Laughter wonderfully balances worry and sadness.

Friends who love us know that motherhood is about transitioning—and adjusting, constantly, to those changes. We must become masters of change because that is what life demands of us. Our children come into our lives, and then they wander away. Sometimes they return; sometimes they don't. Occasionally we welcome the change, but usually it bullies us and we fight back. One thing that we must realize, though, is that fighting transitions draws out the pain. So we must surrender the fight. And one of the best ways to help ourselves surrender is to introduce laughter. That's what good friends do for us—they usher in timely, sensitive humor in order to pull us out of our hurt just a bit and make life more bearable. And in so doing, the changes lose their sting.

FIND YOUR TRIBE

Every woman needs a tribe. Again, I'll mention my dear friend Marie Seiler. She knows. As one of three girls raised by a single mother, she watched her mother strengthened time and again by other mothers who listened to her when she was frustrated and loved her when she felt no one else did.

Marie also knows that we each need our own tribe, because she has one. She knows how much she needs one and works hard to keep them all close. Most of us feel too tired for friends at one time or another. We work hard for our families and when our kids are young, put friendships on the back burner. The problem is, many of those friendships dissolve and before we know it, what little pieces of a tribe we may have once had aren't there anymore. We can't let this happen. Force yourself to pick a few good women who will go the distance with you. Talk with them, write them a note here or there (not an email, but a handwritten note), and tell them what they mean to you. Pick up the phone and chat, even if you can touch base for only five minutes a week. But hang on to those you select for your tribe because you will need them more as you age. And they will need you. As we move closer to the "golden years" we begin to realize that the gold part isn't so shiny. Middle age is tough, between caring for adult children and aging parents. If we have a tribe that's seen our kids recover from chicken pox, graduate from high school, and even get married, they'll be with us by the time we need to check out nursing homes for a parent we adore and who has dementia, too. They—the two or three who have loved us forever—will buoy us through those difficult middle years.

FOOD IS FRIENDSHIP

My mother loves people by feeding them. She stuffs them with good food—meat, usually, with potatoes and dark gravy. The kind of gravy that has become a lost art, perhaps because we spend less time cooking, less time learning our cuts of meat, less time pushing food on loved ones.

For many of us mothers, feeding people is our love language. When we are too intimidated to express our feelings, particularly when sadness is involved, we resort to casseroles. Bake chicken, cut up carrots, and roll out pie dough. These are the hand motions of a friend who longs to soothe a mother's broken heart. And somehow, miraculously, they do.

When Lisa's husband, Brett, was diagnosed with pancreatic cancer, the first person she called was Beth. Lisa's voice was icy with shock, Beth recalls. Then suddenly, as she was speaking, Lisa broke down and sobbed. Beth could hear her heaving, gasping for air between cries, and Beth remembers the quick conclusion she drew as well: "With two small children, one only nine months and the other two and a half years old, I wondered how Lisa was going to make it. What about the kids? I thought about the sadness of those two small kids growing up without their dad, but then I felt sorrier for Lisa. She was so young. No one this young should have to endure this kind of trauma, I thought."

Little did Lisa realize in that first phone call what the next two years would bring or what an incredible friend she had in Beth. Being a good ten years older, Beth knew about life with small kids and life with older ones. She knew the difficulties that lay ahead of her friend in venturing to raise the two all by herself. And because she had a background in medicine, Beth also knew the gravity of Brett's diagnosis. He would have two years, tops, she knew, but she kept it to herself.

"There was nothing I could say to take her pain away. I wanted a gigantic magic wand to wave over Lisa and Brett and their kids. I wanted desperately to make the cancer go away. Then I felt so frustrated and I felt I was going to go crazy. So I did what I always do when I feel madness coming on. I start to cook. I'd make cookies and eat half the dough. I felt if the cookies were going to make Lisa and Brett feel any better, they might as well make me feel a little better, too. I made chicken casseroles, lasagna, and burritos. Lots of them. I'd freeze them and give half to my boys.

"Pretty soon, weeks went by, then months, and Brett continued to progressively waste away. Sometimes I told Lisa to go out and I'd sit and take care of the kids and talk to Brett. But I found that even while I was at her house, the oven would mysteriously come on and before I even realized what I was doing, the aroma of sweet rolls or some other dessert would be seeping out of it. And the funny thing is, I think that subconsciously, I thought that even the smell of food cooking in the house brought optimism. Cinnamon rolls really can counter the smell of death in a home. Or at least, the aroma can make you pretend for a minute that life is normal and good. Maybe that's it. It's all about pretend."

When Brett's last days arrived and he left his home for the last time to go to the hospital, Lisa couldn't let him go alone. So she went, too. And who stayed behind? Beth. Without being asked, she simply arrived at Lisa's door with a packed bag to stay with the children as long as she was needed. She literally stepped into Lisa's shoes and took over where she left off, because that's what extraordinary friends do. She cleaned, played with the kids, put them down for naps, and took them grocery shopping.

"During those last days, we went to the grocery store a lot," Beth recalls, "because I was in a serious cooking mode then. I felt so helpless. I wanted to love Lisa the best I could, but words, hugs, flowers, nothing did it. I don't even know if food did, but I do know one thing, that cooking at least made us all feel that some part of life—maybe the task of keeping alive—was moving forward. We had to all just keep moving forward. That's what cooking meals did for us all."

Not many of us are fortunate enough to have women in our lives who will love us so well. Ironically enough, Lisa was one of the lucky ones—at least in the friendship department. The love Beth gave to Lisa might even have saved her life. And cooking great food was an integral, wonderfully simple part of that love.

Food doesn't soothe, but the intention does. Where love stops, chicken pot pies can take over. There is an understanding that while the blender whirls and the oven preheats, the friend in pain is being remembered in her hurt. The cook is thinking of her, wondering how she is faring, what she is experiencing. While friends cook, they slide their feet into the shoes of the hurting mom in order to participate a bit in the pain she feels. One mother to another. While I bake, give me some of your troubles and I will carry them as best I can, is what the activity sends as intention. I can't be you, but I can be like you in some way. Our common bond as mothers is that we must cook for loved ones. So I will cook for you now, says that friend. I can pretend that you are with me and that I can make life better for you. So let me in, says the food.

THE FRIENDSHIP THAT CHANGED MY LIFE

One of the amazing things about friendship is that it comes back to you, in both big and small ways. You make a casserole for a friend when she's sick, and later she does the same for you. But sometimes you get much more than you expected. That's what happened when I met Patricia. The first time I saw her, we were at a luncheon that a local church puts on every year for the community. Businessmen, pastors, high school kids, and the homeless turn out for the event. I almost walked right passed her. She was the type of person who was easily missed. I think she liked it that way. She was walking out of the church kitchen behind a group of women and she walked alone. I was struck by the softness of her appearance— her fawn-colored, wavy hair, her beige wool coat, and her walk. Everything about her seemed quiet and soft. Certainly, she didn't appear destitute or homeless. A friend of mine whispered to me that she was homeless because her husband had squandered their money and left her for another woman. I couldn't believe the information I had heard.

As I approached her for an introductory conversation, I felt awkward, almost ashamed. The last thing that I wanted to impose upon this lovely older woman was embarrassment—for her or for me.

"Patricia?" I called from behind.

She turned around and dissipated my anxiety immediately with her warm smile.

"Yes?" she said, looking me squarely in the eyes.

"I'm Meg. I don't believe we've ever met."

"Oh, yes, dear," she said, continuing to walk toward the door. "I know who you are. I've lived here a long time. My doctor is in your medical practice."

I didn't know quite how to take her candor but supposed that she knew volumes more than she would ever let on. We chatted for almost twenty minutes as I tried to draw the conversation out as long as possible before broaching the sensitive subject that had prompted me to introduce myself. Finally, I did it. I summoned the courage to ask this stranger to come and live at our home for as long as she saw necessary. As soon as I asked, I waited for the shocked and apologetic look to appear on her face. It never came.

"That would be lovely," she simply said. "Are you sure? I mean, you have small children and I most certainly don't want to be a nuisance." How did she know I had small children? I felt a bit spooked.

We made arrangements for me to pick her up from the women's shelter where she was currently staying. Two days later I packed her small suitcase of toiletries and a grocery bag full of staples carefully labeled with her name into my car and brought her to our five-bedroom home. She came for three weeks and stayed a year and a half. I cried like a baby when she moved out.

Patricia was a sixty-five-year-old mother of four grown children, a registered nurse, and one of the brightest, kindest women I have ever known. She moved in with us because she was homeless, but she was anything but a sorry woman. She had been married thirty-something years when her husband lost all their savings, as well as their home. He drank heavily and found life a bit more welcoming with a younger, wealthier woman than Patricia. So he left her. She stayed in their home until the bank foreclosed on it and she had to watch a perfect stranger auction off her teacup collection, the children's toys she was saving for her grandchildren, her nightstand, and all of her other personal belongings on her front lawn. Not wanting to burden her children, she took a bus to the women's shelter and made a temporary life for herself there. Over the years we spent together, I learned about many of the antics of her skunkish husband, but never from Patricia. In fact, I never heard her complain about him, her children, or her poverty.

When she came to live with us, my children were ages two, six, eight, and ten. We had two dogs, a guinea pig, two rabbits, a parakeet, and a chameleon from Madagascar that lived in my daughter's bedroom. But a peculiar sensation fell over me when she came. I became very self-conscious, almost anxious about my mothering. She watched. She heard my conversations with my children and saw me put them in time-out. She was quiet and she was there—always in the wings, watching silently.

She spoke very little and continually occupied herself with work around the house. I never asked her to help with picking up or folding laundry, but I didn't need to. She was a mom—she just knew what to do and she did it.

After only a few weeks, my anxiety and self-consciousness dissipated. I realized that she, too, had used time-outs, spanked her out-of-control kids on occasion, and even lost her temper. But mostly my discomfort lifted because of who she was. She let me know that she was neither judge nor critic; she simply was a grateful friend.

Sometimes we would draw out our time at the breakfast table just to sit together or talk. I drank strong coffee and skipped the food while she sipped tea and ate, quite ritualistically, oatmeal mixed with raw chopped broccoli. One morning I learned why she ate the odd combo. She had macular degeneration in both eyes and her doctor told her that vitamin E in broccoli stays the progression.

Over our months together, she coerced me into eating fruit every day and getting my hair cut more than twice a year. I lectured her about self-worth and not taking flak from her rotten ex, and rode her to stand up for herself. She never argued back, but nodded her head and smiled at me.

When my kids threw temper tantrums, talked back to me, or tried to sneak out of chores, Patricia hovered on the sidelines and smiled. Her motherly wisdom evidenced itself in her restraint. She never offered advice unless I asked. And even then, she used few words and couched them in layers of love and grace. Never did she want to offend me.

I drove her to doctors' appointments and to bus stops. She read to my kids and soaked them in the tub. When they cried in the middle of the night, I would often go into their rooms and find Patricia at their bedside, singing to them. We celebrated each other's birthdays. I took her to Sears to buy her new clothes or to a salon to have her hair set. One birthday morning, I awoke to find a tiny cardboard box on my dresser stuffed with folded pieces of paper. Each piece had a handwritten message from Patricia to me on it. "Never forget how much you are loved," or "You are an amazing mother."

Eventually Patricia found an apartment at a senior citizen housing complex and she began making arrangements to move into this new place of her own. I was heartbroken, but I knew she needed her space and I rationalized that since the place was only a mile from my home we might still be able to eat breakfast together. Of course, life gets in the way of those kinds of plans and we rarely if ever started our day together again. Her life became her own when she left, although we saw each other weekly.

During our twelve-year friendship, she suffered a stroke and two bouts of pneumonia, and had a defibrillator placed in her heart to correct irregular heart rhythms. Once, shortly after her defibrillator was put in, I was sitting by her bed talking with her and the device misfired. It gave her such a strong electric jolt that she almost flew out of her bed. It hit again, throwing her tiny, soft body off the mattress, and she screamed. I couldn't bear to see her beaten up like that and when her doctor finally came in, I yelled at him in my firm doctor voice. I wanted to choke the man for allowing her to go through that.

With every hospitalization, electric shock, or round of antibiotics, Patricia grew older. Her wavy fine hair grew thinner and her front teeth became smaller. Was it the nighttime grinding or daily stress that caused them to shrink? I didn't know.

Sometimes weeks passed and we didn't talk. But every day I drove by her house and checked to see if her lights were on or her plants were watered—signs that she was still there and alive. When my father was diagnosed with Alzheimer's, I drove straight to her cramped quarters and cried to her. She listened, hugged me, and held my hand. When her granddaughter overdosed, we cried together. Whenever I was on the road, lecturing or doing a media appearance, Patricia told me that she would pray for me. Once, when I returned, I found her in the hospital with severe pneumonia and swore that I would not leave again unless her health was good. "Nonsense," she said. "Promise me that you'll always do what you were put on this earth to do." So many times, like that one, her words puzzled me.

I practiced medicine because I liked it. I didn't do it because of some outside force guiding me. I went to medical school because from the time I was sixteen and watched my dad's best friend perform hip surgery, I wanted to be a physician. I was determined, wildly enthralled with medicine, and stubborn. What did she mean, what I was meant to do? I meant to become a doctor. No one else drove me there.

"Sit down," Patricia told me during that same visit. "I have something to tell you." The tone of her voice was sober but excited. She looked at her nurse and waited until she left before she continued to talk to me.

"I had an incredible dream last night." She beamed. "No. It wasn't a dream. It was something—supernatural. Like a vision, I suppose." My curiosity was sharp, as was my skepticism.

"You must believe me. Promise that you'll believe me, Meg," she said. I nodded my head. I needed to know what she was about to tell me.

She watched my eyes, apparently finding permission in them to go on, so she did.

"I was having a terrible time breathing. I felt like I was going to suffocate before I fell asleep. In fact, I don't even know how I fell asleep, but I did. Anyway, after I fell asleep, I saw myself ready to die. I wasn't afraid. I was dying and all of a sudden I saw the ocean. It was a gorgeous green. I looked at the horizon and I saw a tiny boat and I knew then that the boat was me." Patricia paused and watched my face. I knew what she was searching for—skepticism—so I tried to hide it. I didn't want to disappoint her, and I also wanted her to keep telling her story. I wanted to listen.

"It was being tossed up and down by enormous waves and it was tipping. It looked like it was going to sink." She paused briefly and looked for my reaction. I tried to show enthusiasm, rather than the skepticism that I was feeling.

"The boat was *me!*" she squealed. "The water became calm and the tiny boat was moving closer to a beautiful harbor. As I watched the boat move, I saw the shoreline of the harbor and it was incredible. It was clean and safe. The shoreline seemed to engulf the little boat. Then—and this is the most amazing part"—her eyes grew brighter than I have seen on any person's face, and she continued—"I heard God speak to me."

"You mean, like a voice?" I asked. I wondered to myself what medications she was on. I must check her chart on my way out, I noted to myself.

"Kind of. Yes, like a voice. But more than a voice. But it doesn't matter. God told me that I was like a tiny, beautiful boat all alone and that He would always take care of me. That's why He brought me into the harbor. To keep me safe. When I woke up, I felt a calm that I have never, ever known. Right now, I still feel it. And I don't think I'll ever be the same."

I didn't know what to say. What *do* you say to someone who says that she has just heard from God? "Good. I'm so glad. That must have been neat"?

I can't even remember what I said. The truth is, it didn't really matter. Patricia believed in what she'd experienced and nothing would shake her belief. It was one of those rare moments in life when one learns something or feels some truth that is deeper than can be communicated. I knew that she was experiencing one of these moments. And I am so grateful that she chose me to participate in her moment. That's what friends do.

Several years and a few illnesses later, Patricia recounted the story and conviction of its truth in the same manner she had in the hospital the morning after it occurred. She never wavered. In fact, she talked to me more frequently about her God. Sometimes when we sat in her living room chatting, she would mention Him as though He were sitting in a chair right next to one of us. Once I even glanced at the rocking chair beside me to be sure. Maybe old, lonely people do this kind of thing, I wondered. But not Patricia, I reasoned. She wasn't lonely and she certainly wasn't loopy. What most impressed me was the way in which Patricia talked about God. Her voice quieted and became softer. She used adjectives when describing Him like *kind, gentle,* and *nurturing.*

One dark October morning, I got a phone call from my husband, who was at work. I sensed there was bad news even before I picked up the phone. "It's Patricia," he began. "I'm in the ER with her and she's got a subdural hematoma. She fell this morning. She's still awake."

Before he finished talking, I hung up the phone in my kitchen, jumped in my car, and went to the ER. I almost pulled my car over twice due to the nausea that fear had brought on. Between the phone call and my arrival, Patricia had slipped into a coma. She never came out of it. They placed her in a bed in the ICU and she lay deathly still. I sat by her bed and one by one, her children and grandchildren filtered in to pay their respects, cry, or share stories of this wonderful woman.

We tired of waiting and watching her not respond. I grew impatient and angry at her God, who she said was so nice. Because of a prescribed medication she'd been taking, she was bruised all over. Her body looked like it had been beaten with a baseball bat, particularly her face. I wanted to hide her face—it was supposed to be lovely, not beaten up. Her life had been so terribly hard and the ugly bruises reminded me that she had been, literally, beaten at times. Physically, emotionally, and most certainly by the act of living.

On the sixth night of her hospitalization, I asked a friend to accompany me to the hospital so that I could be with Patricia. I just wanted to touch her, to sweep my hand over her hair, to make sure that she was still breathing. We snuck into her room long after visiting hours were over and heard the gentle puff of her respirator. When I looked at her, something was different. I looked at my friend and asked if she noticed anything different about Patricia. She ever so slightly nodded her head, gesturing that she didn't believe what she was experiencing. "She's not here," my friend whispered in astonishment.

"I know," I answered. We were too afraid to speak more on the subject. Something eerily spiritual had happened and neither one of us understood what. We sensed, if that is an appropriate description, that Patricia had passed into heaven before her body gave out.

The next morning the doctor advised her children that, since there was no hope of Patricia getting better, he be allowed to take her breathing tube out. Pull the plug, and let her go. I watched the four of them talk among themselves and they looked terrified. After several minutes they asked me to join the discussion and offer my opinion about pulling Patricia from life support. Without warning to myself, I began to talk to them.

"Don't be afraid," I told them first. "Your mom does not want you to be afraid. She wasn't afraid to die. I know that, because she told me. I also believe that you should let her go. She would want that." I spoke with a confidence that I rarely, if ever, had felt. The confidence puzzled me.

The four told the doctor to remove the tube. Then they turned again to me. "We don't want Mother to be alone when she dies. Would you mind staying with her?" they choked through their tears.

Of course I would stay. Because that's what friends do. I held her bony hands in mine and kissed them as the doctor yanked the plastic and tore the tape from her face. I heard her kids in the hallway whispering, waiting. I hated the moment but I didn't want it to end. Then I looked up at her frail body and something extraordinary happened. I felt a calmness consume me. Her heart rate was slowing, her breaths were shorter, and soon they would stop. But it was all okay. It was all okay. Someone some-where was telling me that she was safe and well and that I needn't worry. She was already gone and these mere measures needed to happen to alert everyone else to the fact. Was Patricia trying to tell me something that moment? I don't think so. I think that it was God—her God—who had told her so many years before that there was a harbor just for her and it was beautiful and pain-free and safe. Perhaps this was the moment when I would fully believe the dream she had experienced as reality many years before. She had prepared me for this experience by sharing her deepest and most personal experiences—as difficult and risky as they may have seemed to communicate—and allowed me to feel such un-matched peace. She shared; she risked telling me her spiritual thoughts, because that's what friends do.

During our friendship, Patricia taught me to be a better mother. More accurately, she *showed* me—how to sing at night to my kids, how to be patient with them. She taught me to forgive myself when self-contempt consumed me for losing my temper or when guilt over working enveloped my conscience. She taught me better than that. She taught me, in her life, that God is good, because she opened her heart and shared secrets with me. Secrets of an old woman who had lived enough to know that life knocks us around, but we can survive—if we have friends who will listen to our secrets. And in her death, she showed me how good God can be.

Mothers are forced to live deeply. From the moment our children are born, terror strikes our hearts in a new way. We worry, fret, and at times try desperately to overcontrol our kids because we are so afraid. We become mad, really. Crazy women—manipulating events, setting curfews, driving by playgrounds at recess to ensure that our kids are still alive. We'd buy cars with airbags that pop down from the roof if we could. We become intense and protective because motherhood makes us confront the sobering truth that we are not in charge and that at any moment in our lives, we could lose—big-time. We could lose a spouse, a child, perhaps our own lives. And if the latter came about, we would lose influence and protection over our children as they grew up without us. Having children keeps us from pretending that life is easy and cushy. And the stark reality that it can be quite cruel hits us square in the face.

And that is probably the most compelling reason why we mothers who want to do more than simply survive need other mothers as friends who understand the undercurrent of angst we can feel. Friends help us thrive in the midst of emotional tumult and cold. When death snakes its way into our lives and we crash, we have to have women friends who will stay with us, teach us, and, as Patricia so beautifully showed me, show us that it's safe to navigate our way forward. It's really, in fact, more than safe to keep on living.

THREE WAYS TO MAKE THE HABIT STICK

#1: Have an inner and an outer circle of friends

Psychologists tell us that introverts feel drained by being with others while extroverts are energized by it. It would seem reasonable to conclude from this that some of us need many friends and others just a few. In my experience, this is not true. Regardless of our personality type, every mother needs connections with women on different levels. We need an inner circle and an outer circle of friends, if you will; women who satisfy our longing for intimate emotional connection and others who provide us comfort and affection on a lighter level.

Women comprising our inner circle are usually few in number— three or four. These are the friends who can step into our kitchens at dinnertime and take over feeding our kids, put them to bed, and clean up the peanut butter on the floor and the jelly on the chairs when we suddenly fall apart from tragic news. They feel like our right arm or our left leg, whichever we need on a certain day. When we are convinced that we cannot love our husbands because they fail to satisfy the needs on our lists, these friends challenge us to shorten our lists because they know we have fortitude. They fill in the gaps in our lives where we fall short, because they love us. Inner-circle friends have a cistern of patience for us that never seems to dry up, even when we repeatedly forget to call, or say things that sting, or let their birthdays slide by unnoticed.

Inner-circle friends may come from family or extended family and have been in our lives long enough to see our tempers flare, our most shameful mistakes revealed, and the pounds we gained with the last pregnancy get stuck to our hips. And the greatest thing about these friends is that they don't care. They don't take our tempers personally, they don't see the extra rolls across our bellies, and when they catch us berating ourselves over mistakes, they firmly tell us to stop because such criticism hurts their ears. When we complain too much, they tell us to reroute our words because complaining brings about nothing good. And when we act like jerks to our husbands or kids, they gently refrain from scolding but diplomatically help us see that our attitude has soured and then they ask why.

The hallmarks of inner-circle friendships are trust, maturity, and faithfulness, all of which work together to cultivate the deep love between us. And each one of these must flow in two directions: Both friends must fulfill for the other. Jealousy never exists in these friendships because the ugliness of it erects a wall between us, stunting trust and faithfulness. While we might expect inner-circle friendships to simply appear, flowing naturally into our lives, often they don't. They require attention, diligence, and emotional elbow grease on our part. Like a marriage, they need honing, sweat, and time. But the joy they bring to our lives and the peace they afford are immeasurable.

Outer-circle friends, while no less valuable, are nonetheless different. These are the friends who bring casseroles when we are sick, who run our kids to school and soccer games, and who are always up for a brisk walk after dinner. They are companions who bring laughter and comfort and uplift us when we are down. Usually there are more outer-circle friends in a mother's life—about ten or so. These friends will come to our daughter's wedding but may not know when our birthday is. They provide us with a sense of belonging in the woman's world and, no, they don't have to be mothers. We don't need them to commiserate with or understand us when we are woeful. We just need to know that they are around and available sometimes to fill our world with affection and attention.

As is true with inner-circle friendships, these too require work. Outer-circle friends will grow weary if we ignore them too long and they will move on to find another to replace us because they recognize that they need companionship. Our relationships with outer-circle women are limited only by differences in personality. Often one in the relationship may long for deeper commitment, but if the other doesn't feel it, then the friendship will stay in the outer circle and this is fine. Depth in the friendship requires mutual trust and comfort and this can't be forced by one woman to accommodate the other.

#2: Balance the types of friends you choose

One of my mantras to the parents of teenagers in my practice is "Be careful if you have a really nice girl; they are the ones who get into trouble." Girls who are kind, polite, ethical, and bright find themselves doing things that they don't want to do simply because they don't want to hurt others' feelings. An astounding 40 percent of girls ages fourteen to eighteen have unwanted sex because, they say, they don't want to hurt their boyfriends' feelings.

The same warning should be issued to really great mothers: "Be careful if you are a really nice friend." Gracious, ethical, intelligent women often end up with one-way friendships because they are so nice. There is nothing wrong with having friends who need help constantly. You know the friends I'm referring to—the ones who ask (if they're going to ask at all) how you are doing half an hour into the conversation. These women are the takers—the needy ones who are always in crisis mode.

Have a few friends like this, because you have something to give, but never, ever have only this type of friendship. It will suck you dry. Find balance in your relationships. Have a mix in your tribe. Find friends who ask how you are right off the bat and also let you answer. Tell them how you are; if they open themselves up to you, too, you know you've found a good friend. Keep them close. We like to be needed, but we also need other women who will give and take, let us help when they are in crisis, and then move forward so that they will be available for us when we are in crisis.

Often mothers find themselves drained by their friendships and this usually happens because they have no balance.

Since friends bring their own giftedness to relationships, try to find friends with diverse gifts as well. Some friends only help us laugh, and others are best when we are crying, so have one of each. Some stimulate us intellectually but are colder than stone, so find one who is a great listener with a lot of empathy and one who will argue with you. (I do not mean to imply that intellect and empathy are mutually exclusive.) No female friend can meet all of our needs, so we shouldn't expect one to. This is the beauty of friendships between women in our tribes—each can complement the others so that many of our needs can be met.

#3: Love a friend better than you know how

Girlfriends don't break up only with boyfriends. They break up with girlfriends as well. Adult women who love each other deeply sever their relationships with girlfriends *for many reasons*. Most of these reasons are due to unresolved anger and lack of forgiveness. There are other times when we push good friends away because we simply fail to love them well. We become selfish and consumed with our own needs and issues and forget about the friends we love. Sadly, many good friends drift away from each other because one in the party becomes so consumed with her life that her vision becomes myopic. She refuses to see beyond the world of her comings and goings and in so doing, alienates close friends. She simply won't think about another's needs.

Since by nature mothers are women who give love to others, one might think that we would love our friends naturally and easily. The truth is, for many of us, loving friends well is really tough. It requires phone calls we're too tired to make and graciously eating casseroles that taste horrible. Loving friends extraordinarily means interrupting our work schedules when a friend is in crisis, speaking boldly in her defense even when we're angry with her, and being ready to step into her shoes if tragedy makes its way into her life and she for some reason can't function at her normal level. We will be there for her and her children because that's what women who love other women do.

While women friends aren't habits, working hard at friendship with them *is* a habit. Women friends are vital because they help us become or stay emotionally more stable. They lift us out of despair, they make us laugh when we want to sob, they force us to keep living when we don't want to. Friends make our hearts shake like snow globes filled with thousands of different feelings. And when they shake, new feelings land in new places. We are open to trying different behaviors, learning to trust and to love when everything in our person tells us, "Don't you dare." Sometimes our friends push (maybe even yank) and other times they merely give us a nudge. They help us stay on the right track when we want to run away, they help us forgive when we want to take revenge, and they love us when we feel that everyone around us has left.

Perhaps it is the comfort of friendships that allows us to learn so well. When we are free to show our swollen eyes after crying for days, or invite a best friend to a ceremony where we receive an award that she has never received but we know she is as thrilled as we are, we relax in the confidence of the love and we can be completely who we are. I believe that it is just this level of comfort that gives us the nerve to face ourselves and change. With the security of a friend, we can examine our deep fears, critically assess how well we love our families, wrestle with financial issues, and figure out whether or not we believe in heaven or God or Buddha. The deep mystery of friendship is its intense security, which accepts us exactly as we are and at the same time yearns for us to change, to improve and live a better life. And that is exactly what establishing healthier habits is all about.

||||||||||||||||||||||||||||||||||||||||||||||||||||||||||||||||||||||||||||||||||||||||||||||||||||||

Value and Practice Faith

WHY MOTHERS NEED FAITH—AND WHY IT ISN'T ALWAYS EASY

I have a confession. Faith is a struggle for me. Whether it's putting faith in a pilot to carry my daughter safely to Indonesia, asking God to comfort my dad in the deep night hours as he lies alone in his bed at the nursing home, or even counting on myself to deliver a good lecture, faith is just tough. Having an adult daughter live halfway around the world, where I can't comfort her when she's sick, and watching my lovely father lose his mind before my very eyes have challenged my personal faith dearly. Watching them struggle has been very painful.

I think that the toughest part about faith is that it fundamentally requires a lack of control. We need to put our faith in someone else because we are unable to control life. We can't protect the people we love through sheer will. We feel inadequate, because we are. And I, along with many of you, don't like feeling inadequate. It isn't a pride issue as much as it is an emotional one. I want to be able to do everything necessary to ensure the health and happiness of my loved ones, but I simply can't.

There are two levels of faith that are important for us mothers. First, we must learn to put some faith in other people. This is really hard, because at times friends and family members have let us down. We have trusted them to come through for us. Sometimes they do and sometimes they don't. And many times they fail to come through for us not because they don't want to, but simply because they are limited, too. Even the most faithful, loving friends or family members can let us down because they are human. The second level of faith is quite serious. That is faith in God. We can't live without this. Many try, but when our days draw shorter and our bodies wilt, the existence of God is an issue that everyone must face in one way or another.

Many of us grapple with God's existence when we are young, and this is good. Some of us shy away and ignore our spiritual dimension for years because it makes us uncomfortable. But I believe that the sooner we find answers to our spiritual lives, the healthier we will be, because we are fundamentally spiritual beings.

Some mothers put their faith in the Judeo-Christian God, some in saints, some in Buddha, some in Allah, and some more existentially rely on the universe. Even atheists put their faith into something, even if it's just their own ability to reason. Atheists reject an external being and are left trusting themselves and the rules of life that their minds rationalize. Some accept certain moral codes, some accept science alone, but all of these atheist beliefs rely on things born from human knowledge. We all put our faith in something, and we do so every single day. So the real question isn't whether or not we should have faith. The more important question is what we should put our faith in, and why. And further, if faith is such an enormous part of our everyday experience, why don't we pay any attention to it? We hyperfocus on what we eat or don't eat, how much exercise we get or don't get, and what type of clothes we should wear. We intensely scrutinize our kids' reactions, needs, and desires and yet we gloss over the most important aspect of their character—their spirituality. We do this, quite simply, because everyone else does this. It's part of American culture.

Then there's another force at work. We look and see "people of faith" and sometimes we recoil. I know that we are supposed to "know Christians by their love," as the old hymn goes, but at times that love can be hard to see. Gandhi woefully remarked that he would have followed Christianity if it hadn't been for Christians. Unfortunately, I know what Gandhi meant. There are Christians who have brought hundreds of thousands of believers closer to God. Billy Graham is a beautiful illustration of a man whose heart beat after God's own heart. But on the other end of the spectrum, there are Christians whose behaviors have made a mockery of the Christian faith. Some have looked like hypocrites and turned others away from the faith. And extremists, particularly in other countries, have killed in the name of Christianity. These things are tragic and I believe hurt the heart of God. Other religions can be just as difficult to accept. Some balk at Buddha because he is dead. Statues of Buddha remain but he never rose from the dead like Jesus did. While his teachings encourage peaceful living, enlightenment, and inner peace, it takes many years of difficult practice to get there, if it is even possible. Christians reject the teachings of the Muslim faith because they run counter to Christianity and, most importantly, because they themselves have been frightened.

We all feel quite confused, so we shelve our faith. Figuring out the nuances seems overwhelming and, quite honestly, a bit unimportant. Not only do we not want to get into arguments with friends and family, but we are busy. We are tired. Thinking about faith, we reason, can wait because we need to get supper on the table and our kids somewhere. We run and fret and work harder to get things done and at the end of the day, when we feel empty and exhausted, we wonder why. The reasons are clear and simple—we have not taken any time to nurture the deepest part of our beings—and yet even knowing this on a cognitive level, we can't seem to want to do it. Or at least we don't seem to know how. We are afraid that it will be taxing and that we will turn into a kind of person we'd rather not be—one of those preachy people we avoid in the supermarket aisles.

But we need to feed our faith. We need the deep stuff. Our souls are important to us and we need to be strong in all aspects of our character because we are mothers. And more importantly, we need it for ourselves. We deserve the good stuff. We need more than obsessions about our weight, money, clothes, jobs, schools our kids go to, and how much to spend on them at Christmas or Hanukkah. So let us put aside our fears and get to the business of faith. I've seen in the thousands of exhausted moms out there a woeful lack of attention to their deep selves, their spirituality. And I know that once we feed our faith, everything else in life gets better. Everything. In this chapter I'll show you just how to nourish your faith through a few simple steps, including learning how to think before you leap and to make informed choices about your faith; making faith personal; finding a faith community; and finding even deeper faith by serving others.

FAITH—START WITH THE SMALL STUFF

We have faith on two levels. The first, which I think of as "small faith," rests in people that we trust. We put faith in our husbands, our mothers, the teachers who give lessons to our kids at school. Whether we put our kindergartner on the bus and hand her over to the bus driver or shut the door of our adult child's car and trust in the mechanic who rotated his tires, we are much less in control every day than we can imagine. We need other people. We need friends to pick our kids up when we can't get home, and we need doctors to know exactly what antibiotic to give our sick babies. We are needy. We just don't like to see it.

We must recognize that we need other people and we must be wise about our faith. We must pay attention. The truth is, when it comes to the folks whom we trust with our kids, we do pay attention. Many of us have interviewed teachers and pediatricians. We apply sound reason to the decisions we make and when we finally decide to trust, we realize that even though we have done our homework, we are still taking a risk. The teacher may be brilliant, but have a bad temper. The pediatrician may be nice, but know nothing about the latest treatment for ADHD. We know that when we put our faith in someone to do the right thing for our kids, they may fail. So sometimes, instead of taking the risk and trusting but verifying, we decide to not trust at all.

There are those of us who won't put faith in others because we are just plain scared. Mothers with this problem resort to putting people off right up front. They can be edgy, curt, and a bit frightening to others. They're so frightened that others will let them down that they will keep their distance through their attitude. Many women are afraid to put faith in their husbands to make enough money, to help parent their kids well, or to treat them with respect. They convince themselves that they, as moms, can be enough for themselves and their kids. They pull back and wall themselves off into an isolated independence that may feel good at times but in the end doesn't work well for them. They try to live behind a glass wall of distrust and while they may appear competent, strong, and complete, they know that a life devoid of trust in anyone but themselves just doesn't work. Finally, there are those among us who turn the whole problem on its head. We put too much "faith" in people and they run our lives. We trust too much, and forget to use reason when trusting others. Friends, husbands, and boyfriends end up taking advantage of us because we avail ourselves of them far too easily. Usually this happens because we lack confidence in ourselves to make healthy, sound decisions. When we doubt what to do, we defer to others' wishes. Sometimes this works, but other times it doesn't. Regardless of the outcome, the important lesson is that we can trust but we must be wise and deliberate in doing so.

When we stop to ponder how much faith we place in loved ones every day, we can feel overwhelmed, even terrified. But we should never live in fear. We need. We all need something from others and we do so because we are needy from birth. The only difference between us and our children is that they are allowed to express their needs because they are still young. But just because we grow older doesn't mean that our needs diminish. They simply morph into other, more complex needs. Once we needed food and comfort during times when we were scared, but now we need more comfort with an added dimension of patience and understanding. The food thing we can do for ourselves. As children we needed to know that our fathers thought that we were amazing and our mothers loved us more than anything in the world. Some of us got that; some of us didn't. But the truth is, we still need to know that someone whom we love and admire thinks we are amazing. Need sits at the center of who we are and it never disappears. And where there is need in us, there must be faith because that need must be filled. Since we can't fill it ourselves, we must turn to someone else for help.

As mothers, we must examine our relationships and tease out the faith that we place in others. If we are to get better at this faith issue, we must be willing to look at the people we are trusting. Are they trustworthy or are they hurting us over and over? If they are trustworthy, can we expand our faith in them? We must appreciate them and care for them. We must be thankful and thank them, and forgive them if small mistakes are made. But if we are putting our faith in loved ones who are harming us, we must stop. Many don't deserve our trust. If friends take advantage repeatedly and we return for more, we must take a break from the friendship. If we trust our kids to do certain things and they break that trust over and over, we know that they aren't trustworthy yet, so we must take charge and stop putting faith in them for things that they cannot yet deliver.

I am convinced that more relationships are worthy of trust and faith than we think. The problem is, we tend to focus on the unhealthy relationships more than the healthy ones. It's the same dynamic that kids feel with their mothers. If kids have a good mother, they sometimes ignore her. Some kids are even rude or mean to their mothers. The reason for this stems from their comfort—kids feel that mothers have to love them. They have to always be there because in their minds, that's what moms do. So they take us for granted because many of us are the rocks in our homes. We are ever present. There are more single moms than single dads. Moms stay around. This is the same approach many of us have with our healthy relationships. We take them for granted and even become rude to those we love because we have so much confidence in them. Confidence is terrific, but we must also be more grateful.

FAITH FOR THE BIG STUFF

I'm not saying that faith in the small stuff is easy, but faith in someone more powerful and invisible than loved ones can be tougher. For me, it most certainly is. Relying on those who are close to us, whom we can see and touch, is hard enough, but trusting in One who is invisible seems terribly daunting. Trusting in God feels far more serious because it requires faith: faith that He exists and faith that He will hear our concerns. For mothers like me, who like to be in charge, this kind of faith doesn't come easily, but we must try.

Medical studies show that people who have faith in God live longer, enjoy life more, and have better health. They suffer less depression and raise healthier kids. There have been numerous studies done on the effects of prayer on women's health. There are studies on kids and the effects of faith on their lives and even how the faith and religious practices of their parents affect their physical and emotional health. But I'm not sure that medical studies on faith and its effects on us as mothers are convincing enough for most people. We want more proof. We want to know if it really helps and if God is really there, listening to our prayers, because this feels more important than clinical studies. And it feels far more personal.

So let's clarify a few things here. Faith is not a religion. Faith is a belief and it is a very personal one. Having certain beliefs about God leads to specific religious practices and those practices can be extremely beneficial to mothers. For Jews and Christians, for example, the Ten Commandments act as a road map for healthy living. I used to teach in Sunday school that the Ten Commandments were God's lessons on the "Ten Best Ways to Live." Kids could understand that God gave the commandments to His people so that their lives would be happier. Most religions teach monogamy, and celibacy until marriage. There are good reasons for this, particularly in today's culture. Kids having sex too young get really sick. They open themselves to greater risk of depression and disease, and I have written passionately on this subject for years.

But there are many other good reasons to have faith. There are times in our lives when we need to know a few very basic things. We need to know if God pays attention when we pray for our dying child to get better. We need to know if He is kind enough to spare our life if we have breast cancer and we need to know when we bury our parents if this life here on earth is all they get. We need to know.

The Bible teaches us that "faith is being sure of what we hope for and certain of what we do not see." I like that. This makes sense to me. Faith and hope are connected here. Faith implies a certainty, and yet intrinsic in the word *faith* is an uncertainty. I like this passage because the writer seems to know that. He knows that when we have faith in God, we feel uncertain, and so he addresses it. We're going to feel uncertain, but go ahead and have faith anyway.

"Being sure" is a good thing. The passage above alludes to being sure of what we hope for. What do most of us moms hope for? In very general terms, we hope that life will ultimately turn out well for us and for our kids. We hope that good really is around the next corner because life is tough. I have seen a lot of mothers in anguish, and have had my own share of tough situations, and I can honestly say that I am sure of what I hope for—that God is in charge and good will come. I've seen what faith has done for me, my patients, and my friends, and I'll tell you all about it later in this chapter.

We mothers need to be sure of some things, precisely because it is our nature to want certainty—for our kids, if not for ourselves. When it comes to areas of our lives that we have no control over, we need a place where we can turn to find certainty. That's why this passage helps us so much. Because it says that we can be certain of what we do not see. I take that as saying that we can be certain that God is real and that a spiritual dimension exists. It also helps us trust. If we choose to believe what it says, then we can put trust in the fact that God is there and that when we put our hope in Him, we won't be disappointed.

Faith gets tricky, though, because we know that everything we hope for doesn't come to pass. So the natural question is, is the writer of this passage loony? How can we be certain of things that we hope for when we know that there are things that we hope for that aren't going to happen? That simply doesn't make sense. So we must dig a bit deeper. Now, I am not claiming to be a theologian. I'm just examining a few words about faith. Could it be that we become disappointed because we hope for the wrong things? That is the only answer I can come up with.

If we are told that we can be certain that we'll get what we need, then maybe our needs are grander than we think. Maybe when we hope for our kids to get well, what we also hope for is that if they don't get well, we'll be able to endure life without them. Maybe the writer knows that what we really need is the hope for comfort. We need more hope—for comfort, peace, and certainty that a good God is ultimately in control when really bad stuff happens.

If having faith means believing deep in our hearts that having hope is safe and that everything will ultimately be okay, then we can do that. We can allow our hearts to trust that God will come through for us. We can choose not to trust, but what then? Our alternative is to believe that hope is ridiculous and nothing will right itself. I say no thanks to that.

The second part of the passage says that faith is being "certain of what we do not see." Perhaps I'm wrong, but I think that this is easier for all of us mothers. We grasp that there could be a spiritual world we do not see. Our sense of the spiritual is intuitive. In our nature is an imbedded knowledge that there is more to life than we can see. Look at bugs. They crawl on the surface of ponds looking and searching for something to eat. Sure, bugs are small, but they all sense a greater purpose in life, even though they don't know it! I'm not declaring that bugs have a soul, but watching them certainly makes one wonder about something greater than meets the eye, working in all things, causing them to do remarkable things. If this is true for bugs, how much greater is it for humans, all of whom have souls?

FAITH IS NOT RELIGION

Some people who call themselves religious will not like to hear this, but being religious doesn't require faith. It requires discipline. Anyone can learn rules and will herself to adhere to them — or at least try to adhere to them. With all due respect to those who have committed their lives to teaching religion and theology to their followers: Theology, biblical knowledge, catechism, and apologetics are extremely important but they are only one part of the equation of faith. We must simply recognize at the outset that religion and faith are not inextricably linked and, in fact, the two can be quite separate.

Religion is between man and man but faith exists between God and human beings. Certainly God created rules for men and women, but following rules could never substitute for a vibrant faith. Religion isn't always personal, but faith always is. We can talk about what faith is and how it should be enacted, but when the day is done, only the believer knows the true state of her faith. It cannot be used to show off, nor can it be used to compete with another. It is too raw, too much of a secret. I suppose that's what I find so attractive about it.

Religion is about adopting a set of beliefs about God, but faith is a decision to *receive* something from Him. Much as children get love, affection, and sustenance from their parents, mothers forget that they are children, too. We give and give, but faith requires us to be still and "get from God."

Interestingly, research shows that mothers who are poor have higher levels of "religiosity" than their wealthier counterparts.[*] But wealthier women participate more in religious services. This make sense. Women who are struggling with finances or relationship problems have a felt need. Pain causes them to dig down and find what will help alleviate their hurt or help them cope; women who have more financial stability don't

[*]Susan Crawford Sullivan and Theda Skocpol, "Faith and Poverty: Personal Religiosity and Organized Religion in the Lives of Low-Income Urban Mothers" (Ph.D. diss., Harvard University, 2005).

experience a palpable need, yet they may be part of a social group where everyone attends church services regularly. The irony is that every mother has deep needs that she cannot fill alone. We are all very dependent beings but the difference for wealthier women can be that they are blinded to the need by material comfort. Money acts as a false buffer. Poverty acts as a stressor that can bring good into women's lives.

Some mothers I have spoken with have balked at having faith in God, because they perceive it as just one more thing to do in order to be a nice person. They approach the whole notion of faith as a work plan, a series of exercises that will change their personalities, the way they live, or even their identity. Real faith, however, is about opening ourselves to receive love and goodness from God, not simply adhering to a large list of rules. We must never abandon faith because we approach it incorrectly; rather we must change our approach. God was there before we were, simply waiting for us to respond to Him. Our response to believe that God is there is the first act of faith.

In our moments of clarity, when we mothers attempt to untangle what in our lives is good and what is bad, or when we try to find answers to the biggest questions in our lives—questions like Does my life have value in any way? or What is the best thing that I can leave my children?— we see something profoundly true. At the beginning of our lives and at the end, we are alone. At least, we appear to be alone. If, however, faith rests in our hearts at the beginning and at the end, we are not alone. Not at all. God is there. That truth is perhaps the greatest truth of all regarding faith.

WHEN RACHEL TAUGHT ME HOW SIMPLE FAITH CAN BE

Sometimes we avoid faith not because it is complex or requires a willingness to unravel intricate mysteries or theologies. We avoid faith because it is too simple for us. If God exists, then we must trust that He has some involvement in our lives; otherwise faith would be a waste of time. Faith is about seeing the connection between God and us and trying it out. That's it. It is about knowing that God is there somewhere, and that He wants us, for some mysterious reason, to communicate, love, and try to trust Him. The problem with this paradigm is that trust for many of us mothers is really, really hard. We'd rather struggle through problems on our own, find solutions, and then implement those solutions. Trust demands that we recruit the help of another to get the job done. But how can we get help from an invisible God? There's the real rub—that we can't see God. If we could look into His eyes or hear a voice (wouldn't that be frightening?), then we could know, really know that we can trust Him because we would know that He is real. But if we knew for sure that He was real, we wouldn't need faith. And this feels very confusing. But Rachel, a twenty-four-year-old patient whom I had cared for since birth, helped me understand, as sometimes only a young person can.

Rachel and I were talking about God once and she remarked that she had been trying to figure out what God wanted her to do with her life. She was in her early twenties and wanted to excel in her career. She was at a particular juncture in her career as an interior designer where going in one direction or the other felt strenuous and serious. If she chose to work with company A, she would restore low-income housing projects, but if she chose company B, she would design high-end homes and hotels. She would still be a designer, but her lifestyle would be very different. What if she took the wrong path? As she asked me my opinion, I completely understood her anxiety, since I felt as though I had been in the very same situations myself as my career was developing. Since I was quite close to the young lady, I felt myself starting to feel more anxious as our conversation went on. I very much wanted her to succeed in her career.

As a matter of fact, I bet that she was sorry she asked for my help. I believe that the growing concern written all over my face made her feel less confident than ever. My response magnified the seriousness of her decisions. Finally, she looked at me and said, "This is what I'll do. I will spend about one week asking God to choose which job is the best choice for me. Then, whichever job I'm offered first, I'll take."

I gulped. "Oh, that's a good idea," I said. What I really wanted to blurt was "No, no, no! Wait a minute. That's a good idea in theory, but what if God doesn't tell the people He really wants to offer you the job to call you? Or maybe you need to pray the rosary for three weeks? Or maybe there's another kind of prayer you need to pray? Life's not just this simple. It requires thought, study, hard work, phone calls, letters, and discussion. You can't just pray for a week and expect God to answer like that." But I didn't say anything.

Still, she must have seen my concern, because she assured me. "I'm not going to do anything stupid. I've worked incredibly hard. My grades are great. And I guess I just kind of want to see if this whole thing about asking God to help really works. And I suppose that if I take the first job and I got this whole faith thing wrong, God will turn me around. Otherwise, how will I ever know if faith and God are real?"

Indeed, how would she? Her answer was too simple. It seemed too easy to me. She would ask and believe that God would give her an answer. Then, by faith, she would accept that answer and move forward. But there had to be more to it.

This conversation took place about three years ago and Rachel did exactly what she said. She was offered both jobs and took the first one offered, working in the housing projects. I was concerned that she wouldn't get as much opportunity to advance her career, but after one year there, she received a promotion. She now has a higher position than she likely would have if she had taken the job designing high-end condominiums and hotels. And the very wonderful thing is, Rachel loves her job and the whole experience has made her faith stronger. That, she said, was truly invaluable.

Rachel's story changed me. I realized that I had made faith too complicated and at times a bit too heady. Sure, I loved to read the scriptures, peruse the writings of the mystics and great biblical scholars, but when it came to trusting in God, I did so with a "but" behind it. I always wanted to stay in control. But Rachel didn't. She took Him at His word and related to Him in a childlike fashion that was not only refreshing but real. I saw in her relationship with God something that I wanted, and since

hearing her story, I have learned to trust God in a simpler, less complicated fashion. It is from this perspective that I write today.

Could it be that every day presents us with opportunities to rely on
God in ways that we don't even see? Certainly, if we live like Rachel does.
Each one of us has screamed at our kids and needed someone to help bail
us out. We have worried about which school to send our kids to, which
doctor to trust with our child's depression or ADHD. We worry that we
aren't good enough at being patient, or that our kids will resent us because we work too much or because we smother them to death. Mostly
we stew about our kids and whether we are keeping them on the very
best track to help them turn out well.

What if we decided that we were going to parent with a very simple
faith? What would happen if we chose to ask God to help us with our
kids? Not just by protecting them from the big stuff (drunk drivers and
rapists). What if we even brought the small stuff forward? Sure, it sounds
trite, even a bit childlike, but why not? Why shouldn't we mothers ask
God to find our kids a new friend, make his teacher more understanding,
or even help him learn to like tuba lessons?

Could it be that God is involved, that He does see what our kids do all
day long, and that if He really is omniscient, He can see what they're
going to be like when they grow up? Just as someone can stand on the top
of the Empire State Building and watch a VW Bug course through traffic
and make it to the Brooklyn Bridge, God can see where our kids are turning in a good direction or a bad direction and really help do something
about it. And if we don't get the answer right away, is He teaching us a
larger lesson? That's where trust comes in again.

I have seen extraordinary women with faith who have changed their
kids' lives. I have seen mothers living with intolerable pain (such as a sick
child) learn to thrive and even smile because somewhere in their innermost being they made a simple leap—to believe that God would help. I
have seen mothers who decided to give God a chance and ended up very
glad that they did.

HOW OLIVIA LEARNED THAT FAITH NEEDS HIKING BOOTS

As I've gotten older, I've learned to be painfully pragmatic. I don't like to waste my time and I certainly don't relish wasting others' time. That's why I don't accept the notion of faith as an intellectual exercise or another idea meant to quell our curiosity. And faith isn't about being passive, sitting around waiting for God to magically fix things for you. It's about listening, and then it's about taking action. Faith is more a verb than it is a noun. It doesn't work unless you flex its muscles. Faith means doing something. It requires, as we saw with Rachel, action, which boots us from a point of complacency to a place of work. Faith means that we say things that we'd rather not say, that we act on another's behalf when every part of our being doesn't want to act. Faith requires sweat on many levels. First, it requires that we seek God's direction. This is tricky, particularly when we're not quite sure what God's answers sound like or even if He will answer at all. Then, once we believe that we have received an answer, faith requires doing something about the answer. We can't sit still once we know in our gut that we need to press forward and do something.

While my kids were growing up I often told them that life is a series of hard phone conversations. There are many that must be made and every one of us knows the feeling, which gnaws at our gut when we need to pick up the phone but are trying to muster the courage. Faith is very much like that feeling. We can sit and wait. And we can wait as long as we like. I think that God is pretty patient. But at some point we must move our feet. That's just the way faith works.

I need to tell you about a mother who moved her feet across a few oceans. I met Olivia when she and her family were visiting the United States on furlough from their mission work several years ago. She and her husband, Avi, were visiting local communities and churches, telling about their life overseas. When Olivia was pregnant with her first son, she and Avi decided to take one last trip to Avi's religious homeland. (Olivia is

Christian; Avi is Jewish.) They knew that travel would be hard after their son was born, so they decided to go to Israel a few months before her due date. For Avi, the trip was a personal pilgrimage. Before they went, each of them had a strong faith in God.

But when they arrived, something extraordinary happened to Olivia. One night in a dream, she remembers, God said something to her. She can't remember the exact words, but she knew when she awoke the next morning that God wanted her and Avi to stay in Israel for the birth of their son.

"I wanted to go to Israel," she told me, "but honestly, I went more for Avi's sake than my own. I was uncomfortable, I knew that we were putting ourselves in harm's way because of the political unrest, and quite honestly, I could have been talked into staying home.

"A few days after we arrived in Jerusalem, I had an incredible dream that convinced me we needed to stay in Israel until the baby was born. I didn't tell Avi about it because I thought that he would think I was crazy. A few more days went by and the sense that we needed to stay kept growing in me. I was uncomfortable with it. One afternoon, a sense swept over me about making sure that our son was born in Israel and it was something so powerful that I couldn't ignore it. I had to talk to Avi."

"Where did you think that the feeling was coming from?" I asked.

"I wasn't sure. I had always believed in God, and my husband and I spend a lot of time exploring Jewish traditions and studying the Old and New Testaments. God has always been a vibrant part of our lives, but we're pretty reserved people. At least, we always were when we lived in the States.

"So when these feelings came over me, I assumed that it was God. I told Avi that I felt that God wanted us to stay in Israel longer—at least through our son's birth—but I didn't know why. I was sure that Avi was going to look at me as though I'd dyed my hair blue, but he didn't. He just stared at me. Then, incredibly, he said to me, 'I think that you might be right. I don't have a clue why, but I believe you.'"

I had to ask, "Was he getting any kind of premonition? Any compulsions?"

"Oh no," she said. "He just seemed to understand that I wasn't making this all up. A few days later, a very peculiar thing happened. A woman we met in our travels told us, fairly randomly, that she was in financial trouble. She had an apartment that she was renting and her tenant had to leave suddenly. Without the income, she didn't know how she was going to make it for the next few months. She wondered if we knew of anyone who needed housing right away. But she could only guarantee a lease for four months, one month after our son was supposed to be born. Can you believe that?

"We were stunned. Avi and I looked at each other, and although we were supposed to leave the country in one week, we told the woman that we would rent her place. We would commit to four months, no more. I couldn't believe the words that were coming out of my mouth. I know that Avi couldn't believe it, either. But somehow, we knew that we were right. We knew that this was what we were supposed to be doing."

"What about your jobs back in California? What on earth did you tell your employers?" I asked.

"That too was a mystery. My work (I worked for a small clothing manufacturer) said that they were prepared for me to be off for maternity leave, so they took it better than Avi's. He had to quit his job in financial investments and it wasn't pretty. He took it pretty hard. When he quit, he knew that he would never be able to go back to work for his company. Sometimes I still can't believe we did what we did. He had a fabulous job. I think that if things didn't happen so quickly we might not have had the nerve to let go. We would have overthought things. Overrationalized, and we would have missed out on so much!"

Avi and Olivia stayed in a small town outside of Jerusalem, and their son was born. Shortly before he was born, Avi was offered a job teaching at a small school for children who had been ravaged by the effects of war. His work is extremely risky because he has built a mission where he lives, taking in children and sometimes adults who are under political attack. It's a difficult job, but he loves it. As Olivia spoke, she exuded a calm, which felt foreign to me. She described how she and her husband (and now two children) worked together to help others pick up the pieces of their war-torn lives. She told them that God would help them and she showed them His love by starting down that path with them. Avi and Olivia worked around the clock, if necessary, to help the people that God brought their way. And they absolutely loved what they were doing. In a two-bedroom flat, they loved life.

When Olivia described her joy of life in Israel, I believed her. She had no reason to lie to me and, more importantly, I could see that her days were filled with something mystical (I want to call it magical, but that cheapens it). When I heard that in her voice, I felt jealous. I wanted what she had, but I didn't want to have to go to Israel, live in a small home, and put my kids' lives at risk in order to get it. I wanted her level of contentment and I realized that it came because first she had faith. She felt the prompting, the spiritual movement deep inside her, and when she chose to follow that, her life took a sharp turn. Faith kept her where she was and, at the time of our interview nine months before this writing, Olivia said that she and Avi had no intention of leaving. Life was far too full.

While having faith in God doesn't mean that we'll all go to a foreign land, give up our jobs, and bear children in hospitals where physicians can't speak our language, faith does change us. Olivia heard God and she moved her feet. Her husband believed her and, I suppose in his own way, he must have heard God as well. Perhaps he didn't have a dream, but clearly, God had done something in Avi's innermost sensibilities in order for him to be open to leaving his job, his country, and his extended family. And the more they looked to God to provide answers for the next day or week, the more that wonderful opportunities emerged. Avi found reassurance at every step of their life change, such as when they met the woman with an apartment to rent.

"Innumerable times, things would happen just at the right moment. When we weren't sure what to do next, something would happen," Olivia said. "Avi was offered the teaching position when we were sure that we had misunderstood and made a huge mistake. I had asked God that our kids could stay in the safest neighborhood possible and after a few weeks, one family sold their home and we snatched it up before it ever went up for sale. Those kinds of things happened routinely," Olivia said. "Once I really began to anticipate them, I called them 'kisses on the cheek from God.'"

FOUR WAYS TO MAKE THE HABIT STICK

#1: Think before you leap

While faith is profoundly emotional, acquiring and keeping faith cannot be sustained by emotions. It must make sense to us. And it must be grounded in truth that resonates with our common sense and our intellect. Most of us can be emotionally moved to believe many things that seem impossible, but sometimes beliefs can't be sustained because the beliefs aren't grounded in anything that feels reasonable. Real faith requires that we have a knowledge about who we put our faith in and what good it does for us.

We hear the term *blind faith,* but most mothers are far too pragmatic for that. We need to know what we're doing and what we're getting into and that's a good thing. We don't want to be fools and we don't need another chore to add to our list of rules that we need to follow. Each of us has a burning desire to understand the deeper things in life. The only way to come to understand, rather than simply feel, is to recruit our intellect. Still, others don't think about faith at all. They just jump in—to any kind of faith. Sadly, I've seen smart women involved in very unhealthy cults.

When we choose to pursue faith, we must keep our eyes and minds wide open, but we must keep our hearts open as well. We must find the balance between learning, reading, and seeking answers on the one hand and following answers that we feel God is giving us on the other. We should seek and then when God answers, find what He gives.

So where do we start? Read. And then read more. There are countless resources and I recommend starting with the real thing. Read the Bible. If you find it intimidating, Eugene Peterson has rendered the Old and New Testaments in everyday language in a lovely work called *The Message*. If you are Jewish, read the Torah. Go to the learned in your community whom you admire and ask for readable materials that will help you figure out the tenets of the faith. I know that this sounds like a lot, but really, it can be done in little bites—a few minutes each week. Bookstores are filled with "devotionals" that have short lessons you can read while waiting in the dentist's office.

I know that faith requires a leap. Once we decide to put our trust in God, we choose to do something that feels blind and irrational, but isn't. If what we come to believe about our faith is real, then it must stand the test of questioning and critical reasoning. We mothers have too much to lose if we throw our valuable energy and emotions into another thing that will only disappoint. So question the material you read and question it again. If what you're reading is true, you will know it over time. The wonderful thing about truth is that it is hard to talk yourself out of it. I believe that we are all born with a deep ability to recognize truth when we happen on it. And when we come upon truth, we should accept it, not try to rationalize our way out of it.

#2: Make it personal

I have said that faith is not a religion. It is a deeply personal understanding and relationship that must be discovered and nurtured. The reason for this is that we mothers are personal people. We want relationships, communication, and a sense of deep exchange with others. In order for us to foster a faith like this, we must become involved. Reading and study are important, but we must also allow ourselves a certain openness and availability to God if faith is to be personal. Herein is where the exchange begins.

Prayer begins this communication. In the quiet of our rooms, the car, or in bed at 3 A.M., the conversation begins. It is us and God. We begin by asking questions or simply saying "hello." Sometimes we scream or cry; other times we simply ask if He is real or if, perhaps, we are sharing our innermost hopes with nothing but the cosmic void.

Then we wait. Much like the characters in the Old Testament, we wait to see what happens next. Will we feel something or will the night stay deadly quiet, or both? Here's where faith gets very personal. Over time, we pray again and again and tell God that we need to know if He is there or not. We're not looking for magic tricks, though some of us may need miracles, so we go ahead and ask. Then we wait again.

What we learn through the prayer and the waiting is the beginning of faith. Once we have started, we are involved. We have admitted that we will open ourselves to know God and His personality. Much like Viktor Frankl did during his internment at a Nazi concentration camp, we must learn to stay connected to God through prayer, attention, focus, and study of Him so that we will have a person, not just a set of rules, to hang on to. And why do we need to study the scriptures or teachings on them? Isn't that just adhering to a set of rules that seem to twist us in knots?

Here's the difference: Study of the scriptures or hearing sound teachings from priests, pastors, or trusted church leaders helps us understand the personality or character of God. Through prayer and study, we can find God's hand, or touch His face when we are desperate. When the kids scream for the fifth night in a row, when a husband cheats or when a parent dies, we need to instinctively slide into conversation for comfort and help. If we haven't cultivated a prayer or meditation life with God, we will find ourselves at a loss over what to do. That's why it is important for us to get started, so that we'll be prepared when the tough stuff happens.

#3: Find community

A close friend of mine, a woman who is twenty years my senior, once told me that sustaining a vibrant faith all alone is impossible. She said that because faith is hard, it must be done with the help of others who believe as we do. Otherwise, she said, it will quickly burn out, just as an ember that flies from a fire onto a hearth will quickly grow cold. Those of us who are introverted, stubborn, and busy might disagree—at least until we try to have faith all alone. My friend was right. When life is good, getting along with God is easy. But when bad stuff happens, hanging on to our faith can be like holding on to a rope behind a speeding car: It frays and soon we lose contact.

So find a faith community that will help you hold on. Just as we need friends to fill in the gaps, we need women, men, and other mothers who will buoy us and remind us of what we understood to be real about God when we weren't hurting as deeply. When our prayers have dried up, they will pray for us. When we refuse to believe that God is real, they won't beat us over the head with theology; they will simply love us and keep us moving forward because they are going in the same direction we are.

Others in a faith community teach us about the character of God. As believers who long to adopt His character and follow His directives, they will reflect who He is. The love that God feels for them will move into them and then we who sit in the pews next to them or who pray beside them will mysteriously soak in some of His love. I can't explain it, but I have seen it happen again and again. We may chuckle at the little old lady with blue hair in a wooden pew or the teenager with pink hair down the aisle, but we mustn't be so pretentious; for there in the two may be the heart of God waiting to extend us love. In a faith community, each of us learns more about God, people, humility, and acceptance than anywhere else on the planet. Sure, friends in faith communities bring frustration and disappointment, but if we stay long enough and give others in the community a chance, we will find that the blessings we receive far out-weigh the disappointments.

#4: Serve

This is probably the last word an exhausted mother wants to hear, but it is important. Over our lifetime, the only way we will come to understand the value of another human being is by serving him. Giving brings about humility and humility draws us closer to God. In a world that champions diversity, serving should be paramount because in the action of serving, we say to another, you deserve better than what you have at this moment. Nothing elevates the sense of worth to another like being served. And more importantly, nothing grows and sustains the faith of a mother more than reaching beyond her own needs and caring for the needs of others.

So how do we learn to serve in a healthy manner when we feel that all we do is meet the needs of others? First of all, serving doesn't always mean meeting the desires of another person. If we are honest, most of our time as mothers is spent not meeting needs, but fulfilling desires of loved ones in our midst. This is entirely different from service. Real service means asking God what He would like us to do and then doing it. Sometimes, particularly when our children are young, the demands at home are too great to serve anywhere else and this is perfectly appropriate. As they mature, however, we may be freer to spend time working at a food pantry, a soup kitchen, a women's shelter, or a rehabilitation center. Certainly we can serve people in our lives wherever we are, but the service we extend to people whose lives are harsher than ours changes us in a different way. Sometimes we must push ourselves to leave the comfort in our world and step into another person's shoes. Working with those who are brokenhearted allows us to see God reflected in them more easily because there is less in their lives to cover His presence.

Let's face it, when we are at a good place in life, have a good job, happy kids, and a nice home, God gets ignored. But when life throws us a curve and hurt settles in, we need to be able to turn to our faith and let it connect us to God. Nothing gets us there quicker than performing service to His people. This is why faith and service are so linked and so important. Build your faith through service now, and reap the benefits later when you need it most.

||||||||||||||||||||||||||||||||||||||||||||||||||||||||||||||||||||||||||||||||||||||||||||||||||||||||

Say No to Competition

WHY WE COMPETE, AND WHAT IT DOES TO OUR RELATIONSHIPS

Twenty-some years ago, I was driving down the highway very early in the morning. I was a senior pediatric resident at Children's Hospital in Milwaukee, Wisconsin, and was trying to get to work early enough to check on the younger residents' patients before I started morning rounds. It was spring and I was pregnant with our second child. I was driving about 60 mph in a 65 mph zone when I saw, with my peripheral vision, my girlfriend and colleague trying to pass me in the left-hand lane on her way to make rounds. Before a conscious thought was registered, my right foot reacted and my accelerator pedal pressed toward the floor. My car went from 60 to 65 mph. I didn't want her to pass me. No sooner had I accelerated than she sped up to 68. Then I moved to 70 and she to 75. Since it was probably only 6 A.M., we were lucky enough not to be stopped by the police.

The most peculiar part of the exchange is that neither of us would acknowledge the other's presence. Each time I sped up, I pretended not to notice that she was trying to pass me. And she did the same to me. We women are clever at pretending not to notice the most obviously ridiculous things. After nine miles of cat and mouse, we flew our cars into the parking garage, hustled through the emergency room (still not acknowledging that we were racing), and made it to our respective hospital floors. I had to show her and myself that I was more on top of my game than she was, and vice versa.

After all these years, neither of us will admit what we did (at least to each other). How ridiculous can two grown women be? Very ridiculous, because that is what competition brings out in us. Competition has always been part of my life. I grew up outside of Boston, attended private schools (which I loved), and in the fifth grade began worrying about which prep school I was going to get into, because I was worried about getting into a good college. But I was one of the lucky ones. My parents never pushed me or worried about my prep school or college choice. They were from the Midwest and enjoyed an enviably relaxed approach to family and life. Still, I imbibed the competitive juices that flowed all around me.

This is the frenetic mother culture in which you and I live. The voice tells us that we must do *something*. Improve our kids, don't let them miss out. Make them more, get them more, and watch them more. Be a better mom, be a more successful mom, do something every day to improve something about them and us because—that's what we are supposed to do. Our competitive nature is important to contain because it affects how we spend our money, how we love, whether we can simplify our lives, how we practice our faith, and much more. If we are to get other very important areas of our lives healthy, we must tackle this one. But for most of us mothers, the train of competition is seductive and its voice is sweet.

We want to stop competing, but we are scared to death. In our hearts we long to just simply *be*. We know that life is more than producing and competing and we wonder, Why can't we simply live differently? What would happen if we pulled back, slowed down, and rested for a while? Would we be okay?

We want our best friend to jump first. And if she won't, we'll take on any mother. If she—the one who goes first—survives, then maybe, maybe we'll try it. We are frightened because climbing down from the train feels like we are being terrible mothers. As we'll discuss in detail later, in the simplicity chapter, getting off the train requires that we *not* do some things. Refuse to sign our daughter up for one more dance class? Opt to keep our son off the travel hockey team so that he can spend weekends with his dad hunting deer? (I live in northern Michigan.) If we forgo sending Susie to oboe camp in the summer and take walks on the beach, make peanut butter cookies at midnight, and paint the family room all summer, aren't we wasting a colossal amount of time? We mothers want to be productive, not wasteful.

We need to garner some chutzpah and stop. The problem for us is that, as young girls, we learn that competition is good. Being competitive professionally can be good, as long as healthy boundaries are maintained. But when it comes to being competitive in relationships as mothers, we always lose. Always.

The odd highway exchange between my girlfriend and me so many years ago was between two professionals and it looked pretty silly. What were we trying to prove, and to whom? But aside from competing as professionals, I can tell you that that type of interchange hurt our friendship. She had kids and I had kids and I am embarrassed to admit that out of my own insecurity, I put one of my children with whom I was pregnant at great risk by my speeding.

In this chapter, I'll talk about how competition and jealousy corrode friendships, and at the end of the chapter show you how to conquer competition by recognizing the problem, heading competition off at the pass, giving your friends verbal applause, focusing on fullness instead of emptiness, and being deliberate in kindness.

WE ALL DO IT

Every one of us mothers competes with other mothers in some way. The biggest difficulty with the game is that it is usually disguised and deeply hidden from even our own sight. And most of us would never admit that we do it. But if we really want to live healthier, happier lives, we've got to call ourselves on it. We compete not just because it is the "nature" of some of us, but also because we live in a world that coaxes us to compete with one another. Marketing works because it convinces us that someone has something we need. It tells us that if we had what another person has, we would be happier, so we'd better buy her product. We see magazines filled with beautiful celebrities who live the good life and we want a part of what they have. We read gossip columns that breed a spirit of competition because they are founded on the "let's dish the dirt on so-and-so" mentality. We love to read them because they make us temporarily feel good about the fact that we are not in the poor celebrity's situation. When the beautiful people are lowered (and we don't feel we have to compete) then we feel better about our own lives.

We mothers compete in very insidious ways. Examine the feelings you have about mothers you know, and they are probably your friends, and see if you don't happen upon just a bit of jealousy when thinking about them. Think about the thoughts that run through our minds when we first meet another mom. We say hello and subconsciously size her up. We look at her appearance and we make very quick judgments in our minds about it. If she's out of shape or overweight, we may feel better about ourselves. But if she has a lovely figure, we feel a twinge of envy. We do this not because we're bad people, but because that's what we're trained to do—size women up. We do it daily through the media and magazines. Then we politely ask about her life: where she lives, how many kids she has, if she is employed or not. Again, we make instantaneous decisions in our minds. If she has the kind of job we've always wanted but didn't pursue because we stayed home with our kids, we feel jealous. Then we do something worse—we criticize her for not being as good a mom as we, because we chose to stay home.

Or let's flip the scenario. Perhaps we're a full-time employed mother who drops her kids at day care at the beginning of the day and picks them up at dinnertime. We meet a mother who stays home full-time and we quickly rationalize why we work and why we can be better mothers because we do. But it's a losing game, no matter which side you're on. Competition leads nowhere good. I constantly hear working mothers criticizing stay-at-home mothers and stay-at-home mothers criticizing employed mothers. Neither party does it because they feel good about their own lives; rather each does it because of an insecurity resting just below the surface.

This is hard stuff to swallow, but confronting this insecurity is at the root of living a happier, saner, more content life. Breaking the habit of competing helps break many other important habits in areas we're examining: money issues, living more simply, loving others better, improving friendships. If we can't get our drive to compete under control, we will have great difficulty getting the other habits under control as well.

If you wonder if this is a problem for you, examine your feelings about other women friends. If you find criticism, you find competition. If you sense envy or jealousy, it is there again—the sense that she has something you don't and therefore enjoys a better life. Competing with other mothers does three things to us: It ignites jealousy, keeps us in a constant state of restlessness with ourselves, and changes our relationships. Let's tease each of these apart.

JEALOUSY

Let's assume that you meet a mother who has just moved into town. She is your age, has four children, and stays at home with them. She is friendly, outgoing, and vivacious. Her kids are well mannered and two of them are in the same class as your child. Picture her in your mind's eye. You meet her and something in you makes judgments about her. This is natural, because part of you wants to know what makes her tick, what her history is. Perhaps you are simply curious. You find many things about her that make her attractive and subconsciously you begin to compare your life with hers. She has four kids, you have three. Her kids are in the slow reading group, yours are in the accelerated group. She stays home with her children, you work full-time. You make a few lists in your mind, because that's what we do. And we do it so fast that we don't even know when we're doing it.

Then you make decisions about what you see on the list. What is she better at, what are you better at? She may be prettier. She may be more physically fit than you. Her kids may be more accomplished in sports or music. Suddenly you think you should be fitter. Maybe your daughter should play the cello. Because, after all, we live in a competitive world and you want your kids to have every advantage when it comes to getting into college. Suddenly you are prompted to do something—improve your life or your kids' lives because of meeting her. Now you are competing. She has something that you feel you should have or that you want. Her kids have something that you want your kids to have. Since she has it and you don't, you feel a bit of jealousy.

Maybe she has a nicer home and kids who are more active (you forget about the fact that your kids read better than hers) and you feel inadequate. Something in your life is lacking. If you weren't lacking, you reason subconsciously, then you wouldn't feel a need to have what she has. In short, you feel insecure because you lack something. Jealousy flows from insecurity—feeling that you lack something that another mother has.

Jealousy is an enormously corrosive feeling. It makes us feel bad about ourselves. We have even given it a color, green (is anyone's favorite color green?), which is often associated with sickness, even vomit. Jealousy can be paralyzing because beneath it is a sense of self-deprecation and neediness. And jealousy is usually accompanied by obsessiveness. When we want what another person has, we can become fixated on getting it or on how much better we would feel if we had it. The more we wish that we had it, the more we feel that we need it. All of us have seen jealousy in action. We don't have to examine it deeply to understand how corrosive it is. We know that it makes us feel sick and brings chaos into our lives. Jealousy tangles our thinking and makes us do outrageous things, even hurt other people. But here's the great news: Jealousy only has power when it goes unrecognized and unchallenged. Once we acknowledge our jealousy and admit it to ourselves or a close friend, we diffuse the power that it has. And when we confront jealousy and turn it on its head, it can have a dramatic impact on the people around us.

COMPETITION TURNS US AGAINST OURSELVES

If we feel a competitive spirit erupt when we are with a girlfriend, jealousy appears. Then something deeper and more insidious sets in. We feel that we must improve or change something so that we are more like the person we are jealous of. She has something that makes her life better than ours and we feel that if we got that something, ours would be better, too.

Once the sense of need sets in, an accompanying desperation follows. The more we need it, the more desperate we are to have it. And once we become consumed with having it, we live with an angst that we must find it. This causes two more problems. First, when we focus on getting what someone else has, even if it is very small, we aren't able to focus on what we do have. We can't be appreciative or grateful. And we feel constantly empty, not full. This in itself feels terrible. Second, being consumed with getting what another woman has leads us to believe that she knows a secret that we don't. Why? Because jealousy prohibits us from feeling that pure luck could have been with her. "She must have done something to deserve it or she must have worked harder to acquire it." Then we hotly pursue her secret, which will reveal what we must do to have what she has.

When we sit back and see the dynamics at play, we can also appreciate the ridiculousness of our jealousy. Sadly, however, most of us can't see this because we can't recognize jealousy when it stares us in the face. It snakes its way into even our most benign feelings and wraps its fingers quickly around our most fleeting thoughts. The peculiar part of this is that it all exists within our own minds. Usually when we are jealous and want something that we don't have, it's because we are imagining what life would be like if we had the thing, but that vision isn't necessarily the truth. So, in a real sense, all of the jealousy remains a mind-set. We believe our imaginary thoughts, latch onto them, and feel insecure, determined to find the other's secrets in order to find her treasure and ultimately feel less inadequate. This sounds like an exaggeration, but this is precisely what happens inside each of us when we feel the pangs of jealousy. One can see that, in a sense, we turn on ourselves. Once we feel we are lacking, we begin to dislike who we are, which leaves us even more needy and wanting, and the cycle begins again. Therein lies the trap, and it's almost impossible to get out.

COMPETITION INHIBITS GOOD RELATIONSHIPS

It's obvious that when we are competitive with another, we have less than wonderful feelings toward her. We feel inadequate and we perceive her as more adequate. She has the upper hand, if you will. She moves up in our minds, we move down. When this inequality exists, we can no longer relate to her in a healthy fashion. We have pushed her to arm's length because she has become a small enemy. We will compare ourselves and one of us will emerge the winner and one the loser. Since we began the competition in our mind, we will emerge the loser. For all she knows, she isn't even in the game. She has no idea that she has what we want—only we know that.

As competitors guard themselves from friends with whom we compete because life is safer this way. We must stay guarded so that the other woman will not garner any advantage, because then the distance between her excellence and our miserable state would only be greater. So we keep her at bay and we seal a part of ourselves off from her so that we can stay in the game. We withhold personal information. We refuse to grow too close, because we fear that she may see more inadequacy and then our desire to compete would escalate. In a very peculiar way, we refuse to be equals with her. If she has more and we have less, then we have changed the playing field. We are not equals any longer and the great irony is that equality is exactly what our competitiveness is all about. We want what she has so that we can be equal. But when we compete, we declare inequality—we are less than she.

Aristotle taught that when two people are in an equal relationship (such as two mothers), envy naturally grows from it. It is our nature, he seems to say, that prevents us from accepting each other precisely how we are. And the truth is, it is very hard. It is difficult to accept loved ones for who they are, but it is even harder to accept ourselves for who we are. In many ways we are all average people, but we just don't like being average at all. We all want to see ourselves as exceptional, but then we worry that others are more so. I suppose Aristotle was right.

When we compete with other mothers, we pit ourselves against them, ourselves against ourselves, and we do something else: We grieve their successes. We don't like to see women whom we envy succeed, even if their success is good for others or humanity. We can be jealous of women who are just too nice. Think for a moment. Have you ever known a woman who is extraordinarily kind? Have you found yourself jealous of her because she is so kind and patient and then you felt angry when something good happened to her? Sometimes we feel bad when other good women succeed, because it diminishes our self-worth. We revel when they fail, because it makes us feel better about ourselves. That's how twisted we become when competition sets in. How in the world can we enjoy a healthy relationship with another woman when we have these thoughts and feelings floating around inside us? It doesn't take much to see that all of these competitive feelings markedly inhibit our openness and honesty with her. Competition stunts the growth of any healthy relationship. And since we need one another, we must get a handle on this. Mothers need other mothers in a very unique way. One mother understands another's fatigue. We get one another. We are warriors who have fought hard for our sanity or for our kids. And we've got to stick together. Mothers have no reason to be competing with one another. Who cares if another mother has a nicer home, smarter kids, or nicer clothes? Our perspective is skewed, and what does being better really get you, anyway? The definitions are false and the truth is, she's probably feeling the same way about you. We don't need what other mothers have to be happier, and the sooner we accept this truth, the quicker we will be happier and can have good, strong relationships with other moms.

HOW COMPETITION ALMOST DESTROYED A FRIENDSHIP

Margaret and Makrai learned this the hard way. I became friends with Makrai several years after my husband and I moved to Michigan. She is fifteen years younger than I and we enjoy a delightful friendship that occasionally takes on a mother-daughter tone. Makrai has two children and worked in a demanding law office as an attorney when her kids were young. After five years of stressful day-care situations, she decided to take a break from her practice and be home with her kids. She was fine with her move, but unfortunately, her best friend, Margaret, wasn't.

Margaret and Makrai were college roommates. They went to Cornell and thrived in the academically competitive environment. Makrai studied law and Margaret studied medicine. "We met at orientation freshman year," Makrai told me, "and ever since that first day, we were inseparable."

Although I didn't meet Margaret until ten years into their relationship, when she came to visit Makrai, I felt that I knew her fairly intimately because of the struggles Makrai and she had endured. The two women arranged to be roommates their freshman year and lived together through college and even graduate school. They cooked meals together, studied together, and went on blind dates together. Makrai referred to Margaret as her "soul mate" during those years. Then Makrai got married and things began to change.

Margaret was Makrai's maid of honor. Describing the beginning of their troubles, Makrai said to me, "I should have seen it then. When I called her and told her that I was getting married, I heard an awkward pause. Then she told me how happy she was for me. She threw me a beautiful bridal shower. She helped me make wedding plans. But when our wedding day came, she did something very peculiar. She flirted with my husband. I was stunned, but blew it off because I thought that was ridiculous. She would never do something like that. I thought I was imagining things. I should have seen what was going on."

Two years went by and the two women spoke often on the phone.

They encouraged each other in their new jobs, and cried together when Margaret's mother became ill. Their relationship seemed to have resumed its normal intimacy. Margaret dated a few men, but nothing serious evolved from any of them.

Makrai recalled those years to me. "We talked a lot on the phone and sometimes my husband would get jealous. I knew because he would make snide remarks about me spending so much time on the phone with Margaret. I told her about his jealousy and she'd get annoyed. She told me that I was too good for him. But then, a few phone calls later, she would say something really stupid. I remember that we hadn't talked for a few weeks and she called and asked how much I weighed. Can you believe it? Out of the blue. I was always bigger than she was and to tell you the truth, I think she liked that. She always commented on how she was a size six and I was a ten. Even then I thought that was a bit bizarre.

"Looking back over those first years I was married, I can see what was going on. I knew that things were strained, but I loved her and I just didn't want to see it. Then the next bad blow came when I had Miah. She wasn't married. I told her I was pregnant. Again, the pause—but this time it was longer. I'll never forget her first words: 'What about your job? You've worked so hard! We've worked so hard!' I assured her that I wasn't going to quit. It was all going to work out. Now that I look back on it, she wasn't worried about my job—she was worried about herself!" I saw anger well up in Makrai's face.

She continued: "Miah was born and Margaret was one of the first to come see her. She even beat my dad to the hospital. I was so grateful. Everything was okay again. Then I had Sam two years later. By this time she was married and seemed very happy. We were still close. She had a nice dermatology practice and I was working at my law practice. I sensed that there was some tension, but it didn't seem bad.

"Then I crashed. I don't know what came over me. My doctor said that I had postpartum depression, but it seemed like more than post-postpartum depression. It just kept going. I tried to explain this to Margaret but she just didn't get it. She alluded to me getting soft. That really hurt. I was desperate and had to do something. So I told my boss that I needed a break. I didn't know how long I would be out, but I just needed to quit. When I told Margaret, she freaked. I was shocked. She yelled at me. She called me selfish and a terrible mom. What was I teaching my kids? she screamed. Honestly, I don't know all she said because I was really in shock. Finally, I just cried and hung up on her."

I felt sorry for Makrai. Clearly she loved Margaret and her friend's words hurt terribly. She realized that her friend was angry, but what hurt more, she said, was thinking that maybe Margaret was right. Maybe she was a bad mom, weak-willed. Maybe she was a failure as a lawyer. Makrai cried for weeks, she told me.

Over the next three years, Makrai tried to reconcile with Margaret but nothing ever held. Neither seemed to understand the root of the problem. At least, until Margaret came to visit one day. That visit, Makrai said, changed her life.

Margaret came to talk with Makrai. She came to tell her friend that she was sorry for acting so cruel. She had been having terrible problems at work and with her marriage and she was irrational. That helped, Makrai said. Then Margaret continued to talk. Makrai told me that she said something like this: "I know that I was wrong and that I raged at you and you didn't deserve it. I'm sorry. But that's not what I'm really sorry for."

Makrai was confused. She had one ear to her friend and one to Sam, who was teasing the dog in the other room. Even at such an important moment, she was having difficulty concentrating. Margaret went on: "Here's the thing. I have been jealous of you for fifteen years. You are prettier. You are smarter. You got married first. You are a mom and I'm not. Things seem to come so easily to you and, I guess, that's always bothered me."

Makrai told me, "Then she started to cry. I didn't know what to say. I was mad. I was stunned. Where did this come from? Had she felt this way toward me for all these years and I trusted her as my friend? I felt betrayed. I didn't know whether to hug her or ask her to leave. Friendships are just messy, I guess."

After the exchange, Makrai said very little and Margaret went home. Makrai said that she didn't call her friend for many months because she needed time to let Margaret's words sink in. One day, her phone rang. It was Margaret. She was crying hysterically and needed Makrai. Her obstetrician had just told her that the baby boy she had been carrying inside her for seven months was dead. He had been healthy and fine. And then his heart just stopped. What was she going to do? Margaret sobbed to her friend. Makrai hadn't even known that she was pregnant.

"I threw both kids in the car and headed downstate to her house. I had to be with her. I had no clue what I was going to do, but I had to just give her a hug and be there for her," Makrai recalled. "It was a terribly sad time but we both learned a lot about ourselves, our friendship, and about life. Jealousy is a wicked thing. It almost killed our friendship. The scary part for me was, I didn't have a clue that Margaret felt so competitive with me. All those years, she had those feelings and I never knew. To tell you the truth, I don't even know that she realized her jealousy. The great part is, we got over it. Once I recovered from that visit, I realized how ridiculous I was to be mad and she realized how much energy she wasted feeling that way toward me. It's almost as if, once we got it out into the open, it evaporated. How strange that something so powerful as to almost ruin our friendship disappeared so easily."

HOW CINDY CONFRONTED JEALOUSY AND TURNED IT AROUND

Cindy confronted jealousy from the other side, and in very different circumstances. I met Cindy socially many years ago. She was, and continues to be, a quiet, pensive soul. She had six children and lived in a house the size of a shoe box. Shortly after her sixth child was born she learned that her husband had been fooling around for several months with one of her friends (a mother). When she confronted him, he admitted it and launched into a diatribe about having fallen out of love with her. He felt cramped, unfulfilled, and needed more room to breathe. Cindy didn't beg or plead with him. She became enraged. How dare he be so selfish with a houseful of dependent children?

After months of arguing, he left. He didn't go far. He bought his own home a few miles away so that he could "stay involved in the kids' lives." After three months in his new home and only one phone call to all six, Cindy's beliefs about his real motives were substantiated.

Cindy's husband divorced her and married her friend. The new couple bought an even bigger house together since they pooled their salaries. Cindy couldn't afford to move. She cleaned houses for other women on the side but wanted to be home with her kids as long as she could be, so she opted to stay in her tiny home. Years passed. One Saturday she received a phone call from him. He wanted to start having the kids over to his home. She hung up on him. The next Saturday he called again. She argued with him. Finally, she resolved that the kids needed him in their lives and she allowed the Saturday rendezvous. One week followed the next and true to his word, he came to her house and picked up a few at a time and brought them to his house for a visit.

I met Cindy several years into the Saturday visits. As she told me her story (as she would many times) I marveled at her demeanor. She was pleasant. Her rage seemed to have dissipated. Being the nosy sort that I am, I wondered where it had gone and so, eventually, I asked her about it.

"I have to tell you that hearing your story infuriates me. How could he behave like such a cad and get away with it?" I asked. "I would be so furious that I wouldn't want my kids near him."

"At first I was really bitter. I was jealous—of her, mostly. Sure, he was a jerk, but she was lovely. She had a great job. She was gorgeous. Everything about her made me feel like a failure. I know it's not rational, but it's the way I felt.

"I cried a lot. I went outside late at night and screamed. I hated her and I hated him. They seemed to have the easy life, but I had my kids."

"So, how, did you get over your jealousy?" I asked. I really wanted to know. She did it—something that to me seemed an impossibility. She was jealous of her ex-husband's wife and even though her ex was acting like a jerk, the truth was, she had loved him for a very long time. Her jealousy ran deep.

"Here's the deal. A good friend of mine—a really good friend—was talking to me one day and listening to me moan endlessly. Then she asked me a tough question. She asked me if I was ready to face my jealousy. I was furious with her. I said, 'Are you out of your mind? Why in the world would I ever be jealous of that woman?' (My ex's wife.) I had such ugly feelings toward her that I didn't want to admit that I was actually jealous. Asking me that question was one of the kindest things anyone has ever done for me. Because once I recognized what I was doing, I was able to begin to let it go. I refused to stay jealous. I accepted that I was good enough—he just chose to walk away because he was a jerk. I stopped beating myself up because I didn't have her job, her figure, or her house. The great thing was, confronting my jealousy completely began to deflate its power. That's how I'm able to be with him, to encourage the kids to see him, and to be happy with my life. I have so much more than she does. I actually kind of feel sorry for her."

She continued a bit longer. I think that she sensed that I wanted to hear more. "I realized that I didn't want to grow into an old bitter woman. I didn't want it for myself or for my kids. Is he a bad example of a dad to the kids? Sure. But he's still their dad. I also realized that this wasn't going to change. They still needed to know their dad."

Here's the most amazing part about Cindy: She really isn't filled with rage any longer. She exudes contentment and a sense of security. She speaks with self-assurance and a sense that she likes who she is. I began to feel jealous of her, but then I caught myself. Jealousy brings about nothing good, but overcoming it brings outrageous freedom.

Competition is a powerful force, and it has the potential to destroy. But once it's confronted and brought into the open, it can be surprisingly easily overcome. Jealousy between mothers, especially, is ugly stuff and there is no place for it. But like Margaret, we all harbor it to one degree or another because we are women who want life to go well, and when we think we see someone else get everything so easily, we want what she has. But it doesn't have to be that way.

In the end, we need to remember that everything we need comes from within us, or from God. Once we do this, we can be content knowing that who we are and what we have is plenty enough. If we can recognize our value as mothers and treasure everything we do have in our lives, we are complete and can enjoy other mothers for who they are. We can let friendship thrive and let real joy enter our lives.

FIVE WAYS TO MAKE THE HABIT STICK

#1: Recognize jealousy and don't be fooled

The first and most important step in changing any habit is recognizing it. This can be the toughest part of the change for us mothers who are busy. The busyness of life sweeps us away and we often act without thinking. In order to uncover the first inklings of competition in us, we must be able to recognize the symptoms. And these are rooted in the thoughts and feelings we have as we interact with other mothers—particularly ones we meet for the first time.

Think about times when you have met another mother for the first time. As we discussed earlier, you evaluate her in your mind and draw some conclusions. This is natural when we meet someone for the first time, because we're trying to get to know her. As we learn information, we not only paint a mental picture of her life, but we also pull up a picture of our lives and set it right next to hers. Again, this is natural human instinct. The pictures sit side by side and we begin to compare them, and as a result, we elevate a part of hers above our own. And we do the same thing with our lives—we elevate parts of ours above hers. But even this is not a problem yet, because the truth is, she may have a nicer life in some aspects but we may have a better life in others. She may be prettier, or have a lovelier home or kids who don't yell at her. But we may have kinder in-laws and a more understanding husband. Differences are natural. The problem comes not in the comparison, but in the wishing that we had what she has. When that first tiny eruption of desire wells within our hearts and whispers in our ears that life would be better if we only had her job, income, figure, whatever, we have crossed into dangerous land. We have entered a destructive state of competition and those feelings will only grow stronger unless we stop them.

So think about the voices in your mind that gently articulate the desires you have for something that she has. Is it her figure you want? Her ability to eat all that she wants and never gain a pound? Or is it something more serious? Do you want your kids to behave more like her kids—to excel as they do, to get into an Ivy League school, to go to law school? The list of desires that may well up in our hearts is endless because we are mothers. We want better for ourselves and better for our kids. We compete in two arenas because we have our lives as well as their lives to watch out for.

Sometimes feelings erupt before the verbal utterances. We experience a general sense of discomfort in the presence of a mom who has what we want. Jealousy can be as benign and gentle as an irritation. I have found myself annoyed by a mother (even if she's really nice) when I am jealous. Recently, I found myself criticizing a friend of mine who is an excellent parent because her daughter was marrying a wonderful man and I was concerned for the welfare of my own daughter. I wanted for my daughter what her daughter was getting and so I became critical of my friend. But here's the most insane part of my thinking: I didn't even know her daughter's fiancé! For all I knew, he was an ax murderer. Not really, but the point is, her daughter's greater happiness than my daughter's happiness was all in my head. My daughter is very happy and is perfectly capable of making good decisions about men. My jealousy was rooted in a belief that her daughter had what I thought my daughter should have. And to show how really twisted things become when jealousy sets in, I was agitated at my friend (who had done nothing to me) because she was her mom. How ridiculous can we be?

There are twinges of irritation, anger, and annoyance, as well as a desire to gossip, backstab, or criticize, when we first feel jealousy. The tricky part is that we don't identify them as jealousy, so that's why we must be on the ball. For once we see that jealousy is at the root of the feelings, then we know that we are already competing with another mom. Only when we see this dynamic can we begin to stop it.

#2: Head competition off at the pass

Once we have recognized the initial rumblings of jealousy, we must act. This is war because competition with other mothers serves only one purpose: to take us down. We who are jealous hurt more than anyone because it is a dull state of self-torment. Once we feel criticism, gossip, or agitation at another welling up, waiting to erupt, we must tell ourselves that we will not compete. We need to say it out loud to ourselves, or at least own up to it in our minds. We must speak to ourselves boldly and refuse to compete. We must initiate an internal dialogue that helps us to reject jealousy and the need to feel that we must have what she has. We need to be very clear with ourselves regarding what it is that we want. I did this when my friend's daughter got married. As embarrassed as I was to tell myself that I was jealous over the marriage (yes, I was even embarrassed in front of myself), I was then able to think through my feelings. They were ridiculous. Jealousy is ridiculous, but more importantly, we must follow our self-confrontation all the way through to resolution. We can admit our feelings, what we are jealous over, and then we must admit to ourselves that we don't need the thing. I didn't need my daughter to have a nice husband (as my friend's daughter had, or so I thought), because my life was complete and so was my daughter's. So there are several steps to this process. First we recognize the feelings, then we get very specific to ourselves about what we're jealous of, then we remind ourselves firmly that we don't need the thing for which we are jealous. The final step is very important. If we only identify jealousy and what we're jealous about and forget to firmly tell ourselves that we don't need it, the jealousy can dribble on and on.

Many mothers can do this exercise successfully with their jealousy. But there are times when we feel so competitive with other mothers over large issues that confronting ourselves alone is not sufficient. We need the help of a good friend. We need an objective person who loves us enough to not think ill of us even when she hears our stupidity verbalized. That's what good friends do—they accept what we think and feel and take it all in stride.

We need our friends when jealousy has sunk deep roots in us. For example, if we are constantly angry at other women, frequently defensive of our behavior, our kids, our work, or some other activity that we do. When we are jealous of other mothers because they seem to have life perfectly balanced and figured out, we find ourselves wanting to be with them and hating to be near them, all at the same time. We want to see how they do it, but since we feel that we can't do what they do or have what they have, we leave angrier than ever. Sometimes jealousy gets such a strong hold on us that we have difficulty having any good relationships with other mothers. We always feel so inadequate or guilty when we are with them that we just scrap the whole friendship thing altogether. That's when we really need to pull a good friend close to our side and get competition under control. It is insidious and can be profoundly destructive.

How can a friend help? In several ways. First, she may be able to see your jealousy and competitiveness when you can't, and if she is a really good friend, she can gently tell you that. She will ask if you are having problems feeling jealous or competitive with anyone or someone specifically. Or, if you already know that you are struggling with jealousy, you can recruit her help to work through it. Once you understand what you want that another mother has (even if it's something small, but it's got a strong grip on you), you must tell her what or whom you are jealous of. This is a wonderfully powerful exercise that defuses the jealousy. As you hear yourself state your wishes out loud to a friend, you objectify them. Sometimes, this can be funny. My sister admitted to me once that she was jealous of another mother's hair. As ridiculous as this sounds, her own hair bothered her for a long time and she felt thorny and critical of another mother she knew who had gorgeous hair. My sister knew that she felt irritated around this woman, but her ugly feelings never went away until one day she told me that she thought she was jealous of the woman's hair. As soon as she admitted it, we burst out laughing, and guess what happened to her? She got along better with the beautiful-haired mom and she began to like her own hair more. All from saying something out loud.

Openly articulating our thoughts and feelings to a good friend about even the tiniest ways in which we compete is the best way I know to head competition off at the pass.

#3: Give frequent verbal applause

My same crazy sister told me many years ago how to encourage my husband to do what I want him to do. She said, "Clap for him." (I think that this will work for almost any man.) Her point was well-taken. When we give verbal applause, we give others a boost. And everyone needs a boost.

When it comes to stopping our competitiveness with other mothers, this same rule helps accomplish something very different. We know that we don't want mothers whom we are jealous of to do anything for us, but we know that we need to change the way we feel about them so that our jealousy will disintegrate. One of the best ways I know to ward off jealousy is to speak well of the woman who has something we want. This is akin to praying for our enemies, if you will, and it is really tough to do. The more competitive we feel with another mom, the more we subconsciously dislike her and the harder it is to not criticize her, let alone say nice things about her. But this is exactly what we must do. And, after a while, it feels good. Giving praise to someone you have hard feelings for—particularly when you do it sincerely and to her face—heals all sorts of ills. It is remarkable.

Many years ago I worked in the hospital with a brilliant but very angry colleague who was also a mother. She was a no-nonsense, tough woman and seemed to want everyone in the hospital to know it. She had a reputation for cutting people down to size in front of patients and colleagues alike. Many who worked with her routinely said negative things about her. They called her names behind her back, said they felt sorry for her son, and criticized her as a physician. I found myself on the receiving end of her anger on many occasions. I had to agree that what many said about her was true. I didn't want to engage in gossip so I devised a plan to deliberately say positive things about her when I could. I can't say that I was jealous of her per se, so my reason for applauding her was a bit different. Still, it accomplished the same positive outcome as it would have if I had been jealous.

One night, a mutual patient was critically ill. She had placed the child in traction to heal a broken leg. I was called to see the child in the middle of the night because she began having seizures. I called my colleague and told her that we needed to take the child out of traction and get an MRI of her brain because I was afraid that she might be hemorrhaging. My colleague flew off the handle. She yelled at me that I was stupid, didn't know what I was doing, and furthermore, if I took the child out of traction, I might face a lawsuit since her leg might never heal. Hmm, I thought to myself, I am more concerned about the child's brain than her leg. I simply told this doctor that I was ordering the child down from traction and she was going to get an MRI. The doctor got out of bed, came to the hospital, and continued to berate me. I stood quietly, refused to engage in a fight, and did what I believed needed to be done for the child.

About a year later, one of this colleague's patients was in serious trouble. She didn't know what was wrong and needed help from another pediatrician. Since she had made so many enemies, she didn't know whom to turn to. She came to me. Very humbly, she called and asked for my help. I have to say that I felt pity for her but also a twinge of glee. I gave her the help she needed and we helped her patient get through his illness (I can't remember what was wrong). Several days later she came and thanked me for helping. More importantly, she said, she wanted to thank me for being kind to her. (She never learned that I wasn't really as kind to as I was scared of her, but she didn't need to know.) After that, we became friendly and another year later she divulged to me a deep-seated insecurity she had as a physician and mother. She never felt that she was doing either job very well and wondered how other working mothers balanced their lives. Her insecurity prompted her anger and a need to compete with other physicians (particularly those who were also moms) to feel better about her own life. Never before had she said this to anyone.

Was it my forcing myself to say nice things about this woman that helped her? I don't know, but I do know that it helped the two of us have a relationship. She ultimately felt less jealous of me and the negative feelings that I had about her earlier in our relationship went away altogether. Saying nice things, praising other mothers, and encouraging one another whenever possible changes us. Jealousy goes away and relationships grow.

#4: Focus on fullness, not emptiness

Happy people are fun to be around. If you listen to them for a while—a day or a week—you'll see that happy people rarely complain. Why? Because they focus more on what's positive in life rather than on what's negative. This can be easier or harder for some mothers, depending upon our personality type, life circumstances, or health issues. But each of us can cultivate a more positive attitude. Regardless of who we are, it requires work.

Competitive mothers have many things in common and one of the most glaring is an intentional focusing on what they don't have rather than the great things they do have. And so much of what competitiveness in us prompts us to focus on is silly, if not outright ridiculous. I have seen mothers with fabulous children and kind husbands bemoan the size of their homes, their figures, or their lack of nicer clothes.

We all choose what thoughts will fill the spaces in our minds, if you will, at the beginning of the day. It is a simple mathematical truth that if we spend more time pondering what we don't have, we will have far less time to feel grateful for what we do have. So when you find yourself bemoaning something small, or even something larger like your health or job, make a deliberate effort to refocus on what you have. Write down what you are grateful for. Look at it in black and white and if you do this small exercise consistently, your thinking will change. Feeling competitive with other moms will fade away over time. And positive thought patterns will become more routine, more second nature.

Many women feel defeated before they start such an exercise because they believe that it is too simple to work. Or they feel negative and down and wonder why in the world they should go through such a simple exercise when they don't feel grateful. Here's why: because actively focusing on what we have, regardless how we feel about our lives, makes us feel differently. We won't feel more grateful or more content at the outset, but I have never met a mother who has done this exercise and not felt more positive about life. So regardless of your attitude, focus on what you have, not what you don't have. Do this for three to four weeks and wait to see what happens to your mood.

#5: Be deliberate in kindness

Doing kind things for others is always good, and acting kindly toward a mother with whom we compete helps our relationship and curbs the desire to compete. Sometimes we have difficulty finding positive things to say about another whom we envy. We can become so wrapped up in feeling negative, in finding fault with another, that the only banter we engage in is negative. That's why we have another option. We can act on their behalf. We can do well by that person. And sometimes this works to improve their love, our lives, and our relationship with them even more powerfully than simply praising them. Words can be cheaper than actions, though not necessarily less sincere.

Being kind to loved ones is easy, and it makes us feel good because when they are happier, we feel happier. Helping good friends and loved ones can be a bit self-serving because we usually reap great rewards for our kindness toward them. Either we directly benefit from it, or they return the favor. But the real test comes when we reach out on behalf of those we don't really like. And most often we don't really like the mothers whom we're jealous of. So if we want to get rid of our jealousy, the best way to shovel out the rot of the feelings is to find something very nice to do for the other mother.

If there is a mother you know who just had her third baby and you desperately want a child but can't have one, cook her a meal and bring it to her. If there is a mother who works outside the home in a job that you think is fabulous but know you can't have, ask to take her child to the park one day while she's working. Perhaps there's a mother whose kids are number one and number two on the varsity tennis team at your son's high school and your son can't play any sports well because he's, well, clumsy. Send her a note telling her how well her kids are doing.

This is tough stuff. I've done it myself and I know that it works. It requires that we dig deeply and act against our natural instincts. But this is the only way to get off the train of competition. It feels severe at times and a bit gut-wrenching, but as I said earlier, this is war. We are at stake. Our sanity, our happiness, and our contentment. If we want these things, we've got to be willing to accept that we live in a tough world and that left to our own nature, we will follow some pretty ugly paths in that world. We will jump aboard the train and frantically go after what we really want, we think. We will pull a part of her—the other mother's—life into ours in order to make ours better. We will challenge ourselves to find out how she got what she has and get the same, somehow, some way. If we choose this, we will end up miserable—guaranteed. Part of you is on that train, wanting to be better, look prettier, be more successful in something. So get off. Right now. Take the hard road and abandon it altogether. Confront your nature to compete with other moms and rise above it every day, every week. Doing this is the beginning of reconciling with yourself that what you have and all you need lies within you, not outside of you. All of it.

||||||||||||||||||||||||||||||||||||||||||||||||||||||||||||||||||||||||||||||||||||||||||||||||||||

Create a Healthier Relationship with Money

I CARRY FIVE different shades of plum-colored lipstick in my purse at all times. There is silvery plum, plum dandy, perfect plum, violet berry, and my favorite—viva glam. The peculiar thing is, each looks exactly like the other when smeared on my lips. So why do I carry all five, all the time? Because having them makes me feel good, even chic.

The five shades will stay zippered in my purse because, in addition to making me feel better about myself, they are luxurious and fun, and they make me feel good about life. When I have extra cash in my wallet, I buy a new tube of plum lipstick. Other mothers buy shoes to splurge; I buy color for my face.

But maybe there's really more to the five tubes of plum in my purse. First of all, having them makes me feel secure in a very small way, and I like that. I know that at a moment's notice, I can take charge and look better. But the lipsticks also remind me that I have cash and the ability to buy something for myself. I can do something for me. More importantly, the tubes of shiny paste represent the work that I finished in order to buy them, and I like my work. I love to see patients, to write and encourage mothers, and, to be honest, to have the ability to make money. In one activity, I can find personal and professional satisfaction and receive financial compensation in return. This means that I have money in the bank and a feeling of control over my own life. I like this. Most mothers do because we like to be in charge, to make decisions, and to not feel that we have to depend on others all the time to make life move forward. Lipstick seems to represent a lot to me.

But what does that say about my relationship with money, or any of ours, if lipstick can literally buy happiness? Let me ask some tough questions. If money gives us a sense of control and independence, and maybe even boosts our self-esteem, shouldn't all mothers who are wealthy necessarily have a greater sense of all of these? If it were money that really did this, the answer would be yes. But we all know mothers richer than us who aren't necessarily happier. Clearly, there's more to this money issue than meets the eye.

The complicated business of money stems from the fact that we all have relationships with it. And these relationships are complicated. If we don't pay attention to our relationships with it, its power can swallow us and take over. If we allow it too much power, it can turn us into crazy people. And we don't have to have a lot of money for this to happen. If we allow it to become a god, if you will, it can take over and bring us misery. But if we keep our relationships with it balanced, life will be far richer. In this chapter, I'll show you how, and give you three tips that will help the habit stick: opening your fist and grabbing someone else's hand to find *real* security, asking yourself why you're opening your wallet each time you do, and looking close to home for true contentment.

MONEY, MOMS, AND OUR WORTH

Parenting critics love to hammer mothers (and fathers) about why we give our kids so much. Boys have too many video games and electronic gadgets and girls have far too many clothes. Modern-day teens and college students travel the globe the way we used to travel to Florida for spring break. Mothers harp about other mothers who spoil their kids by indulging them with cellphones, cars, sometimes exotic vacations. And the funniest part is that those who criticize others are succumbing to the same indulgences as all the rest. The truth is, most American kids are spoiled, and I fully understand why. I've done the same, because when it comes to giving to our kids, what mother isn't going to struggle with how much and how soon to give? Giving things to our kids is complicated. We give because we love them and we want them to feel good. We give because that's what mothers know how to do. We give until it hurts and then we give some more. Then experts come along and criticize us for doing what feels quite natural.

The tricky part in being a mother is that giving is good and it is natural, but we forget to give what really matters to our kids (our time, attention, and affection) and instead spend our energy paying for things for them. We do so because we believe that things matter more to their success than we do. It's not that our motives are wrong; they are simply guided in the wrong direction—the same direction that all of our friends are headed in. We are stubbornly convinced that providing nicer homes, schools, clothes, tutors, piano lessons, etc., makes us better mothers. This is not a conscious belief; rather it is a strong subconscious feeling that drives many of our parenting behaviors.

Have you ever walked into a friend's beautifully furnished home and found shoes lined up neatly in the mudroom, towels folded with only the rounded edges showing in the stack, and children playing quietly in the basement? In a moment, you feel wholly inadequate as a mom. The familiar bantering inside your mind quickly taunts you. "If I had this kind of money, my house would look like this and my kids would be happy." Of course, your thoughts are ridiculous. You know this, but somehow you still kind of wonder, because you want to believe that having this lovely home would make your life happier.

The voices chant on, convincing you that the other mom is a better mom, because she has more money. She can afford to buy her kids what they need to be happy. What kids wouldn't play quietly in the basement of such a gorgeous home if they had it? The chirping in our brains neatly outlines for us that in order to be better mothers, we need only have a little more money to get nicer things for our kids. Yes, having more purchasing power for our kids makes us feel that we are more valuable as mothers.

Consider the frugal, hardworking mother we all compare ourselves to. She is the one who scrimps and saves to pay for the private tutor, ice-skating coach, and piano lessons. She pushes hard to get the promotions in order to earn more so that she can send her daughter to the Ivy League college of her choice (after she pays for the tutors, private secondary school, travel soccer, and SAT prep). We see her as the great mom—the sacrificial mother who worked hard to acquire enough wealth in order to give her daughter a leg up in life, to get her on the best path possible toward success. That, of course, is a noble goal. But could there be a bit more to this scenario? Could she do all of the above in order to make herself feel like a better mother? Certainly. If this is true, then her worth as a mother is directly connected to her purchasing power. This is hard to hear, but the truth is, many of us moms are guilty of getting more money not because we are performing well at jobs we love, but simply because we believe that getting more will make our kids more successful and ourselves better moms.

Providing the right stuff—opportunities, shoes, private schools, skating lessons, etc.—has become the gold standard for many parents when it comes to excellent parenting. Since each of us longs to be the best mother possible, we quickly ride the same train in order to be better. The problem is, we are duped. Rarely do kids describe their mothers as being fabulous moms because of the material things they provide. When I ask adult children about their parents, they talk about their mothers' greatness in terms of their kindness, affection, and caring. (Yes, and they even describe their favorite foods their mothers made.) Young kids talk to me about their moms' moods, how fun they are or whether they are crabby. They don't boast about their shoes, their schools, or the sports they play when talking about their mothers. They talk about their moms, not what their moms give them.

As far as kids are concerned, good mothers are known by their character, not by the education, clothes, or coaches they supply. So why, then, do we so frenetically chase and pay for so many things for our kids?

I think we do so because it makes us feel better about our own worth as moms. We compare ourselves relentlessly to our friends and their parenting, and if we are honest, we certainly don't want to be outdone when it comes to providing for our kids. Never underestimate the power of peer pressure in mothering.

There's more. Spending on our kids is profoundly emotional. It is very much akin to feeding our kids. If our toddlers eat well, we feel more successful as mothers. (The most stressed mothers I see are mothers of children who fail to gain weight as infants or who have eating disorders as teens.) First, we believe that we are doing our kids a favor, making them happier and giving them at least momentary pleasure. Second, when we feel bad about life, buying things for loved ones can make us feel momentarily happier (until the credit card bill rolls in). Buying and giving can be mood altering.

WHY DO WE SPEND?

Let's face it. Understanding our own worth as mothers in a healthy and truthful way is tough. We tend to lean on all the wrong things to make us feel valuable and while our rational brains tell us this isn't true, we tell ourselves that our kids will be happier if we buy them more stuff. It's an emotional, not a rational, choice. So we must focus on reality and what our kids tell us about ourselves, which is that what they really want and need is more of what we do best—talk, encourage, and spend time with them. And the great news is, once we surrender the potent temptation to be more for our kids by providing more, we open the door for joy and sanity to return to our minds.

Interestingly, most of us mothers would unequivocally state that we are not spending to boost our self-esteem as mothers, or even to boost the self-esteem of our kids. No, we'd say we're doing it because our kids really need what we buy. But the truth is, it really is all about (artificially) boosting self-esteem. We are afraid to stop because we are afraid what we will feel about ourselves if we do. Many times we say that we don't want to stop, because we don't want to disappoint our kids, and this most certainly is true, but it isn't the whole picture. In fact, most kids would much rather have our time than the stuff and opportunities we kill ourselves in order to provide.

Here's the great news: We can stop. No, we don't have to stop spending money on our kids, but we can stop evaluating our worth as mothers by the material things we give them. This is real freedom. We can extricate ourselves from the feeling that we have to give just a little more, provide a nicer vacation, or take that second job to pay for the private school. The truth is, our worth as mothers is *not* tied to doing those things in our children's eyes. A study of adolescents completed in 2003 was conducted to find out how successful they felt their mothers' parenting was. The researchers also asked the mothers to rate their own performance. The results were fascinating. The teens gauged the success of their mothers most clearly by the amount of time that their mothers spent *talking* with them and *doing* things with them. Teens whose mothers spent ten or more hours talking and doing things with them gave their mothers much higher scores on parenting.

And how did the mothers feel about themselves? When the study was finished, the researchers found that mothers, too, feel that spending time talking with their kids has the greatest impact on how well they are parenting.*

I hear what kids think about their mothers because, as a pediatrician, I am a professional listener. When I ask a seven-year-old boy to tell me about his mother, he never tells me what she buys him or what her profession is (usually he doesn't know because he doesn't care). He uses phrases like "fun to be with," "mad a lot," "squishy to hug," "pretty," or "really nice to be with." Even as our kids grow older, they use similar although more grown-up terminology. Think back on your own mother. Were you impressed as much by what she bought you as by her character? Of course not. The part of her that caused you joy or pain came during the exchanges that you had with her, for example, when she made you so mad that you wanted to put your fist through your bedroom door, or

---

*P. Strom, et al., "The Success of Caucasian Mothers in Guiding Adolescents," *Adolescence* 38:151 (2003), p. 501.

the time she made you feel better by picking you up at school after you vomited in front of your classmates, and brought you home to lie on the living room couch. These are the memories that really last.

HOW LEXI STOPPED WORRYING ABOUT MONEY AND FOUND CONTENTMENT

Many years ago, when I was working ninety-hour weeks at Children's Hospital in Wisconsin, I had a conversation with a male colleague that I will never forget. It was 2 A.M. and one of our patients had died. We felt despondent. We were pediatricians in training and began asking whether we were working in the right field. Why would one pursue such a career? It was filled with heartache and, contrary to popular belief, it wouldn't make either of us rich. Almost any other type of physician would make more money.

After much complaining and commiserating, we came to conclude that our work was our mission. We loved kids and we loved making them better. It was that simple. Our work was in us and we needed to let it out. We were the lucky ones, we concluded, because our work, as painful as it was, gave us great joy and satisfaction. When we worked, the dam was released. Something inside each of us felt relieved. But things become much more complicated when we stop working for the satisfaction, joy, and release, and start working (or working more) simply for money. Rationally, we know that money can't buy us happiness, contentment, or peace of mind, or assuage a darkened conscience. If we know this, then why do we continue to hope that if we can just afford one more thing, or hold on until our proverbial ship comes in, *then* life will be good? We hope and chase because, although we realize on a cognitive level that money doesn't satisfy, we have formed serious habits regarding spending and hoping. A nicer home, better clothes, a more progressive school for our child, you name it—we are convinced that something out there will make us a bit more content.

Many of us mothers chase contentment by buying things because that's the only way we think we can get it. Unfortunately, we set ourselves up for frustration and disappointment. We can even land in a cycle of repetitious compulsive behavior that Freud articulated many years ago. This happens when we feel a need for something (peace of mind, happiness, or contentment) and we try to fill that need by doing something (buying things) that won't satisfy that need. After we purchase an item and it fails to bring the result we wanted, we become even more frustrated than we were before. Then we react to that frustration by trying the same behavior (buying) over and over in hopes that the next time around we will feel satisfied (our need will be met).

As you can see, this can become a truly compulsive behavior. As the compulsion becomes more severe, it can increase one's frustration level virtually exponentially. I don't doubt that there are mothers trapped in this pattern of spending, but one thing that I am sure of is this: Many of us are trapped emotionally and psychologically by this same type of thinking. We may not spend the money, but we hold on to the belief that if only we had . . . something else . . . then life would bring us much greater satisfaction and peace. Until we give up this frame of mind, we cannot escape the toxic belief that more money brings more satisfaction. Some mothers will go to great extremes with this. Lexi did.

I met Lexi a few years ago when she brought her kids in to see me at my office. We bonded quickly because, as middle-aged mothers (though her kids were born later in her life than mine were), we had already learned immensely important lessons. We both love to work and we love our kids. Each of us felt the sting of time that passes and can never be retrieved—particularly important time with our families. Like seasoned warriors, we became close because of our private battles. Before we met, Lexi lived in Chicago, and she moved to my town in Michigan shortly after her lifestyle change.

When Lexi graduated from college, she immediately took a position in her family's marketing and development firm. She was young, bright, and extremely likable. She did well and worked hard to earn her own way. She never wanted any other employees to feel that she got special treatment because she was the owner's daughter. By her thirtieth birthday, she was making excellent money and had become vice president. She had her sights on becoming president one day, and she loved her work and her family's company.

Lexi fell in love and married a man seven years her senior. He had no children and was anxious to get started on a family. Lexi became pregnant, had one child, then soon had another. Her husband was a broker at an investment firm and felt strained by his job. The stress of his job made Lexi worry about him and their relationship, as well as the impact of their careers on their children.

By the time Lexi was about to turn forty, she was president of her company. She scaled back to fifty-hour workweeks from the sixty hours she had needed to earn her position as president. Her husband tried to cut back on his workload, but every time he tried, something else came along that put him back to fifty hours per week.

Lexi would have told you that her life then was the classic dream of many American mothers. She had a dynamic career, she had two healthy, thriving children and a 6,500-square-foot home in the suburbs of Chicago. She said that she should have felt like one of the luckiest women alive. She admits today that she wasn't necessarily unhappy then, but she lived with an aching sense that something was deeply wrong.

"I'll never forget the day that the limo picked me up from O'Hare and drove me home after I went to San Francisco for a meeting. I got out of the car in my gorgeous suit and looked up at my beautiful home. When I got to the front door, I heard my kids inside giggling at something and my heart sank. I missed them. But that wasn't all. When I went to put my key in the lock of the front door, I had this overwhelming sense that my life was profoundly empty. I should have been content and I knew that very moment that I wasn't. With all I had, something very deep was missing in my life.

"Maybe it was a midlife thing, I wondered. But once the recognition came, it never left. It haunted me. I started asking myself, What am I doing? I had a hard time finding answers, but I wasn't going to give up until I found out what I was missing and how I was going to figure out how to find some peace and joy in my life. I was terribly restless."

For Lexi, that epiphany came four years ago. After much soul-searching, she decided to take a sabbatical from work and spend some time in contemplation, reading, and solitude. During that time she reflected on her frenetic lifestyle and the toll that it was taking on her health. She was missing out on fun, her kids, and her husband. She had no friends because at the time she didn't find them important—a huge mistake, as we learned in the friendship chapter. Lexi decided to take charge of her life and her schedule and bring sanity into them both. She scaled back her work, hired another vice president to take over some of her work, and reorganized much of the business. She learned that she couldn't do it all herself and traded money for time—and was able to keep a job that she genuinely loved. Her change made home life better, and it made life at work far more pleasant as well. She made room for life.

"I think the thing that shook me the most is that I really believed that all of that stuff—work, money, travel, lovely home, and clothes—would give me something which it never could. I knew it, but I hung in there trying harder and harder to feel satisfied, content, but the feeling never came."

Indeed it couldn't, because peace can't come from stuff we do or get. It comes from inside ourselves. Fortunately for Lexi, she found that joy. It just took time and a lot of faith.

WHAT GRETCHEN LEARNED: TO GIVE MORE BY MAKING LESS

Gretchen learned a similar lesson, but she found a different path. And it was a chance remark by her daughter, surprisingly, that got her started. I met Gretchen ten years ago at a Christmas party. She is five years younger than I am but looks ten. When she talks, she commands attention, but not because she is abrasive or demanding; rather, she has an air of wisdom about her. Her demeanor causes one to feel that she has something important to say.

After Gretchen graduated from college she embarked upon a very successful career in finance. In five years she made more than most women do in twenty, but she quickly became bored. So she applied to medical school. At the time I met her, she was in private practice and taught part-time at a medical school in Boston. Since the Christmas party was at her home, I met her four children and two golden retrievers, and got a tour of her lovely, enormous home.

As much as I wanted to be jealous of my friend, I found that I couldn't. She was so down-to-earth and kind that she was impossible to criticize. (Isn't it peculiar how we often catch ourselves looking for the faults in our friends who seem to have everything?) Over the next few years of our friendship, I got to know her sons and daughters, ranging in age from seventeen to ten. Lily was her youngest.

During lunch one afternoon, Gretchen confided in me that she had convinced her husband to move to a home half the size across town. Immediately I suspected financial troubles. Since we were close, I asked if everything was okay.

"We're moving because of Lily," she told me. Was the child having problems at school? I wondered.

Gretchen's explanation surprised me. "Everything with the kids is fine," she said. "It's me. I'm going over the edge." One thing I have always admired about my friend is her brutal honesty about herself. "My personality was driving everyone crazy." I was taken aback.

"Here's the thing. I'm driven. And I'm a perfectionist. I get onto something and I just can't stop. The more I do, the more I want to do. It's painful, really. Part of it stems from my personality. My dad's just like me, but part of it comes from a deep sense that I need to be financially and emotionally ready," she said.

"Ready for what?" I asked

"Ready for bad stuff to happen. For Quentin to leave. For my kids to leave. For my parents to pass away." I wasn't getting it initially.

"Making money is who I am. Buffering myself gives me security. My mother always taught me to be able to take care of myself in case trouble came. She was right, but her words took over and I felt like they owned me." I began to see Gretchen's dilemma unfold. Perfectionists desire perfection and this appears good on the outside, but beneath it lies a deep fear of imperfection. They often equate error with personal defectiveness and believe that by attaining perfection, they will receive personal acceptance.

I was beginning to understand but had to ask, "What does this have to do with Lily?" I had met Lily on several occasions and she appeared to me to be well-adjusted and happy. She was polite and respectful when she spoke (unlike other very wealthy kids who can often be demanding with their mothers).

"About six months ago I overheard her talking to a friend. They were in her bedroom and her door was shut, so I know that she was trying hard for me not to hear. Her girlfriend was talking about her problems with her parents and Lily piped up and said something that stung. She said, 'I know what you mean. I used to love being with my mom. When I was little she was really fun. She had this laugh that made me feel that everything was okay. She used to laugh a lot and she used to take me places alone. She doesn't laugh anymore. We never see each other. I really miss my mom."

"She's just a kid," I said. "All kids say things about their parents they don't mean."

"No. She meant it. So I did some soul-searching and took inventory of my attitude, my stress level, and how I am to my kids. The truth is, I have been so absorbed, if that's a strong enough word, with making more money and working harder, that Lily has lost a huge part of me." I was moved by her candor.

"So, we're moving. I decided to change our lives. Quentin's not really happy, but we're going to do it. We're downscaling. We're going to move into a much smaller house—and by the way, the boys, too, admitted that they never liked this house. They said that it doesn't feel like home. I'm cutting back on my extra hours, too. If all this stuff that I've worked so hard for is making my daughter feel like she's losing a big part of me, then I'm going to scrap it."

Whatever respect I had for my friend before quadrupled in that moment. Her words almost took my breath away. Talking about change is easy, but doing something so dramatic took guts and that was one thing she had.

Two years later, I am happy to report that Gretchen did just as she said. Her kids, particularly Lily, loved the move. She and her husband sold their huge home and downsized into one they could afford on her husband's salary. Gretchen told me that Lily loved having the smaller house because her bedroom was closer to her parents'. Best of all, Gretchen told me, she was spending more "upbeat" time with her daughter. She worked hard at relaxing more and at being more relaxed with Lily. Her daughter seemed to respond.

And Gretchen? She said that it was a real struggle for her. Internally, she continues to fight to quiet her compulsion to work more and keep her savings growing. She said that she feels like a race car with the choke on constantly. Was it worth it? I asked her.

"Well, let me say this. I think I laugh more. And that makes Lily very happy."

Working hard and acquiring nice things wasn't Gretchen's problem; having it occupy too much of her mental, physical, and emotional energy was. She had a belief instilled in her when she was young that she needed to be prepared for bad things to happen. To her, that meant that she needed to have financial security. When her belief was coupled with her very intense personality, a fuse was lit. She began working to get more and more security, but earning more didn't give her that. Otherwise she would have been able to stop. She became obsessive about earning and it cost her and her relationship with her daughter a lot. It stole relaxed, enjoyable time from them.

And isn't that true for each of us mothers? When getting things or having things becomes more of a priority than people, we're in trouble. And if we are truthful with ourselves, most of us have fallen into this trap. Her story reminded me of Pierre Bezukhov in *War and Peace*, who learned that "man is created for happiness; that happiness lies in himself, in the satisfaction of his natural human cravings; that all happiness arises not from privation but from superfluity."

There was another lesson that I learned from Gretchen. She taught

Lily that she could have joy, contentment, and a great life with less. Lily had a smaller bedroom, but it was closer to her mother's. The pool was gone, but she still had a swing set, and more importantly, her mother came out to swing with her. Gretchen confided in me that she got rid of many of Lily's toys during the move and that her daughter didn't seem to notice! Isn't that a lesson that all of us mothers want our kids to learn, particularly in a world with a fragile economy? What a tremendous gift to give her daughter—the knowledge that she could live well with much or with little. By selling their gorgeous home and moving into a smaller one, Gretchen handed Lily the personal freedom that accompanies such knowledge.

The relationship that we mothers have with money isn't about how much we earn or store away. It means so much more. Earning comes to define us and the power that it gives us makes us feel more independent and secure. The truth is, it does give us more independence and some security. But we must always remember that those two things aren't made complete by money. We need people: our spouses, our kids, our friends. We are dependent on people for emotional satisfaction, for mental and intellectual stimulation. Many of us don't want to feel dependent because it is frightening. What if others let us down? Sometimes making money helps us live with the illusion that we really are less dependent than we are.

We will never be completely independent or secure because of our jobs or how much we have in our savings. Never. We can lose our jobs or the stock market could tank. If we lose money or our jobs, does that mean that we cannot enjoy security? No. That's where friends, family, and faith come in. These are the real things that give us about as much security as can be found in our lifetimes.

But most importantly, we need to remember that whenever we pursue money and material gains there is a cost. When we work very long hours outside our homes (and inside as well, but that doesn't generate income and that's what we're focusing on here) we take something away from our families. Many times we must work so hard and long because we need to put food on the table. Other times we must because we will lose our minds if we don't have a break from the stresses of home. But we must always be careful to weigh the cost and benefits and feel comfortable that we are striking a balance. This is extremely hard because making money and having a job or career is emotionally complex and can be a large part of a woman's identity. Still, we must get past this so that we never lose sight of what is lasting and what is fleeting.

It wasn't easy for Lexi and Gretchen, although it was worth it. And it won't be easy for you, either. For us mothers, there is nothing simple in our relationship with money. Like food, money is something that is a part of our everyday lives and there will always be tension surrounding it. Whether we are single mothers carrying the extraordinary burden of full-time employment alongside 100 percent of the parenting responsibilities, married mothers who stay home full-time, or working mothers who share the work of child care, making money or having money means far more to us than meets the eye. We play games with it psychologically, dancing around it and with it, trying ever so painstakingly to get it to give us something it can't. If we are going to break free from the hold it has on us, we must be honest with ourselves regarding its real meaning in our lives, then be bold enough to peel away that power and forge a whole new relationship with money, which I know we all have the power to do.

THREE WAYS TO MAKE THE HABIT STICK

#1: Open your fist and grab someone's hand—therein lies real security

Money offers limited, if any, security. If it is there, we can use it to buy a better life insurance policy for loved ones, pay the mortgage, or buy long-term care insurance. There's saving for the future, too, of course, but keep in mind that there's a big difference between saving for the future and saving for a bigger house. The problem is, money can disappear as quickly as it came. The stock market can crash, our business can fail, or we can lose our job. Those who rely on money alone for security sooner or later find themselves disappointed. So don't do it.

Place your trust in real things—in yourself and in loved ones. Real security comes from solid relationships with people who will never leave you. If the economy is strong, they will be with you, and when the stock market tanks, they will still be with you, helping you through anything life throws at you. Many of us rationally know that we can't find security in the size of our bank accounts, but we look for it there anyway. It's a deeply ingrained habit.

So break this bad habit. Challenge yourself to focus on the good relationships in your life and put your energy into loved ones. Solidify those relationships and you will have no regrets. Certainly, people can't ultimately keep us from dying, but they can do just about everything else. So, where loved ones reach their limit in the security they bring, focus on your faith. Those who have a strong faith can face difficulties with greater peace and less fear because they learn to rely on sources beyond themselves for security. Even when any semblance of security is gone and we face death, there are only two things left that will help us face the end of life—faith and love. Money can't, and won't, help.

#2: Ask yourself why you're opening your wallet

The next time you have an impulse to get something for your son or daughter, ask yourself what your motive is. Do some soul-searching here and find out whether you are doing it because your best friend just bought something similar for her son, or because you believe it to be a genuine need. If you realize that it is because you are doing it to feel better about yourself as a mother, don't spend the money. Challenge yourself instead by giving your son something more long-lasting. Carve out an evening that the two of you can spend together. Go to a play or a movie, or out to dinner. If your budget doesn't allow that, spend the evening together doing his homework or reading, but do something where there are few distractions—turn the television and computers off.

Then do a test: See how you feel about life the next day. Chances are excellent that you will feel a deeper sense of satisfaction about life and about yourself. And if the evening went poorly and the two of you ended up arguing about something, repeat the scenario. Try again—work on your communication, get through to him, find a way to establish a healthier connection, but don't give up, because the way to really boost your sense of value as a mother is through improving your relationship with your son (or daughter). Nothing else compares to success in connecting with a child when it comes to experiencing satisfaction in your parenting.

Remember one truth about children. They develop by watching, listening, and then internalizing what they see into their beings. This is how they form their identities. This means that every day your child watches you like a hawk looking for prey. Your daughter studies your moods, your decisions, and waits to see how you will behave in certain situations. Your son keeps his eyes and ears open to see if you are honest, courageous, or timid. When he sees something he likes, he pulls it into his own character. Your daughter does the same.

The legacy you pass on to your children is your character, not your stocks or bonds. So dig for the best parts of your character and make them surface again and again. When you do this, you will begin to feel your worth and your children will have the added benefit of learning from you.

#3: Look close to home for contentment—not to money

If we make a habit of focusing on the clothes in our closet we are less likely to desire more clothes. How many times do we get something new only to ignore the item a month or two later? Turnover is a way of life for many Americans. Newness is attractive so we are trained to discard the "old" and fill its place with something fresher. And of course, it takes money to accomplish this.

So purposefully examine what you have in front of you and determine to like it. We really can train ourselves to like what we have and be content with it. My patient Laura spends a fair amount of time helping on medical mission trips to South America. She told me recently that whenever she returns from a trip, she has to wait two to three weeks before she can go to a mall. She says that she feels completely overwhelmed by the mere volume of new clothes, DVDs, shoes, and everything else that she sees. She describes a feeling of total sensory overload if she goes to the mall too soon after returning from a trip. But Laura also said that once she's been home for a month or two, the feeling of being overwhelmed disappears and she finds herself once again enjoying going there with friends.

Interestingly, she says that when her normal state of "mall excitement" returns, she feels frustrated and agitated. "I get into this mind-set of constantly figuring out what I need to change or what I need to buy next. I don't like that," she told me. "When I'm in South America doing my work, all of my attention goes to other things, like people and their needs. I feel so content when I'm there and the irony is that I have so much less! We eat the same food over and over and I wear the same few pairs of jeans all the time. How weird is it to come home, where I have so much more stuff, and find myself anxious and feeling like I need more?"

The wonderful thing for mothers is that we can train ourselves to have this same sense of contentment. It will never come if we continually look outward at the next thing we want to get. It will only come if we acknowledge that we struggle in appreciating what is in front of us. So take a challenge to not buy anything new for one week, one month, even six months. It will change you and I guarantee it will cause you to feel happier.

So let's do it! Let's strip money of the power that it holds over us as women, as mothers. Rather than simply devising scenarios whereby we can make the balance between work and mothering teeter perfectly, let us shatter the notion that making money defines our worth (or part of it), ensures our independence, gives us complete security, and grants us power. Is it outrageous to shatter the money paradigm altogether and embrace the belief that, as mothers, our worth stems from something far deeper? Can we believe that our independence erupts from our human spirit, our power comes from our female humanity, and our security is born from something more significant than money? If we believe that money is part of life but not the driving force that can make us happy (although it never really does) or make us miserable, if we take bold measures, we'll see that real contentment never has a price tag.

HABIT #6

|||||||||||||||||||||||||||||||||||||||||||||||||||||||||||||||||||||||||||||||||||||||||||||||||||||||||||||||||

Make Time for Solitude

ALONE. *ALL ALONE.* For us mothers, the thought of being alone arouses feelings of elation. Whether we spend the day at home chasing toddlers or in the office attacking deadlines, we all dream of peace and quiet at the end of the day. The truth is, we need solitude. While we can't survive without friends, community, and family, we also need a healthy balance of time alone in order to recharge physically, mentally, emotionally, and spiritually.

You might read this and think, Are you kidding? How in the world can I find time for solitude when my kids, job, and husband demand all of my energy? For many of us busy mothers, that's just the point—we think that everyone, and everything, other than ourselves is a priority and has to be done right away. As a result, our health suffers. Our moods change and we feel more overwhelmed than we should. If you learn nothing else from the entire book, I hope that you are encouraged to do this: Take a hard look at what you fill your days with and find ways to slow down. Find time to be quiet, to hear less noise, and to enjoy your own company.

Let's look at what solitude can mean. Obviously, most of us don't have large chunks of time we can set aside to be alone. So don't frustrate yourself by looking for lots of time if you have small children. Solitude can be as simple as turning off the radio while waiting for your daughter to be done with her soccer practice. It can mean going to the grocery store alone, or sitting on the deck alone for fifteen minutes after the kids are in bed. Moments of solitude can be caught in numerous small places throughout the day. Personally, I find the car a great place for solitude. Other places? The bathtub or shower, the office, even the backyard. The point of solitude isn't just to be alone for a few moments, it is to be alone without noise from the radio, iPod, cellphone, or kids in the room. Solitude means not just pulling ourselves away from people for moments during the day (or week); it also means deliberately finding moments of quiet.

Why is solitude so important? Solitude is a necessity because it changes us. It strengthens our relationships with loved ones, it sharpens our sensitivity toward ourselves and others, it brings peace and healing, it helps us stay centered and sane in the midst of "choice overload," and it may even help us live longer. Real solitude is a lost art. I am not referring here to simply making time for ourselves, because these times usually involve time with friends, workouts, or running errands. I am referring to aloneness and quiet. Solitude involves relaxing, thinking, and, very often, not thinking. It is a time of stillness, reflection, or meditation. Even as we think of these types of activities, we see them as un-American because they involve not doing something. In solitude, nothing is visibly accomplished and this idea feels foreign to most American mothers. But we need to refamiliarize ourselves with it because we need it.

I think of wonderful friends and colleagues who are so overloaded with kids' schedules, work schedules, and frenetic lives that I worry how long they can keep up the pace. One friend of mine, Alexis, has a high-profile job in media that demands spur-of-the-moment decision making, travel, and grueling hours. She has two small children at home and is not one of those moms who leave their kids easily. That means she frets on the job about how her kids are doing and grieves that she is missing out on many of their "firsts." She is an exquisitely sensitive mother. While Alexis is young now, and a self-proclaimed high-energy person, I looked at her squarely and said, "How long do you think you can keep this pace up? Five years, ten years?"

I didn't mean to seem cruel, but I firmly believe that we must watch out for one another and this demands honesty. She paused. The glint in her eye disappeared and worry flushed across her face. "I honestly don't know. Not too much longer, I suppose." In a way, I'm writing this chapter for Alexis.

Here is what I fear even more than her health: I am concerned that she will not know when too much is too much. She won't recognize the clues that her body or her mental state are giving her. When she gets gradually more agitated at her kids and husband, she will pass it off as hormonal rather than work overload. When she develops irritable bowel problems, migraines, or elevated blood pressure, she will blame herself for not being able to "handle stress" as easily as she used to. The truth is, she may even ignore cues from loved ones that she is burning out because she will be so used to pushing herself that she will be too afraid to listen to them. She will feel that they are wrong in encouraging her to slow down, because the idea will be overwhelming and foreign to her.

Alexis doesn't need me to harp on her. Sure, she needs time for herself, rest and relaxation, but more than those things, she needs solitude. Quiet. Time to slow her thoughts and clear her head of others' voices. She needs to hear herself think and whisper. She even needs time to not think. She is wired with fabulous instincts that will help her know what to do, but without solitude, her instincts don't stand a prayer of being able to surface. They will be constantly drowned out by the noise of her job, coworkers, husband, and children.

Solitude is not a luxury for any of us women—particularly women like my friend. It is a necessity and will become an even greater necessity in the years ahead because solitude is the antidote to "choice exhaustion," the fatigue that comes from being overloaded with too many choices: from types of bread to which classes to take to styles of blue jeans.

Of course, you may wonder how to balance this with the friendship chapter. You have to be a good friend, spend more time with friends, and then turn around and spend more time alone. Does this sound crazy? Yes, on the surface. Here's the point. The habits discussed in the book are not to be practiced all at once. Many mothers define balance as doing a little bit of many things every day. The balance is different for each of us. For instance, I can't live doing a little of many things each day. I am not good at multitasking, because my personality is a bit too intense. I concentrate on one thing at a time. Consequently, I go hard at one project for as long as it takes to finish, and then I watch *Monk* reruns for several days at a time. When I'm with my kids (who are now grown) I try to keep focused on their needs and enjoy them. When I'm at the office, patients have my full attention and if other things need to be done (errands, chores, etc.) I find someone to help me. In other words, balance for me occurs over a long period of time. At the end of a year, I've gotten many things done, but most have been done one at a time.

Still, how do we balance friends and having time alone? It's different for everyone, but when it's time to choose, most of us ambitious, enthusiastic mothers are working hard on the relationship end but are falling down when it comes to ensuring that we have carved out times of solitude for ourselves. There really is room for friendship and solitude, but you may have to let go of some relationships, commitments, and things you think you "need" to do. We'll talk about that more in the simplicity chapter. But for now, I'm going to talk about why solitude is so incredibly important, and about a few women I know who have successfully enriched their lives through solitude. And at the end of the chapter I'll give you specific tips on how to make the habit stick, including how to start with bite-sized moments, how to find a specific place for solitude, how to quiet your mind, and finally, how to go deeper.

WHY MOTHERS NEED SOLITUDE

Why do we need solitude (and silence, which often accompanies it)? We need it because solitude makes us more sensitive mothers. Removing ourselves from constant stimulation and noise actually sharpens our sensitivity. Also, solitude forces us to face ourselves. In solitude we learn to like ourselves better because we are faced with our own company. It helps us heal from old hurts so that we can be free to enjoy the present and it refreshes us in ways that the company of others can't. Finally, solitude centers us and brings about a deep peace that cannot be achieved while staying immersed in either the good noise of friends and family or the awful noise of raucous media. We must retreat into quiet aloneness so that we can learn to be the women we were meant to be.

We need aloneness because it allows us to step away from the stresses we face and take a look at them from a different perspective. Aloneness almost allows us to get away from our situations and look at them as though we were an outside observer. Many things look different to us when we step back from them a bit. And aloneness helps us figure out what we really want. When we are with our kids, families, or friends, we hear their opinions and feelings constantly. But solitude allows us time to think more deeply about what we want and why we want it. Ours is the only voice we hear and this is important because all too often, our voices get drowned out. In order to work where we should, to parent the way we feel we should parent, and to be a good friend to others, we must be able to hear our own voices. In solitude, we can use meditation or prayer as an opportunity to explore our deepest thoughts, feelings, and beliefs. No one can influence us in alone time except for us and God. There is the loveliness of solitude.

But of course, it's still hard to make time. Are we really too busy for solitude? Mothers are champions of busyness. You name the activity, project, or challenge and we will make sure that it gets done. We sign our kids up for too many things because we are afraid they will miss out on something. Then we sign ourselves up for too many things (and this includes job-related activities) because we are either afraid that they won't get done without us (we are indispensable) or that they won't be done well (we are control freaks). In the midst of our frenetic busyness, we resist spending time alone. And we resist because we believe it is selfish.

But for many of us, the word *alone* also strikes a cord of anxiety. Being alone reminds us that maybe others don't want to be with us. Perhaps being alone reminds of lonely periods we spent as children, feeling that no one cared enough to be with us. Solitude smacks frighteningly of abandonment and this feels wholly unacceptable. As a matter of fact, many of us mothers subconsciously craft our days in such a way that we are rarely alone. We do this because deep down we are terrified to settle down for a moment, to reflect on our lives and our feelings. You can recognize us from a mile away. We are the extremely busy ones. The moms who constantly exude frustration because we simply can't seem to get enough done in a day, even though half of that stuff doesn't really need to get done. We clean too much. We stay at work too long. We complain that we can't slow down because too many issues are pressing down on us all at once.

Or we could be the moms who socialize constantly. We don't work outside the home but can't stand being home too much, so we pack our days with volunteer work, athletic endeavors, and meetings with friends. Whatever the venue, we make sure that we are with people constantly. We know that we should be able to spend time in our own company and we feel guilty because we don't want to. And we don't want to be with ourselves because we may learn something that we simply haven't time for, and none of us mothers needs something else on her plate. But could we give something up instead? Or would that somehow seem selfish?

IS SOLITUDE SELFISH?

In advocating regularly scheduled times of solitude, I am not advocating selfishness. Neither am I advocating increased self-absorption. Solitude embraced in a healthy manner does not encompass either of these. Solitude is a time set aside for introspection, reflection, meditation, and prayer, for the purpose of making us better people. It is a necessary component of healthy human survival because when we are alone, we separate ourselves from good activities as well as bad activities and influences of other people. We mothers are in the habit of staying caught up in frenetic busyness for a lot of bad reasons. First, because everyone else is doing it. If you're not as frantic as other mothers, you wonder, Am I doing something wrong? Then we stay this way because it makes us feel more important. Finally, we stay so busy because we are afraid not to be busy. Quiet can be scary.

I do feel strongly that most modern mothers are exhausted because we do a lot of things we don't need to do to be good moms, but we do them because we believe they are expected of us. That's why I encourage every mother to take a hard look at what fills her days and grill herself on why she does what she does, just as we did in the money chapter. Ask until you find an answer that you feel is right. Does each child really need to be in two sports at a time? Do you really need to stay at the office longer than your colleagues? Are you staying late because you have work that needs to be done, or are you just trying to impress your boss? Do some real soul-searching here because you are important and where you put your energy is just as important.

But there are mothers who have soul searched and concluded that their lives really are in balance. Mothers who are single, especially, simply can't cut anything from their schedules. Necessity is necessity and food must get on the table. To you I say, hold on. Get through the tough years when your kids are young and demanding and look forward to a period in your life when you can pull back and have some aloneness. It will come someday. In the meantime, seek as much quiet as you can. Turn your electronics off at the end of the day. Put your BlackBerry recharger in the basement so that you won't be tempted to pick it up every few minutes. Or do what I did and hire a babysitter so you can have a precious quiet hour.

Being busy can be a bad habit and a crutch, a way to make yourself feel important and ignore the real questions that trouble you deep inside. But we must change this bad habit because our stubbornness is slowly corroding something deep within us. It is dulling our sensibilities, chipping off the edges of our sensitivity toward others, and it is killing our spirit. The more we avoid quieting ourselves, the colder we become to ourselves. And this is a dangerous place to be. For when we grow insensitive to ourselves, we can become filled with self-contempt, and that is a very painful state.

So let's be bold enough to change. We need to change for ourselves and because it is the right thing to do. A life devoid of quiet is a cruel existence and it is wrong to be cruel to ourselves. And being kind to yourself will improve your relationship with your family, too.

LIVE THE SECRET THAT MOTHER TERESA KNEW

This all may seem good in theory, but how do you actually find time and learn to prioritize solitude? One of history's greatest women is my inspiration. While I never had the privilege of meeting this extraordinary person, I can glean from her lifestyle and writings that Mother Teresa truly understood the power of solitude. The secret she had was that spending time alone with God, in silence or prayer, energized her. And what mother isn't looking for more energy? Pulling away from noise and craziness for even a few moments during the day offers benefits on many levels. It can give us emotional refreshment, more physical energy, greater mental clarity, and as the mother saint revealed, greater spiritual depth. It gave Mother Teresa strength to get through her grueling days. Some of us may look at her daily routine of cleaning, encouraging, consoling, and caring for the overwhelming number of poor people and think that she had supernatural energy because she was so holy. Maybe, but I don't think so. Mother Teresa was extraordinarily ordinary. She was small and physically frail. But she had her priorities clear. And those priorities included regular solitude with God.

Every morning, before Mother Teresa went into the slums of Calcutta to minister to the poor, she spent time in silence and solitude. Quieting herself in prayer, she received the Eucharist and asked for God's help. In fact, she asked for a lot more. She asked that He do the work for her so that greater healing would come to the sick than she could give. Before she bent down to wash the sores of a leper or rub the back of an elderly woman with tuberculosis, she silenced herself before her God.

Think of the image of this tiny woman clad in her famous white headdress with blue stripes. We remember her face first, with the ever-present grin. Then we remember the hand gestures she used when speaking to the street people. She always touched whomever she was speaking to. Often she would cup their faces in her frail hands and look straight into their eyes. This gesture was profoundly personal. They were present, they were seen, they were important, and they were loved. Mother

Teresa's sensitivity and compassion were the hallmarks of her great work. And how did she become so sensitive and compassionate? She spent hundreds of hours in silent prayer.

Well, we mothers say, *that* worked for Mother Teresa because she had no children of her own (she would beg to differ), she had no husband (though she claimed to be married to Jesus), and she wasn't juggling home life and a career (she was doing something much more difficult!). As an American mother, this doesn't seem relatable. We have day care, bills to pay, grocery shopping to do, kids to drive around. Time for solitude? Perhaps we can find a bit in the car, we reason.

None of us can be Mother Teresa, but that's not the point. We can learn from her life and extraordinary behavior that solitude shapes character. She demonstrated profound sensitivity toward those around her. When she approached someone, she appeared to see no one else but that person. She cried with people and tended to their most basic needs. Then she retreated to a quiet place to pray in solitude.

I would think that living with the dying day after day might make someone callous. I've seen that among my medical colleagues. Caring for people with illness and pain is deeply disturbing. And most health-care professionals cope with their discomfort by shutting themselves off emotionally to that pain. We become desensitized in order to go back to work the next day. We become distant so that the sick person appears to experience hurts that we never would. We conjure up a world where we feel protected from the pains we treat.

Mother Teresa never did this. She drew herself closer to another person's pain. One could say that she lived more deeply. She never ran from hurt; rather, she engaged it. And she was able to do so because she didn't absorb the negative chatter around her. She didn't listen to those who berated the sick and left them to die. She withdrew herself in order to maintain her sensitivity toward them and gain strength from God to continue to love them and heal them.

FINDING TWENTY MINUTES A DAY FOR SOLITUDE

Carrie's life couldn't be more different from the outside, but she did much the same thing as Mother Teresa. Carrie is a good friend, and she's a psychiatrist now and a mother of three. When she was doing her medical residency and working ninety-hour weeks caring for geriatric patients in the hospital, she told me that she would often become so overwhelmed with sadness that she had to leave the floor and find a place where she could be alone.

"Sometimes, I just needed to go off and have a cry. Other times, I just needed to eat peanut butter and jelly sandwiches and listen to silence. Sometimes I stayed in the quiet space for ten minutes, sometimes for half an hour."

At first I wondered if Carrie really needed to go off alone because she was just plain physically exhausted. Maybe that drove her to be alone more than an emotional need, I wondered. So I pressed her on it.

"No," she answered. "It really wasn't that. Maybe at first it was, but after six months of regularly retreating to spend time alone, I realized that I liked it because I felt like a better physician. I came out of these times alone feeling more refreshed, but also a little more compassionate, less hardened toward my patients. In a weird way, I felt closer to them, not more detached."

Carrie described a more acute sensitivity toward her patients very much like what I have seen other mothers experience toward their children and families after they have begun a habit of carving out time for solitude. I asked Carrie if practicing solitude years ago has had any impact on her parenting.

"It has," she confided. "I was so amazed at what even the small bits of solitude I got during those years of residency did for me, and my attitude, that I wanted to continue to incorporate it into my life as a mom. I honestly don't know what kind of a mother I would be if I didn't have my 'alone time.' I know that this sounds weird, but starting every day with twenty minutes of quiet reading, prayer, or meditation helps me be a nicer person. And believe me, there are many days that I need to be a nicer person for my kids! Even when my kids were small, I'd get up before they would or take my alone time during their naps. I even arranged my work schedule so that I could make it happen."

How does this work? Solitude makes us more sensitive to people and our surroundings because it banishes noise. It cuts out good noise and bad noise. Television, music, coworkers talking, friends calling, children crying, or husbands demanding our ear as they recount their day keep us drenched in constant chatter. Stimulation can be pleasurable, but constant stimulation just isn't healthy.

And the wrong kind of stimulation can desensitize us. Hearing criticism, gossip, or fighting on television makes us duller. Watching violence, or people arguing or in pain, causes us to detach ourselves so that we can cope with the situation. If we are to become more sensitive—or at least renew our sensitivity—we must withdraw from all desensitizing things. This is precisely what monks and Buddhists do to sharpen their keenness toward the outside world. Retreating from too much stimulation, even positive stimulation, is necessary for a healthy sensitivity. Isolating ourselves periodically from others is not a weakness; rather it is an activity requiring extraordinary strength. It is certainly a lot easier to remain in an overstimulating environment and feel detached than it is to remove ourselves from stimulation. When we are alone, we talk less, watch less violence because it bothers us, or gossip about friends less because we know it is hurtful. Then our sensitivity returns. When we are overstimulated, we become less sensitive to our environment. This happens because we know that since we must stay in it, we must find a mechanism for coping. Thus we "shut off" parts of our emotions that are being overstimulated. We become dulled to our surroundings. We care less. We hurt less for others who are upset or sad. We fail to hear what others are saying because cognitively we can't process too many statements at once. In a very real sense, we shut down a very wonderful part of our being in order to simply survive the day.

This is precisely why we need solitude and silence. Stimulation changes us in good ways, but also in destructive ways, so we must plan to pull ourselves away regularly and determine to refocus on what is important. We must recenter ourselves so that we can stay sensitive to our words, to those around us, and to ourselves.

FINDING A PLACE TO BE QUIET—LONDA'S STORY

There is more to solitude than understanding who we are and sharpening our sensitivity to others and ourselves. Solitude helps us connect with a deeper part of our being, called the divine center. Philosophers, mystics, and religious leaders have described this as the part of our being that is spirit. It is the invisible, intangible center of who we are. We can neither feel it nor see it, but we know that it exists. Our spirit, or soul, gives us value and meaning beyond what we can articulate.

Interestingly, mothers who have grappled with terrible pain often speak openly about spiritual matters. Women who struggle with chronic illness (physical or mental), alcohol or drug addiction, post-traumatic stress disorder, depression, or other serious problems are forced to seek answers about their pain. In the seeking, they make decisions about their abilities, their humanity, and the existence of a part of themselves that connects with God. Desperate for relief from emotional, physical, or mental pain, many mothers intensify efforts to find something or someone who offers help beyond what they or anyone else they know can bring.

It is no surprise that mothers who struggle are also more likely to pray or meditate. They do this because they fastidiously search for help. Here again, solitude and silence brings about prayer and causes some to face truths about their struggles. It helps them become more sensitive, more understanding of the intricacies of the struggle, and finally, it helps them reconcile their lives and their hurts. But there is more. There is the encounter of their spirit with another—God. Herein lies the secret to the peace that many mothers describe as flowing from solitude. When we feel our spirit connect with an invisible God, we know it to be true, but we cannot articulate it. It exists as a deep, very personal knowledge. Londa knows what this means.

When I first met Londa, I liked her immediately. We took our kids to the same preschool and during our first chat, we seemed to click. Looking back at that first meeting, I think that what I was attracted to was her ordinariness. She wasn't a perfectionist—she was a mom who brought store-bought cookies or undercooked brownies for preschool snack. She had tremendous energy. She took her kids with her everywhere and whenever she had hauled them on too many errands, she would stop at the park on the way home and play with them. She looked like a really fun mom.

Over the succeeding two years, I noticed that Londa was losing weight. She wasn't a dieter; on the contrary, she loved to cook and eat and frequently joked about her exercise regimen, which she followed, she admitted, solely because she liked to eat. Otherwise she would have ditched it. Her moods shifted frequently and I saw them take a toll on her kids and her family. A gently escalating anger began somewhere in her and she hid it as well as she could for many years, she later told me. She was becoming increasingly anxious and agitated over those two years. Her anxiety seemed to appear like a coiled leopard silently waiting behind a tree for the right time to attack its prey.

One Saturday morning her husband called. He had taken Londa to the hospital during the night with an acute anxiety attack. The doctors told him that she was having a nervous breakdown and needed to be hospitalized. I felt sick to my stomach. My friend was hurting, confused, and probably terrified. For five days she stayed hospitalized and tranquilized with medications. After she was discharged from the hospital, she went home and spent the next two years seeing a great counselor.

I will never forget a conversation we had several years after the event. Of course, I desperately wanted to know what had gone wrong. Had something bad happened to her that no one knew about? What precipitated such a violent explosion of emotion in her that caused her to break?

When I posed just that question, she quietly said, "I'm not quite sure."

Frustrated by her answer, I pressed her. "Well, what did the doctors say when you were in the hospital. What has your counselor said?"

"Well, my first doctor thought that something from my past might have been welling up inside, triggering the anxiety. My counselor thought that I had never adequately learned how to express certain emotions and that this may have contributed to my anxiety. Actually, I think I just come by it naturally. My brother has it and he has had it all of his adult life. I really can't pin it to anything in particular. But I guess that's because I don't feel the need to. What's more important to me now is how to handle it. And I think I've learned a pretty good way to do that."

My interest was piqued. What did she know?

"I learned over the years that my mind and my body seem to race. Sometimes I feel like I have the motor of a Porsche in my head. Thoughts, ideas, things that I think would be fun to do came in my mind and circled around and around. When they did, I would act on them. When the motor revved up, so would I. Physically, it wore me down. I did everything and—this is the weird part—I kind of liked doing it. The problem was, it didn't work. I couldn't keep up."

She continued. "I was too involved, started sleeping less, and when that began to happen, everything went downhill. I got more tired and my mind raced. Everything around me felt like it was racing. I ate erratically. So what I learned to do was catch the racing as it was gearing up. When I felt my mind starting to grab hold of another thing that I was going to do (and there were always more and more coming), I pulled back. I shut myself away from the kids and Dan. I took twenty minutes to myself and learned to quiet my mind, and it made all the difference."

There it was. Solitude. Londa first identified something internally that was going to get her into trouble and at once, she sought aloneness. I wanted to know more.

"Here's the thing. As soon as I could feel anxiety and racing thoughts welling up inside and I took myself away—even into my bedroom while the kids were watching television—I began to calm down. I slowed my breathing. I sat in a chair in my bedroom and closed my eyes. Call me crazy, I began to pray. I began to concentrate on God. Sometimes I'd recite the Lord's Prayer. Other times I'd ask for help. Sometimes I just blurted out whatever came to my mind. The cool thing was, I always felt calmer after I went into my room."

That's great, I thought, but what about times when she was at the park with the kids, in the grocery store, or out to dinner with friends? What then?

"I've actually learned that even the tiniest moments alone are so important that I may leave a full grocery cart in the aisle and get to my car for ten minutes. Or maybe I'll excuse myself from the table and go to the bathroom. It sounds crazy, but it works."

Many of us don't struggle with the severity of anxiety that Londa had, but that doesn't matter. What helped my friend control her anxiety can help any one of us mothers with other things: frustration, mental fatigue, irritability. That's what is so crucial about solitude. It helps alleviate a multitude of stresses. And we all need a little more peace in our lives.

And solitude will bring, at last, peace. Peace doesn't come through needless chatter, figuring life out, or reading about peace. It comes through stillness. Not idle stillness, but active stillness. Truth be told, I have not personally encountered a mother who has experienced profound peace without making room for it. No one has claimed to have gone out, decided to find it, and then grabbed on to it. Peace is elusive and nebulous. Like our spirit, we know when we have it and we certainly know when we don't have it. But it is a profoundly precious commodity and has been down through the ages. Deep inner peace comes as an infusion from another place. The key, as Londa related to me, is that one must make a way for peace to enter and then clear a spot in which it can rest.

FOUR WAYS TO MAKE THE HABIT STICK

#1: Start with bite-sized moments

Medicine is replete with studies illustrating the profound benefits of solitude. Quieting ourselves through meditation or prayer has been shown to lower blood pressure, reduce anxiety, and restore energy. We hear doctors, friends, and parents telling us to slow down, but usually their words bounce off of us because we already know this. We just aren't convinced that we want to.

I have heard just about every excuse we mothers can contrive when told that we should spend some time alone. You name it, I've heard it. From "Maybe when my kids are older," to "Sorry, alone time is a luxury for moms who have nothing better to do," to "I could if my kids and husband weren't so demanding of my time." Really? Are the excuses we come up with really why we avoid solitude or is there something deeper going on?

Here's the bottom line: *We find time to do what we really want to do.* We are stubborn, driven, frightened, and too easily manipulated by our loved ones. So we must make some changes if we want our lives to change significantly. We need more. Not more stuff or money, opportunities or challenges. We need more authenticity. We need more peace. We need more healing and a keener sensitivity to ourselves and our world. All of these come through solitude.

So do it. Find time—anywhere—for a little solitude. Any mother who drives a car can find solitude. Yes, it can start in the car. Even better, it can start in the bathroom, though many mothers of small children dispute this. We can find moments of solitude and silence when we are scrubbing floors (I write books best while painting walls or vacuuming), driving to pick kids up from school, or coming home from work. The first challenge is simply to determine that you will find moments for solitude and then that you will take advantage of them.

#2: Find a place for solitude (and let everyone know)

Just as my kids had a time-out chair when they were growing up, I had a chair in a tiny study off my bedroom designated as my "quiet time" chair. The kids knew that when I was there, I wasn't to be disturbed if at all possible. Of course, when they were little, I would have to leave them with a babysitter downstairs while I was in my chair because they might have killed themselves otherwise.

This quiet-time chair became so important to me that I would do just as I said above. I would hire a babysitter after school to come to my house and play with my kids while I was in the chair. Sometimes I read, sometimes I prayed, sometimes I took an accidental nap.

Solitude for mothers with young children isn't easy to come by, so we have to make it happen just like anything else in our lives. Kids used to have playpens to keep them safe and now, well, we mothers need a chair, a pillow on the floor, a closet, a study—just a safe place where we can be all alone. As my kids got older they realized that it was good for them for me to spend time in my chair. I was a nicer person when I emerged.

I have known women who have incorporated small rooms into their homes during remodeling for the specific purpose of meditation or quiet. They understand, as we all should, that the benefits of retreating to a special spot that is easily accessible on a daily basis improves many different aspects of our lives. Having our own spot, beanbag chair, or easy chair reminds us that we will have quiet soon. With a visible object, we have a reminder that spending time alone is doable and important.

#3: Quiet your mind (yes, you can)

When you are alone, the next challenge is to break the habit of thinking about all of the things that you should be doing rather than quieting yourself. This is a tough one. Shutting your mind off can be done, but it takes training. But we are all trainable, particularly when the outcome benefits us and we can feel the benefits readily. Once you have carved out the time for solitude, prepare yourself for the onslaught of worries.

When the thoughts flood in and the guilt about being alone, silent, and not "accomplishing anything" sets in, wage war. This is precisely what girls with eating disorders are instructed to do. Wage war with unwanted thoughts in your mind. Reject silly worries, but if they are legitimate concerns, tell yourself that you will deal with them later. Give yourself permission to worry about things later, like in thirty minutes, but not during your solitude.

#4: Go deeper

Once you have begun moments of solitude, have rid your environment of noise and cleared your mind of unwanted thoughts, solitude finally begins to be fruitful. In the deafening silence you may become frightened, but don't run. Stay in it. Meditate on something that you like. Think about the joys in your life. Even if you hate your life, focus on something positive that you have. Here some mothers simply sit and enjoy silence. Others meditate and others pray. Sometimes your mind will wander (particularly at the beginning) and this is all right, but be careful. Dwelling on your problems without constructive learning can be harmful. In other words, if you are prone to look at your problems and become stuck in self-pity, solitude does you no good. If worries constantly surface in your mind, tell yourself that you will worry about them in thirty minutes, but now you want your mind to be quiet. Or even better, approach your problems with an attitude of resolution and healing. Here's where faith can also come into play. If you get stuck on thinking about your pain or a bad situation that you are in, ask God for guidance.

Beyond staying still, we also begin at this point to connect to our divine center. Don't let this idea frighten you. It is not magical, but it is mysterious. Doing so demands that we think more deeply, that we grapple with our limitations as women, as mothers, and as humans. Going deeper in our solitude means that we must challenge our spiritual selves and find some answers. Those who need answers in this area are fortunate, in a way, because they are forced to look sooner than those who are not so desperate. But who among us mothers, if we are honest, has not felt desperate? We need answers because we love intensely and we are frightened of losing loved ones and those relationships. We are desperate to figure things out—for example, should we spend more time at home or at our jobs? We want answers when our kids are sick, when we are fired, or when we simply hate our lives. Perhaps, then, we are really more desperate than we think.

I can assure you of one thing. In our frenetic, noisy world where we tell too many lies about ourselves—mainly that we must be thinner, kinder, busier, smarter, harder-working, more perfect mothers—we need solitude more than ever. We cannot live without it if we are to keep our wits about us and not lose our minds. Saying that we deserve it doesn't cut it. We *need* it. Our survival as moms depends upon it; otherwise we will become merely reflections of the messages that we hear every day.

We will lose any hope of authenticity. And when this happens, not only do we lose, but our children and spouses do as well. Finally, we mothers need to learn to wait in our solitude. We must wait for refreshment. We must learn to be patient for answers, understanding, healing, and finally, peace.

||||||||||||||||||||||||||||||||||||||||||||||||||||||||||||||||||||||||||||||||||||||||||||||||||||||||||

Give and Get Love in Healthy Ways

MOTHERS AND OUR LOVE

I am one of the fortunate women who has a large, extended family of in-laws whose company I enjoy. My mother-in-law, in particular, is an extraordinary woman. She is eighty-three and has Ronald Reagan black hair and an indomitable spirit. Three years ago she rolled her SUV into a snowbank and laughed out loud when describing herself and her girlfriend "hanging upside down" waiting for help to arrive. She is tough, outspoken, and very good to me. She has shown me how to be gracious to friends regardless of their behavior, and loved me when I was acting pretty impossible. She loves fairly and graciously. And I am convinced that she loves so well because she has worked hard at it. For the thirty years I have known her, I have seen her work at love more times than I can count.

Several years ago, I received a very generous but unusual Christmas gift from her. She bought some property and gave my husband and me two parcels of land abutting her own newly acquired piece. It was situated on a hill next to a cherry orchard off a quiet country road. The only problem was, it was small—very small. It was my very own cemetery plot. A place for my tired bones to rest for eternity.

I wasn't exactly sure how to feel. It was expensive, it was beautiful, but a cemetery plot for Christmas? That left me emotionally stumped for a few moments. But only for a few moments, until my uneasiness wore off. When it did, I began to laugh and hugged her. I shook my head in amazement for hours. I laughed because I know my mother-in-law well. She is the quintessential gift giver with a heart that is unstoppable. She loves our family and her friends with great intensity. And the primary vehicle through which she loves us all is gift giving. But she has German heritage and remembers the Great Depression. She has learned to save tinfoil and reuse paper plates, and she composted years before it was fashionable. We have all come to realize that her gifts smack of no-nonsense utilitarian purpose but they are no less gifts of great love.

We mothers are lovers. We give love in our own peculiar ways and we receive it the best we can. Sometimes, though, as natural as love is to our mother hearts, the giving and taking ties us in knots. Before we bring that first child home, we envision our life with him and our love for him. We will glide back and forth in a mahogany rocker wearing a gown of white pima cotton. There will be no signs of pads soaked with witch hazel for hemorrhoids or bra inserts for drippy breasts. We won't know the names Tucks and Spanx because nothing significant will have impacted our figures or veins. (After four kids, Tucks and Spanx became two of my best friends. If you don't know what Spanx are, you aren't eating enough.)

The mystery of love is that it gives us life, but it can also throw us into a pit of pain in nanoseconds. That's exactly why we need to stop and take a hard look at how we do it. Giving love well takes a lot of work and receiving it is even harder for most of us. Sure, we feel love intensely and we do the best we can in loving our kids, but the wonder of how well we are doing threads its way through the recesses of our minds with unrelenting regularity. We *need* to know that we are doing it right. Because if we fail at this—giving love in a healthy, meaningful way to our children— we feel that we might as well hang up this whole mothering thing. Sure, it sounds simple, natural, romantic, and easy. But it isn't. It is gritty. It makes us feel crazy and exhausted but we must continue to work at it because without giving or getting love, life simply wouldn't be worth living. In this chapter, I'll show you how to make it easier to give and get love, how to take smart and calculated risks, how not to take loved ones so personally, how to read loved ones (and let them read you), and finally, how to express love even during the toughest times.

THE GIVING—WHY WE MUDDY LOVE WITH NEED AND EXPECTATIONS

Let's face it. We all became mothers because we wanted something. We wanted more love, a sense of purpose in our lives; maybe we simply wanted to upset boredom in our lives. We birthed or adopted these creatures into our lives from a sense of selfishness. Sure, we may have adopted a child from a third-world country, but if we were completely altruistic in our motives, wouldn't we have adopted the neediest of the bunch?

Wanting children and the love that comes with having them is fabulous, because loving kids can make us more complete women. Love for children really is different. Romantic love is wonderful, but it is entirely separate. It behaves differently and constricts in ways that we believe motherly love won't. Romantic love, which we usually experience before we love as mothers, has conditions. In order for it to work well, we must be something, look a certain way, or excel in certain areas in order to attract and keep the best of our romantic love, at least initially. We want to escape from the pressure so we choose another route—motherhood. I believe that fathers do the same.

Our beauty is born. Round, swollen, and red. She screams and our heart jumps in our chest. At the first cry, we are smitten. She hasn't even done anything, and we are in love. Why? Precisely because she hasn't done anything yet. Loving is easy. She isn't supposed to do anything. She gets a pass because she's a baby, entirely dependent and needy. But in the back of our mind, we know that this will change and the good stuff will get going. Our dreams become crystallized in our conscious and we are off and running. We will give her everything so that . . . she can . . . be . . . president, winner of a Pulitzer Prize, first-chair violinist with the Philadelphia Philharmonic. But that will come later. First, she needs her baby shots.

We start to dream about her future because we want more. Maybe we want more than we had, whatever that was or wasn't. We want her to be polite because we weren't. We want her to want to come home during her summers in college because we never wanted to. She'll have a perfect mom. Our daughter will be the lucky one. We'll give her everything that we missed.

Can you see what we do? Early in our son's life, we lay out our hopes and dreams, not based on who he is, but on who we are. While we say that we will let him be who he wants to be and that we will love him unconditionally, the reality is, none of us mothers can actually do that. When we go to give him our love, our own needs become kneaded into that love and pretty soon, love can feel messy. But it doesn't have to be.

We adopt or have our own children because we have a hope that we will experience love on a different level. And we expect in having kids that we will give love and receive love back from them in new, wonderful ways. I would like to address some of these expectations that we mothers have, because they can be very confusing for many of us.

Before our children are born, we begin painting pictures of what they will be and what they will give us. After we have them, our expectations continue. We want them to behave a certain way or excel at certain things. We want them to be academically strong and physically strong. High expectations are good for kids but they are not synonymous with love. One of the most difficult challenges we mothers face is separating these two things. This is extremely important because when kids feel that they need to meet our expectations of their behavior, appearance, or performance in order to get love from us, they feel trapped. None of us mothers ever wants our kids to feel this way, and usually we connect expectations and love quite innocently and unknowingly. Every child should know that regardless of what she does, even if it means that she sits in her closet for the rest of her life, we will love her and express our love to her. When we do that, we love unconditionally.

Loving our kids gets really messy when we see someone else inside of them. Usually, though not always, the person who we see inside is another form of ourselves. Psychologists report that many mothers have the most tumultuous relationships with their oldest daughters, and I have seen this in my own practice. It is primarily because we identify ourselves in them. We see our own character traits in them, and some of these traits we like, but others we can't stand. Her behaviors become personal because she is not only herself; she is very often a smaller, younger version of ourselves and this rubs us the wrong way. So we fight. We don't really fight her; we fight ourselves in her. We see in her another woman—our mother, our sister, or (tough break for our daughters) ourselves. We see the prepubescent little girl who was ridiculed in sixth grade and we think she's ugly. So we have difficulty hugging our fifth-grade daughter. We were ugly; she is ugly. She becomes our substitute and we are completely unaware of this fact. We are blocked from loving her for who she is because we have unmet needs, unreconciled pains.

The most frustrating part is that we don't realize we're doing this. That's why it is important to recognize, so that for her sake and for ours, we can give love better and enjoy our relationship with our daughter so much more.

We love less well when we are disappointed. And we are only disappointed when the expectations that we had are dashed. So the problem really isn't our disappointment; the problem is our expectations. If we cut the list of expectations we have for our kids in half, I can guarantee that our disappointments will be cut in half and life will be a lot less stressful and a lot more fun.

When we expect our kids to be less than perfect and we are prepared to love them that way, our parenting rises to a whole new level. We become better at parenting because we are cleaner at loving. And the best news of all is that when we change the way we talk, think, and act toward our kids, we feel more affection. We feel less strained, less heavy at the end of the day. When we free ourselves to love in a cleaner way, we enjoy our relationships infinitely more.

THE GETTING—PROBLEMS WITH ANGER, LACK OF TRUST, AND A DIFFERENT KIND OF EXPECTATION

Giving love is hard, but getting (or accepting) it back is just as difficult for many of us mothers. The main culprit is anger that has hidden underground. And many of us moms are experts at being angry and neither showing nor feeling it. Anger is tied to too many other emotions. We feel pressure, particularly when our kids are young, not to show disappointment, anger, or frustration at the young people they are. But we need to address this issue because we are the ones who live with the smoldering suffocation of latent anger. We are the ones who miss out because we don't want to give it up and allow the great infusion (or even trickles) of love from all sides and from all sorts of people in our midst.

As kids grow older, they begin to smile and also snarl and sometimes scream. They get bossy and belligerent either because they are smack in the middle of a difficult developmental stage or they are just plain ornery. Sometimes they ooze love; sometimes they refuse to show it. In short, the love they express toward us is fickle at best. We can't depend upon any steady flow. This is where the anger begins. We want more from this relationship because we invest so much in it. We pour our hearts and souls into these creatures and what do we get? Temper tantrums and doors that slam. They park their hands on their hips and let us know exactly what they think about us at any given moment. Since there is no internal filter, what they feel is what we see, including the bad stuff. Since we are women, we want a steady, consistent stream of love. We need it (we think). We get extraordinarily frustrated and that frustration, growing more each day, can turn into a slow-burning bitterness. How do we know? Listen to the way we talk. Our tone of voice says volumes about our deep feelings. I hear it in my own voice and I hear it in the mothers who come into my office.

There is something else operating with regard to anger. Before our kids are born, we see them in our mind's eye. We see what they look like and what our relationship with them is like. We sit in a rocking chair with a baby who doesn't vomit on our white pima cotton nightgown. We pick up our kids at school and they are glad to see us and run to the car so that they can give us a giant hug. When our daughter is fifteen, we take shopping trips and have luncheons at nice restaurants and chat about anything and everything. She is happy just to be in our presence. Each one of us has a vision of how life should be with her. There will be warm, consistent exchanges of laughter and love.

Then life comes along. Her personality is different from ours, and when each of us fires love at the other, the arrows miss in midair. One goes up and the other goes straight into the ground. We get mad at ourselves because things just aren't working the way we hoped. So we try harder and when love bounces back to us and our son won't talk, we get more frustrated and begin to feel like a failure. Now we're mad at ourselves as well as our son. We're the perfect setup for rejecting love. Our hearts get crusty. When he is ready to be nice or show affection, we don't want it. We're ticked—at him, at ourselves, and at this whole mother thing.

Here's why this tangle of frustration gets to us. First, we don't see it. We simply don't want to face the fact that the relationship is messy. We want to love our kids and get that love back. We want each of them to have a personality that works with ours so that the exchange of emotion and affection will be natural, consistent, and smooth. We fear that if we admit that it's going any way other than what we'd hoped, we'll also have to admit that something is broken in our children, or that something is off in our mothering. Neither of these is a fun thing to accept and so when it comes to feeling humbled or hanging on to a slow burn, we opt for the latter. Being angry is safe. It is easier to swallow than admitting that something is cracked. And it protects us from further hurt. Since love isn't coming from the kids the way we want it to, or we are failing to do a good job at loving, anger keeps us from feeling the deeper hurts of loss and sadness. It sits there like a slimy coating over our hearts and keeps us emotionally distant enough to get through the next day. The problem is, this doesn't work. The smoldering upset eventually makes us old. It makes us mean, old, resentful women. The tragedy is that not one of us mothers needs to live this way. Not one of us.

These are general aspects of the isolation that anger produces. Add to this the death of a parent, abuse from a spouse, loss of a job, or failure of a marriage and sadness piles on top of that deep disappointment. It goes deeper underground and before we know it, we have protected ourselves against taking any form of love not just from our kids, but from many more loved ones. We don't want touch, affection, help, or even words of encouragement. We just want to be safe and angry.

Lack of trust can also be a huge issue. As new and fresh as we believe our relationship with our young kids to be, it isn't. We hope at the outset that this time, love will be better. Kids won't do what Dad did or our best friend did. As we venture into this relationship, we have a renewed hope. Additionally, since we are the adult, we can massage the relationship in a determined, effective way. We are excited to be able to move the love in a direction that feels better and works better than it ever has. We have the power to do that. We will raise kids who are honest, trustworthy, and good. They won't let us down the way others have in the past.

At first this may work, if we're really, really lucky. But then the little monster tells a fib. We told him to pick up his room and he said he did. But he didn't. He came over bubbly and excited to tell us that he was finished. He hugged us as he said it. Our daughter got in trouble at school for fighting with a boy at recess. Our teenage son stayed out all night with his girlfriend when he said he was at his buddy's home during that time. As we look in our daughter's backpack to get the permission slip we need to sign, we find a bag of weed. There it is—unsafe love staring us in the face. She, he, they—the whole lot of our children are like all the others we have loved in our past. They too are not trustworthy, at least as far as getting emotionally close to them is concerned. They will disappoint us and when we open our hearts to take the overtures of love they express (as inside out as they may be), we balk. Nope. We will keep that love at bay because we will not be burned again. No more hurt.

If we believe the letter our daughter wrote describing her remorse, how much she misses us, will she really mean it? When our son texts from soccer asking us to make his favorite spaghetti (yes, this is an expression of love), will he be home to eat it or will we sit at an empty table eating meatballs all alone? Perhaps we have a teenage son who lives with his dad, who parents very differently than we do. He allows our son to play video games at all hours of the night and that's just the beginning of the chaos. Our son loves being there because Dad is the nice, understanding parent. We are the Nazi mama. He has sent out college applications but we are a bit worried because all of the partying has cost him good grades. But we are wrong—both he and his dad know that. So we keep our mouths shut. Then the rejection letters come. One after another and suddenly we are his best friend. He calls us despondent on the phone and needs us. He loves us and wants to come live with us for a while to "get his head clear." When he does, we have a new kid on our hands. He's helpful and he even hugs us. Do we dare take his affection? We've seen this pattern of behavior before. He loves us, he loves us not. Just like his dad, the expression of his love is fickle and erratic. Can we trust it?

Finally, expectations, which we discussed in the last section, can cause enormous problems in reverse, too. Our love for our kids gets tied up in our expectations for them, but we also have expectations about how we feel we should be loved in return. We must confront the fact that when they fail us (in our minds) our natural instinct is to emotionally retreat from them. No, we don't do this dramatically, but we do it just enough to throw our kids off balance. In our disappointment, our body language tells them things. It says, "No thanks, I don't like you very much. Don't even try to be nice, hug me, or pretend that you like me. I am off-limits." If kids are extremely self-confident, or extremely lacking in confidence and needy, they will drive right over our negative messages. They will pursue us. They will coddle us or make us dinner. They will assume full responsibility for making sure that we feel loved and they will try to press it into us. But that shouldn't be a kid's responsibility.

I have heard many parents say that they love their kids but I have heard those kids tell me that they honestly don't believe their parents do love them. What is going on? When kids feel that they must do well at certain things in order to be loved, they don't feel loved, regardless of how successful they are at those things. Kids need to feel it.

The extraordinary irony about our expectations of love from our kids and spouses is that they act as a self-protective device. Our expectations protect us from seeing our doubts and insecurities and they protect us from being disappointed in love. When we expect others to love us and they don't, we blame them, the lovers. They let us down and they are to blame. When we blame them, we can hold on to whatever illusions we had about love. It was supposed to be great, but it wasn't because the other person failed. In this way we prevent ourselves from seeing that maybe being loved is not really what we thought it was going to be. Maybe it feels good and bad at the same time. Expectations of others to love us well and expectations that it will make us feel extraordinary all the time keep us from the reality that many times there is little in love that we can control. If we don't get too close, we won't have to face this truth. But we need to, both for our kids and for ourselves.

HOW SUE LOVED CORBIN JUST THE WAY HE WAS

Sue demonstrated this beautifully with seven-year-old Corbin. During Corbin's well visit, Sue told me that he was having some temper issues. I asked her to describe them. "Well," she said, "sometimes he just has meltdowns. For instance, if I tell him to do something as simple as picking up his toys, he screams!"

That sounds kind of normal, I thought. I waited for Sue to elaborate. "I mean, he *really* screams—at the top of his lungs for an hour. It's exhausting."

I was surprised at Sue's calm demeanor. She wasn't upset or even asking for advice. My curiosity prompted me to ask, "So what do you do when he has these episodes?"

"Well," she said, "at first they really shook me. I wondered what in the world I was doing wrong that would cause him to do this. I never knew any child this old who did. Then I realized that maybe it wasn't something

I was doing; maybe it was something deep that was bothering him. Maybe something bad had happened way back at the orphanage. I don't know. But we got him so early, this probably wasn't the case. Then I came to the conclusion that maybe this is just him. Maybe he gets emotionally overcharged and just needs to erupt every once in a while. There doesn't seem to be any rhyme or reason to his episodes."

Well, that makes good sense, I thought, but it still didn't seem clear to me, so I asked her for more details.

"When he erupts, I just think, 'The volcano is coming.' I take him into the family room and sit him on my lap facing away from me. He used to scream for me to hold him when he first started. Then I cross my arms over his shoulders and hold him tight until they pass. Over the months they've gotten shorter. I just sit there and wait. That's what he needs."

Now, if you have never been in the same room with a wailing seven-year-old boy, you might not appreciate the emotional fortitude required to sit and hold a screaming child, particularly when you're the mom. Let me tell you, it pushes all of a mother's buttons, hammers at her patience, and makes her wonder—even fleetingly—if she did the right thing in having this child. Mothers take everything their kids do personally, and when it involves emotional outbursts, we can't help but believe on some deep unconscious level that we're doing something terribly wrong in this love process. After all, we conclude, normal kids with good moms don't do this kind of stuff. But I have some news—oh yes, they do.

Here's where Sue got the giving of love to Corbin just right. She reduced her expectations about normal seven-year-old behavior and resolved early on that regardless of what other kids did, this was something her kid did. It wasn't Corbin's fault or Sue's as a mother. She refused to take Corbin's behavior personally. If she would have sat and stewed about what she was doing wrong, she would have gotten angrier with her son. She didn't. She separated herself out and viewed these tough episodes very matter-of-factly. In this manner, she didn't set herself or Corbin up for failing. Then she was able to step back and think about what she needed to do in order to love Corbin through his temper tantrums. Expressing that love came down to sitting on her couch with her strong arms crossed over Corbin's chest for some very long minutes.

Love is so much easier to give when we don't let it get too messy. So often we overanalyze our kids' behaviors and our own. We mothers make everything personal. We have expectations for every one of our kids' behaviors, and when they fall short, rather than stepping back, as Sue did, we get angry with our kids or ourselves. Oftentimes the best thing to do is let go of those expectations. Sue really wanted a seven-year-old son who played Go Fish with a smile on his face. What she got was a sensitive little boy with volcanic eruptions. That was all right with her and life went on. This is when the loving part gets challenging but good.

WHAT MARYBETH LEARNED ABOUT HER DAUGHTER'S LOVE

Marybeth was a mom with an even greater challenge. Eight years ago, she came into my office in tears. Our conversation and her character were so poignant that it seared me with an indelible impression. She was crying because she had recently gone with her daughter to a well-respected psychiatrist at a large teaching hospital. Marybeth told me that she took her daughter, Lupe, to the psychiatrist because she wouldn't make frequent eye contact or let Marybeth hug her. She even became violent at times. Marybeth, still shocked, told me that the psychiatrist had advised her and her husband to send their daughter back to the country from which they had adopted her. They refused.

Marybeth and her husband had adopted the five-year-old girl from Guatemala. She was beautiful and quiet, and had seemingly hundreds of espresso-colored ringlets of hair that barely brushed the tops of her shoulders. When they first saw a picture of her, they knew they had to bring her to their home. So they did.

Lupe had spent the first five years of her life in a terribly poor orphanage. She was neglected, only rarely removed from a crib, and had inadequate clothing and food. At night when the staff went home, the older kids cared for the younger ones, and since they had been emotionally starved, they didn't attend to the younger ones well at all. In fact, some of them abused the younger ones.

When Lupe arrived in Marybeth's home, she never smiled. She had not smiled for five years. She didn't laugh, hug, or show any affection. She had what psychiatrists call a severe attachment disorder. Lupe was comfortable with only one emotion—anger. The reasons were complex but boiled down to the fact that she could not trust anyone to give her anything but pain. She feared love, affection, and any feeling of joy.

When Marybeth and her husband began parenting Lupe, she refused to respond to their kindness. They were patient for one year, then another and another. Lupe never smiled and stood like a wooden plank when they attempted to hug her. After five years, Marybeth was at her wit's end. She could not reach Lupe in any way and wondered if having Lupe ever feel loved was hopeless. Her well-known psychiatrist told her that it was. She should send Lupe back because she might hear about her daughter on the evening news one night for being "the next to shoot kids in her school."

Lupe's teachers wanted her kicked out of school because she hit others. She even sent one boy to the hospital after hitting him with a baseball bat. The boy's leg was broken.

"I can't give her back. It's out of the question," Marybeth cried. Quite honestly, I didn't know what to say. I knew this psychiatrist and respected his opinion. If he thought there was no hope for Lupe to have any intimacy in a relationship, he was probably right. Who was I to disagree? But as a mother, I agreed with Marybeth. I wouldn't send any child back, either. We sat together for a long time. Mostly, I listened to her pained heart. After she unloaded her hurts and disappointments about Lupe, the conversation took an extraordinary turn.

"You know," she said, "I didn't go into this relationship with Lupe naïvely believing that all we had to do was shower her with love and then she would change. I knew better. I read about troubled kids. I've read about attachment disorders. I've been patient, firm, loving, and kind. I've made her do things and I've asked for nothing. Now I'm told to stop, to remove myself from her life, and that's not going to work. What Lupe needs is for me to move in closer. That's the only thing that makes sense and it's our only chance." I agreed, and that's exactly what Marybeth did.

She reined Lupe in. She quit her job and homeschooled her daughter. She kept Lupe by her side constantly. She read to Lupe and made Lupe read to her. They listened to music, did math problems, and swam at the YMCA. Marybeth took Lupe to the grocery store and asked for her help. Lupe didn't complain that none of the other sixth-grade girls had to spend so much time with their mothers. In fact, she didn't seem to notice. Friendship was not on her wish list. Marybeth was unrelenting in her pursuit of Lupe. She said that it was grueling most of the time. I gave Lupe antidepressants, and when one didn't work, we tried another. And another.

When Lupe turned fourteen, Marybeth brought her in for a checkup. When I opened the door to the exam room, I saw Lupe first. She looked up at me and smiled. She smiled! I had never seen her smile. She sat in the yellow plastic chair next to her mother. Her hair had changed from the color of espresso to a deeper ebony and it was longer. Her shoulders weren't as slumped, and when I asked her how she was, she looked me in the eye and said, "Fine."

Marybeth beamed. Did Lupe hug Marybeth yet? No. But she would tolerate a kiss on the top of her head. She made eye contact. She didn't hit anymore. She laughed on occasion and played board games with her sister.

Marybeth was winning at love. Lupe was no ordinary fourteen-year-old and no one would say that she was affectionate. But more importantly, she was learning how to be loved by a mother who did it extraordinarily well. While Lupe's prognosis is guarded (and Marybeth would be the first to admit this), Marybeth beat the odds at love. Unstopped by an expert's medical opinion, she kicked her best mother instincts into gear and got very serious about love. And she was winning. Her daughter's life was changing.

In order to give love in a perfectly healthy, mature fashion, the giver (mom) must be fairly emotionally and mentally mature. Most of us pass those two criteria. In addition, the giving of love works best when the giver is not broken too terribly herself. There's where the messy part begins—we love in convoluted ways that sometimes work and sometimes don't. Our intentions are good, but kids on the receiving end don't respond to good intentions; they respond to love that makes sense to them. We may overprotect, overcontrol, and drive our kids crazy in the name of healthy love. We may withhold affection, buy them too much stuff, or forgo rules because it makes us feel that we are loving them well.

The good news for us moms is that usually our love goes awry not because we don't want to love well, but because something is tripping us up. Usually we are completely unaware of that something. Once we identify it by looking at behaviors, we can correct ourselves and make life a whole lot more fun for us and for our kids and families. Let's look at the most common areas where we trip ourselves up when it comes to giving love, and see what we can do.

FOUR WAYS TO MAKE THE HABIT STICK

#1: Take calculated risks

Nothing is tougher than loving well. As mothers, we are surrounded by people we want to love better, so in order to do better, we must decide to work on it. As much as we want love to naturally flow into and out of our hearts, the truth is, it just doesn't. But we know that we are workers, so here are some ways we can start working harder at the business of love.

Taking charge in our love relationships means that many times we will "go first." We will be the ones to tell loved ones how we feel, we will apologize first, and we will let them know what we need. This is terribly hard and feels risky because when we do each of these things, we give people a peek into our hearts. And every intuition we have tells us to guard our hearts—don't let others see. We want them covered over and protected. But having a child is like living with our hearts outside our chests, and that makes us feel even more vulnerable.

The truth is, we are very vulnerable as mothers who love, but that's okay. We can be vulnerable and take risks with our hearts, and if they are broken, as they certainly will be, we can handle that. We don't take blind risks, but we take them on the people we know deserve a chance, as Marybeth did with Lupe. We are strong and we need that strength. So whatever relationship in our life needs help, we must take that strength and be the first to make amends. Sometimes this means thinking through the problem in the relationship. Is it communication? Is it stubbornness and an unwillingness on someone's part to let go of getting her way?

If you can't figure out the breakdown in the relationship, have someone else help you. Ask a close friend or go to a good counselor. Trust someone to help you and then when you can wrap your mind around the problem, even if it's just part of the problem, figure out what you can do to bring about resolution. When mothers moan about their kids in my office, I repeatedly ask them, "So tell me what *you* can do." I do this because rarely is there a situation where a mother can't do anything. Rarely. So find out what measure you need to take and risk it. Go to the loved one and begin to resolve. Don't walk away, because you don't need to. If you lay your heart on the table and the person doesn't respond, you can handle that. In reality you can handle far more disappointment than you think you can.

When we speak truthfully to loved ones, we not only do something important for the relationship, we do something very important for ourselves: We give ourselves a strong voice. This is extremely important for mothers because we feel that we are invisible most of the time. Stating how we feel in the relationship gives us a presence and causes loved ones to hear us and take us more seriously.

#2: Don't take loved ones so personally

Imagine that your son is in third grade and a classmate begins to bully him. The classmate calls him "fatty" or "retard." At first, your son doesn't want to tell you, for two reasons: He doesn't want the bully to now call him a "mama's boy" and he's not sure that the bully isn't right. Is he fat? Is he a retard? Words hurt because we who receive them wonder if they are true.

When this happens to our son, we sit him down and talk about the bully. He is hurting, we say, because kids who are happy aren't mean. Our son doesn't really care how the bully feels, so we continue to explain.

Most importantly, bullying has nothing to do with him—he just happens to be in the bully's way. We try to help him see that the kid's meanness has nothing to do with him—it is the bully's character flaw. Depersonalizing it for our son helps him cope by shedding truthful light on the relationship.

But this isn't always easy to do. One of the biggest mistakes I see mothers make (and I certainly have made this mistake myself) is to take an altercation with a loved one too personally—particularly when it occurs between us and our kids. When a loved one hurts our feelings, fails to make us feel loved, or forgets our needs, 99 percent of the time it isn't because she doesn't love us. Rather, it is just her personality quirk or something going on in her life. For instance, if a teen yells at his mother, saying she never loved him, or a daughter complains that her mother just doesn't care about her, most often the mother believes the kid, at least in part. The problem is, mothers feel that kids do these things because they don't love us, so we rack our brains trying to figure out what we did wrong or why we deserve to be shunned.

Think about how we respond when our kids are toddlers. They have temper tantrums, throw themselves on the floor, and scream countless and ridiculous streams of accusations against us. Do we respond by apologizing to them? Or do we pick them up and put them in a safe place— their room or a time-out chair? Hopefully, we do the latter.

The truth is, teenagers and even adult loved ones act much the same way. They have temper tantrums directed toward us and try to pull us into their private tornadic whirl. Peculiarly, we get sucked in because, as conscientious and sensitive mothers, we believe the angry slurs that they force from their throats.

We can't afford to do this. When we are hurt by a loved one, we must stand back and assess their words as if we were mothers of toddlers. No, they aren't toddlers, but this helps us be more objective about the problem. When a loved one hurts us, the best thing for ourselves and our relationship with him is to do a simple exercise. Review the words as though they were directed at a friend, not at us. By removing ourselves for a moment, we can objectify their words and try to see if they are reasonable or not. So many times the words really have nothing to do with us and everything to do with the angered one.

This is tough, but it is important if we are to grow in our relationship with a loved one. If a spouse is depressed, he will view his wife in a profoundly negative light, focusing on and exaggerating the negative parts of her personality. This is painful for a woman because she believes the depressed husband's complaints. If a teen is hurt by being bullied at school, she will direct her anger and fear at her mother because she knows that her mother will never leave. And if a close friend feels jealous about her girlfriend's well-adjusted kids, she will lash out against the mother of the kids. How many times have we grown distant from loved ones because we allowed hurt words to drive us apart when we did nothing wrong? We were simply available when a loved one felt hurt and we got caught in the crossfire.

#3: Learn to read loved ones, and let them read you

The best way to express love is to figure out what, specifically, makes a loved one feel loved. Kids in my practice frequently tell me that their parents love them, but they then go on to reveal that they really don't feel loved. This is important. Love works best when we feel it, and every one of us needs to feel it at different times. So how do we make our kids and spouses feel loved?

We need to do some investigative work. We need to watch them and see what makes them feel good about their relationships with us. Does our daughter calm down after a long talk? Does our son smile to himself when we mow the lawn for him when he's overloaded with homework? Every child responds to different gestures we make. Sometimes those gestures come in the form of words, physical affection, or work we do for them. Gary Chapman wrote a very instructive book called *The Five Love Languages*, which shows how to figure out a loved one's "love language." It really does work.

Many mothers show love to their kids by cooking their favorite meals, driving them everywhere, or buying them gifts. While our intentions are good, these gestures don't ensure that kids feel loved. Certainly kids learn to appreciate the work we do for them as they mature, but in the meantime, it is important to find the small things we can do to let them know that they really are loved by us. While they are growing up in our homes, much of our interaction with our kids is negative because we are correcting them or disciplining them. So find out what makes each child feel loved. When you do this and express it, it will come back to you tenfold.

While it isn't appropriate to ask our kids outright what they can do to make us feel loved (because this isn't their job), it is very important to communicate this to our spouses. Raising kids feels like a thankless task many days so it is very important that we get refueled with love somehow. Women can read other women and figure out what they need, but men can't. They think differently. When we hurt, they frequently don't see it, not because they don't care, but because they are wired differently. So tell your spouse what makes you feel loved and that you need it from him. Most of us need someone to ask us simply and sincerely how we are at the end of the day. Then we need that loved one to listen (or at least pretend to listen). This simple task makes an enormous difference in our sense of feeling loved. But since others can't read us, we need to be very specific and divulge what makes us feel loved.

After we have done this, we must be patient. Usually, asking another to give something takes time. They are not in the habit, so we must gently remind them that we need them. Tell a husband that you need love from him (not just love from anyone, because then he may get his feelings hurt and tell you to find it elsewhere), and when he shows it in a specific way, it draws you closer to him. It's frightening to help him read you because you risk him not responding. But try again gently. Don't badger, because that never works.

Since you are helping him learn to "read" what makes you feel loved, you must reciprocate. It won't work if you ask for things this intimate and then fail to give back. While he may not know what makes him feel loved, you may have to do the same detective work you did with your kids—find out what works. One thing that I have learned about men is that sex makes them feel loved. Most mothers need emotional connection before sex and have difficulty going without it, because it feels impersonal. We want to smooth things over before sex. Many men are quite the opposite and this isn't a character flaw; it's the way they are wired. Sex helps them bond and it helps them resolve emotional conflict better after it is over. So remember this when you have lost a connection with your spouse.

Reading clues about loved ones and revealing clues about ourselves is risky but it is the only way to let love grow between us and loved ones. Whether it's our kids, our spouses, or even our mothers-in-law, learning their "love language" and using it works like nothing else. Give it time and mental energy and you won't be disappointed. You have little to lose and a whole lot to gain by practicing it.

#4: Express love even when you don't feel like it

Most mothers have parented through enough turmoil with kids to realize that love gets very gritty. It is a discipline, really. When we look at friends who laugh with their kids at the park or in a movie theater, we fantasize that they must enjoy such smooth relationships with their kids that love flows naturally and easily between them. Let's not be so foolish. The best love relationships require rolling up our sleeves again and again and saying a lot of things that we would really rather not.

Love requires that we take a deep breath and ask loved ones to forgive us for acting like jerks. It requires saying no to our kids and then being willing to reinforce the "no" for hours afterward. It means telling daughters that they can't wear teeny tops and skirts to school even when they wail and cry that kids won't like them. And it demands that we have the "talk" with our sons and daughters over and over about sex too soon with too many partners because hurt always follows. We do these things because we love our kids, but nothing is easy about doing any of them.

Love requires emotional and mental fortitude, particularly for mothers who are on the front lines with kids every single day. Somehow staying in the grit seems easier when it comes to loving our kids than it does with our husband. We give our kids a pass when they let us down because, we reason, they're just kids. But when our husband fails us, we get tied in knots. We get mad and bitter because he should know better— after all, he isn't a kid, he's a grown man.

It's sometimes easier to be more tenacious and disciplined in our love with our kids than it is in our love with our spouse. We must try to avoid this because we need our spouse more than we need our kids. Think about it for a moment. Our relationship with our spouse goes two ways more equally than do our relationships with our kids. We parent kids, give to them, and expect little in return. A spouse, on the other hand, can become our soul mate if we work at the relationship. He can become a well of support and comfort whereas our kids often drain us. This isn't a criticism of either relationship—just an understanding of the different dynamics.

So when a spouse drives us crazy, we must draw on the same internal grit that we use with our kids. Instead of complaining, we need to focus on appreciating him. Focus on the big stuff and let the small stuff go. We create barriers for ourselves if we constantly allow ourselves to criticize our spouse or our kids. Complaining takes us nowhere good. Rather, it always pulls us and the relationship down, so we must train ourselves to stop. Mothers can be much happier if we learn to dismiss character flaws, sullen attitudes, or temper tantrums and focus on the goodness in loved ones. Doing so doesn't mean that we are blind; it is quite the opposite. It means that we are willing to see the faults and frailties of our loved ones but appreciate and love them anyway. This is gritty, deeper love, the kind that brings great joy not only to our loved one, but to us as well. Love that comes easily satisfies only a little. Love that requires us to say things that are right and good, to extend comfort and forgiveness to a loved one when he doesn't deserve it, or to refuse to give up trying, is the kind that truly makes life worth living.

||||||||||||||||||||||||||||||||||||||||||||||||||||||||||||||||||||||||||||||||||||||||||||||||||||||||||||||||||||

Find Ways to Live Simply

WHY MOTHERS NEED SIMPLICITY

I get overwhelmed easily. Noises, crowds, too many good things to do in one day, too many types of potato chips, or too many people in one room make my head go hot. I'm sure that psychologists would have a field day with my brain. The good news for me is that I know this about myself. Too much of anything at one time throws me into a neurophysiological storm.

You probably know exactly what I'm talking about because you too have tried to pick out pantyhose and tossed plastic eggs on the floor of the grocery store aisle in exasperation, murmuring that it is simply wrong for pantyhose to come in so many sizes and toe types. And picking out pantyhose is simply the beginning. You have tried to keep up with answering personal emails, work emails, cellphone voice mails, and landline voice mails. You have tried to multi-multitask and beaten yourself up because trying to do so only makes you feel disorganized and frustrated. Other women can somehow do it, you imagine, but not you. And not me. We get overwhelmed by choices, noise, tasks, and demands at home, at work, and even when we try to relieve a little stress at the gym. We plunge into self-flagellation as we eye the gal on the treadmill next to us whose thighs don't sway in four directions when she runs. And we can't even run. We trot.

Okay, maybe this is an exaggeration, but I know that's what happens to me when I feel overwhelmed and overstimulated. Everything feels blown out of proportion. And I know it's not just me. When things get crazy, our thoughts seem faster and harsher. Life seems more frustrating and, unfortunately, we end up taking that frustration out on ourselves. Let's face it: Most of the time, we feel entirely overstimulated.

The cost of too many demands and too much stimulation is emotional and physiological chaos. Many of us end up with depression, high blood pressure, migraine headaches, or stomach ulcers. And these are just the beginning of the list. So if we want to live calmer, richer lives, we must take these types of overstimulation very seriously.

Let's examine the domino effect of overstimulation. The continual onslaught of visual stimulation via television and the Internet; the auditory stimulation of radio, iPods, and television; and the demands made on us at work and home cause us to live in a state of perpetual readiness. When we hear constant conversation, noise, or demands made on us by people in our lives, we quickly learn that we must be ready to respond or react. When we read emails, we react. When we hear kids arguing, we react. When our boss demands more overtime, we react. Our minds, emotions, and bodies learn by experience that we must be ever on alert.

When this happens, our bodies move into "fight-or-flight" mode, just as we'll discuss in the fear chapter. Our heart rates rise and blood moves from our intestines to our muscles. We are mentally on edge, now ready to make a decision quickly. We can sustain this state of readiness for a time, but when it becomes persistent, our muscles fatigue, our minds become less clear, and our emotions become blunted. In short, different parts of our bodies burn out because they were not made to be in constant alert mode.

Our ability to appropriately process messages becomes overloaded. When we try to process too much too fast, our sensibilities become dulled and we lose our way. Decisions we make become erratic and often meaningless. We overthink insignificant things and underanalyze very serious issues. No longer can we tell what is important to act on and what is trivial to worry about. It isn't our fault, because we are simply attempting to accomplish tasks (react to too many things at once) that the mother psyche is not wired to accomplish. And this isn't simply a mother issue. It really is a human issue. But it's even harder for moms, because we're responsible for both ourselves and our kids.

And the result is physiological, mental, and emotional burnout. We become weary but we don't know it. All we feel is a chronic, unrelenting irritability. We want people to go away. We are too tired to go out with girlfriends. Perhaps our kids bother us, or our husbands annoy us, and we long to retreat somewhere to rest our bodies and to turn off our thoughts. Even that is difficult because anxiety has become our bedfellow even though we never saw it move in. And where does this anxiety come from? It comes from feeling that there is too much to do and that we just can't keep up. No matter how hard we try, we feel behind in some area of our lives or another. This isn't fear per se, which we'll learn about later in the fear chapter; rather it is unrest and a feeling of being "behind the eight ball," if you will. Restlessness keeps us from relaxing, and soon we wonder whether we even have the ability to relax at all.

Then the real trouble starts. We are not tolerant of emotional, mental, or physical fatigue, so we subconsciously push away whatever part of us wants to slow down. We simply demand more and more of our minds, our bodies, and our emotions. And we push because of the onslaught of information and the decisions to be made. The noise in our lives never lets up.

Life becomes far too complicated for most of us mothers even when we have the very best intentions. Slowly we add more to our plates and pretty soon we feel trapped. We feel pressured to be better mothers, so we push ourselves to do more for our kids. We doubt ourselves as women, so we compensate by trying to improve who we are. We change our bodies, our jobs, or the things we own. And last but certainly not least, we complicate our children's lives because we believe that in order for them to be successful, they must be given a myriad of opportunities and material goods. And all of this drives us crazy.

That is exactly why each of us needs to embrace a simpler life. In the midst of our fatigue, we crave simplicity. There is a small voice within each one of us mothers that gently whispers, "Let go of the madness." We hear it and we know that it prods us in a better direction, but as soon as it comes, it is drowned out by the other voices we hear telling us to hurry up and accomplish one more thing. React. Respond. *Do something*.

So right now we must take the opportunity to explore that still voice and pay attention to it. It is the voice nudging us to a simpler, richer, and freer life. In this chapter, I'll help you do it, through identifying and really living your priorities, changing the way you talk, and loosening your grip. So let's get started!

INWARD SIMPLICITY—FIND YOUR TRUE PURPOSE, AND LET THE REST GO

Inward simplicity refers to an attitude of the heart, an inner resolution. Each of us holds key priorities in our lives that must be defined and acted upon above all else. Once we recognize what those priorities are and deliberately live them out, our sense of being constantly overloaded with demands, choices, and information dramatically lessens. Why? Because when we take our priorities seriously, everything else that comes at us feels a lot less important. It loses its ability to spin us into chaos. And this is wonderfully freeing.

Inward simplicity begins with some soul-searching. It begins with asking ourselves the deep questions in life and coming up with answers. We're not used to pushing ourselves to ask tough questions but if we really want our lives to be different and we're serious about living richer, more satisfying lives, we must begin right here. Every mother must ask herself, "Why have I been put here on earth?"

This is a tough question to answer for many mothers. Some haven't a clue. Others I have spoken with answer the question far too easily, stating something sarcastic like "I exist to drive my kids around." While this may be a cute one-liner, the truth is, there is an underlying tone of sadness in it. Of course, she knows that this isn't why she was born, but many who quip such a response genuinely feel like mother robots who really don't understand a deep sense of purpose. But every mother should have a deep knowledge of who she is and why she was born.

Developing inward simplicity means being unwilling to accept trivial answers to such a deep question as the meaning of our existence. It means taking time, study, reflection, conversation, and real soul-digging to clearly define what we think our purpose is. It means asking questions until we find answers. And I don't believe that we can come to real answers unless we deliberately pull ourselves away from the constant influence of our culture. We are simply too easily affected by toxic messages all around us. Let's take a hard look at the most frequent of those messages:

Get thinner. People will admire you more (men and women) and you will be a better person. And if you are admired more, then you will have more value. With feminism in full swing, one might think that we mature mothers might have progressed past the compulsion to get thinner. But studies show that a whopping 71 percent of women ages 30–74 want to be thinner, although 73 percent of the women studied were at a normal weight!

Be busy, get more done. Women who are important (we are told) are extremely busy. They are productive. Full-time mothers run their kids everywhere because they are conscientious and committed. Working women exhaust themselves juggling work and home life and their exhaustion is a sign of success. Busy women don't have enough time for friends (even family) because they are busy doing important things.

Make more money. No matter what your income, get it higher. As we discussed in the money chapter, we think that money gives us freedom and power, and most importantly, it gives us complete independence. Having more money gives us more buying power, but it also gives us power in our relationships. The more we have, the less we need to depend upon others.

Look hot. Mothers who have it all together show it and one of the best ways to show it is through how we look. We must look sexy (even in our

sweats) and we must never look our age. Middle age is for past genera-
tions and we must look more like our daughters than our mothers. We
should aspire to wear our teenage daughters' jeans and be proud when
we can.

Be cool. Good mothers listen, understand their children's difficulties,
center their lives around their children, and, most importantly, never assert their authority in their kids' lives (everywhere else is okay, though).
Setting rules for children is a no-no for cool mothers because this im-
pedes children's growth and causes them to resent our controlling nature.
So don't impose your beliefs or morals, set boundaries, or expect your
child to be a disciplined person. She can learn those if you simply let her
find her way. ·

Now I ask you, after years of imbibing one or all of these messages, how
can we begin to feel good about ourselves? Our thoughts about who we
are as mothers and women get gnarled and perverted. We find ourselves
overwhelmed and bound up on many levels. Eventually we learn to live
against our intuitions and chase our sense of "inadequacy" relentlessly.

Listen to how we talk to one another. One mother may report how she
must start working out at the gym and another laments her discouragement with her latest diet attempt. Or one may bemoan how she can't
keep up with her kids' schedules and she must get to her doctor to figure
out why she is just "tired all the time." Of course, this one makes sense,
because feeling overwhelmed and overstimulated does cause fatigue.
Her friend may concur, remarking that she too is behind in *something*.

We hear about peer pressure on our kids and how messages from
movies, music, magazines, and locker room banter change their self-
perceptions and their behavior. But what about us? If we are honest with
ourselves, we are no less vulnerable. Each of these messages above has
changed who we are, not because we are weak, but simply because we
feel pressure to be the best.

That is precisely why we must stare these messages down and learn to
quiet those voices in our minds. We must take them apart one by one and
adopt a simpler, healthier way of thinking about ourselves. It is painful to

admit, but most of us spend the majority of our time caving in to these beliefs and living far too superficially. Inward simplicity begins by removing ourselves from their influence. But this can't happen if we haven't the brutal honesty to admit that each of these toxic messages has affected us.

Soul-searching, which illuminates answers to the attendant heart, must be done in a semi-vacuum because we are vulnerable, hurting, and too often desperate to hang on to the first and easiest remedy that comes our way. Finding answers to the purpose of our existence only comes when we are able to block out peripheral noise and meaningless conversations. Read the solitude chapter to learn about finding quiet and how it can help. But the good news is that when we find answers, life takes on a new clarity. We see our kids and spouses differently. We envy friends less and argue less with our bosses. Kids who ignore us don't ruin our days and losing our job doesn't rattle us as easily because we get the bigger picture when we know and live our priorities. I know this can happen, because I've seen it. When I catch a glimpse of a mother who knows what her priorities are, I see a true lightness in her.

Living simply means living bigger. It means letting go of things in our lives that we want to be less important and becoming women of singular focus. It means establishing serious priorities and then committing ourselves to live those out. This doesn't mean that we should make a wish list—this will only lead to more complicated lives. Priorities are different. The ones I am referring to embody a sense of calling. Some women feel that their purpose is to bring relief; others feel that they are gifted at teaching or bringing music. The list is as varied as the characters and personalities of mothers. But what a joy it is to watch women who purposefully live large. They are focused, streamlined, and rarely filled with self-doubt.

The second component of living a life of inward simplicity is accepting the belief that life is a gift. Our lives, our children's lives, and the lives of all those with whom we have relationships are gifts. We didn't participate in the creation of our existence. And while we did exert influence over the timing of our children's existence in our lives, we can understand that personality and health are far beyond our control. If we adopt this perspective, we begin to shift our sense of responsibility about those lives. If we weren't responsible for creating them and bringing them into our presence, then we are not responsible for everything that happens to those lives—for good or bad. Far too often we live as though our lives are a chore to be endured, not a gift to be cherished. The great irony is that when we see life as a gift, we can loosen our grip on it.

As we'll see in the fear chapter, we mothers can be the most controlling creatures on the planet. We are mothers because we were assigned charge over little ones. We want everyone in our sphere to understand that we fully intend on taking that charge very seriously. We decide when we will have children, what they will wear or eat, where they will go to school, and whom they will play with. And that just gets us rolling. When our kids are in grade school we really ramp it up. Some of us become room moms in order to keep our fingers on the pulse of classroom dynamics, and others join the PTA. As our children mature, we invest more effort and money to make sure that we maximize their opportunities. While this is good, it can be harmful to us because it fuels our sense that we have more control and influence over our kids than we really do. Before we know it, we begin feeling responsible for every aspect of our children's future.

For instance, if we fail to push a son hard enough in high school and he doesn't get into his (our) dream college, we feel responsible. If our daughter discovers too late in high school that she has a gift for music, we blame ourselves for not starting piano lessons earlier. If we had only gotten those lessons going when she was five, she might have become a professional.

In short, we live with an overriding sense that we have ultimate control over who our kids become when they are adults. We therefore believe that every decision we make can potentially alter the outcome of their lives. And this is an enormous burden to carry.

I want to be clear here. Parents are the primary influence in a child's life concerning character development, but the truth is, even our influence is very limited. I have cared for thousands of kids over the course of my career, and I have come to realize that children are born with very distinct personalities. Some are strong-willed and some are passive. Boys react very differently to certain stimuli than girls do, even at birth. Our job as parents is to blunt harsh edges and help kids release their talents and gifts. We can steer them in one direction or another, educate them, and love them. But kids are who they are. We must come to grips with this so that we can begin to release the false guilt we carry regarding the choices our kids make. Inward simplicity as mothers begins with this very release. Our children are fully different creatures than we are, and we are in their lives for a time in order to nurture them, love them, and nudge them in certain directions. We simply must accept that they are loaned to us for a time and then they are released into adulthood. When we believe this, we feel more joy and contentment in parenting them, we simplify our expectations of ourselves regarding parenting, and we experience a welcome levity in our relationships with them.

Inward simplicity also demands that we adopt a similar attitude regarding other loved ones in our lives. They, too, are gifts loaned to us for a period of time. We are to love them and provide what care we can and then let go of feeling completely responsible for what they experience. If we simplify our expectations of loved ones and we simplify the expectations we place on ourselves regarding caring for them, contentment seeps into the relationships. We feel the same levity and enjoyment because we learn to hold loved ones and friends more loosely. We lessen our grip on them and learn to give them and ourselves room to breathe.

Finally, inward simplicity means releasing our clamped fist from all that we own. We even try to control the material goods we have. We buy and sell, move, clean, and reorganize matter. In fact, we spend so much time attending to the stuff we have that *it* begins to control *us*. We worry about things being stolen, damaged, or lost. But our worries only reflect the fact that those things hold such power and meaning in our lives. If we learn to care less for the things we own, they begin to lose that power. We must learn to need them less. This is the beginning of living a life of inward simplicity.

OUTWARD SIMPLICITY—LIVE WITH LESS AND PLACE LIMITS

Outward simplicity naturally follows a heart that has learned inward simplicity. It is the act of changing the structure of our lives in accordance with inward simplicity. It means ridding ourselves of unnecessary things, activities, and concerns that only serve to keep us in a state of constant anxiety. This sounds severe, but sometimes in order to get sanity back into our lives, severe measures are required. Just as we saw in our decisions about money, we must learn to keep the important things in our lives as the most important. Having stuff and caring for it takes time. Is that what we really want to be doing?

Living with less of something frees up more time in our lives so that we can be about the business of really living life. Consider the stay-at-home mom. Often mothers who don't have a job outside the home (a paying job) feel guilty. They might compensate by overscheduling their kids in an exhausting number of activities. They place more pressure on themselves to be better parents because parenting is their "full-time job," but they end up weaving a complexity into their lives that suffocates everyone. The way to avoid this terrible trap is to commit to living more simply by placing limits on our kids and ourselves. Mothers in this situation must learn to incorporate relaxation, downtime, and even a bit of boredom. Mothers and kids need quiet and unscheduled slices of time so that they can recharge.

Let's put some feet on the idea of simplicity. First, take a long hard look at what drains you each week. Is it running your kids around after school? Is it going to evening meetings? Is it your job? Is it constantly feeling behind? When we stop to examine the biggest sources of strain in our lives, we can find a good place to begin the process of simplifying. For mothers, there are four areas in our lives that get out of control quickly and rob us of joy: expectations of ourselves, schedules, work, and spending. Let's look at each one.

First, let's make a brutally honest (and private) list of what we expect from ourselves. We must bare it all to ourselves on paper because we can never change what we don't know exists. List what you expect of yourself and be very specific. The list might go something like this:

Be patient with my kids and husband and never yell,

Get more physically fit,

Be nicer to my friends and in-laws,

Be ready to invest more (time, energy, and effort) into my kids,

Work harder at being prettier—wear nicer clothes, keep my hair nicer, etc.

Every mother's list is different. Now keep that list and write an entirely new one. Write a list of the goals you have deep down for yourself. These are your secret hopes, the things that you would do if time and money weren't an issue. List them in order of priority from 1 to 10. The two lists probably won't line up, and that's all right. The first list should flow from honest feelings you have about yourself—these are the things that you think you should do and they haunt you regularly. The second list erupts from a deeper sense of what you believe—or want to believe— goes into being a great mother and woman. It's tangible evidence of inward simplicity.

Review the first list a few times. Now tear it up, burn it, or throw it into the trash compacter. Take the second list and scratch everything but the top three items off (remember, these should be the three most important expectations you have for yourself as a mother). Commit to yourself that you will work on only these three things for six months or a year and let everything else go. Everything. All other expectations of yourself are on hold. Now you have given yourself permission to work on three things. Just three. So when you hear the old voices whispering in your mind that you should really do x or be better at y, you can let them go because you made a conscious decision to do so (temporarily or permanently). If working on your temper, being content, and being more patient form the top three, that means you will not feel guilty if you don't exercise, get nicer clothes, find a new job, or cook really good dinners. When it comes to anything below the top three, you are off the hook.

This exercise is the most powerful way I know that any mother can simplify her life and de-stress. It works so beautifully because it helps us deliberately push extra noise out of our minds. It allows us to relax and accept where we are in our lives. If we suffer from anything, it is the ugly noise in our minds that causes us to beat ourselves up without even realizing it.

The second problem I see frequently is overscheduling. Most mothers I see allow their kids' schedules to get completely out of control. Evenings and weekends are spent racing from one music or athletic event to another. I know because I made the same mistake when my kids were young. If this is a struggle for you, simplify life for everyone by adopting the "One Rule." Tell each child he may choose one after-school activity per grading period. This sounds outrageous to some parents who want their kids to excel in many different areas and who most certainly don't want to deprive them of opportunities. But remember one thing: Whenever your child is on the soccer field, he's deprived of time with you and the family. And which does he really need more time with in order to grow up emotionally and mentally sound?

Cutting activities from a child's schedule seems heretical for a modern-day parent. Let's face it, we are competitive with the parents in our child's class and it's hard to be home watching the other kids' parents pulling out of the driveway on their way to ski practice while you and your kids are sitting down at the kitchen table to tuna noodle casserole. But whenever your neighbor takes off with a car full of kids at dinnertime, remember that you and your kids are the real winners. You aren't doing nothing with them; you are building stronger relationships with them. And kids need better relationships more than they need more practice at any sport or extracurricular activity. They will never regret time at home.

If the area of great stress for you is overscheduling yourself, apply this same rule to your own time. Commit to only one activity outside your primary work (your family, and your job, if you have one). That means, if you're committed to exercising, no PTA, choir, book club, volunteer time. Nothing. You are home in the evenings with the kids you have said no to when it comes to their schedules as well. At first, the quiet evenings are strenuous because if you and the family aren't used to them, you and they will probably argue during the transition. If this is the case, it's a good thing that you are all home, because constant arguing means that you haven't been spending enough time together. This sounds like an oxymoron, but the truth is, families who spend more time together learn to work their differences out. So if the tension at home seems higher after the initial transition, hang on, it will get better. It takes time for your mind and body to adjust to slowing down, and we all adjust at different rates. Some do so within weeks; for others it may be months.

Getting out your BlackBerry or Day-Timer and scratching off evening activities takes tremendous discipline. But any of us can do it. Doing this feels good and bad at the same time. We feel good because we are taking charge, but guilty because we have chosen to live differently than our friends. Every mother wants to simplify—we just want the other mother to go first. Don't wait for anyone else. Be bold and apply the One Rule for yourself, your kids, or both. You will never regret it.

The next problem I want to discuss is work. Perhaps being over-scheduled socially isn't a problem for you, but your job is. You may have a demanding boss or a career that has grabbed you by the throat and won't let go. You leave home and step into your office and the migraine starts. Or you come home from work each day only to snarl like an alley cat to your kids because you have nothing left over for anyone. Take charge. Do some soul-searching and simplify your work situation. Maybe you need to work one or two days less per week. Maybe your job description needs shoring up because you have taken on more than your own proper load. Perhaps you need to hire an assistant or two in order to free up some of your time. Pare down however you can and if cutting back doesn't work, then maybe you need to find another job. Or no job at all until you feel more balanced with your home life. Whatever it takes, you must decide to make one or two changes with your work.

This gets frightening for many women and I understand why. We fear that we can't live on a smaller income or without job security. There's the money issue again, as we examined in the money chapter. The truth is, most of us can, but we just don't want to. We can do without the second car, the pool, the vacations, or the second home. And deep in our hearts we know that we would love to have the pressure of providing these off of our backs. The truth is, when we give up something at work, we add something else to our lives. We add more time with loved ones or more relaxation to our very stressful lives, or we even extend our lives. Simplifying work and reducing stress can literally add years to our lives. Then there are those mothers who feel most stressed not by job, income, or overscheduling, but from more insidious and hidden causes: expectations of themselves. In fact, most mothers suffer from this. At one time or another every mother believes that she should do more, provide more, and produce more for herself and her family. We mothers are our harshest critics and simplifying life must occur for every one of us. Can changing our expectations really make us happier? Yes. Studies show that while stressed mothers often change their work schedules to simplify their lives, they can also reconstruct their expectations about mothering in order to alleviate stress.

Finally, let's talk about spending. Money can really complicate our lives! While having more money can be a gift, it can also make life more work and it can muddy relationships. Buying kids too much (and every one of us mothers is guilty) drains us. We give because we want our kids to be happy, and when we see that the happiness is not commensurate with our gift, we feel bad. Some mothers spend because they are sad and buying things acts to alter their moods, just as drinking can. One of the best ways we can spare ourselves from the complications brought on by spending money is to cut back. We can buy less for our kids or buy less expensive things. Taking charge of expenses is extraordinarily liberating, and spending less gives mothers a tremendous sense of control and power. Ironically, mothers who have money and choose to withhold spending can have a greater sense of power than if they spend their money. This is because saving takes more discipline than spending.

If spending is a real problem for you, cut back slowly. Take ten or fifteen dollars off your budget each week. When the urge hits to buy your son new sneakers, wait a few weeks and see if he really needs them. Take a look at your checking account and review what you spent money on over the past few months. Find one item to cut out next month. And, like dieting, if you fall off the wagon, move on and start right back up the next day. My friend Dave Ramsey has written and lectured extensively on gaining control over your money, and in wizardlike fashion, he has helped hundreds of thousands of women and men simplify their lives through good budgeting. So rather than give more tips, I refer you to his excellent collection of works.

If we successfully take charge and simplify these areas of our lives—our expectations of ourselves, our schedules, our attitudes about work, and our spending habits—we will experience far greater contentment. The weight will lift from our shoulders and we will find that, wonderfully, we have energy to focus on what we really want to matter, the things we might have put on our "real" list, such as our relationships with loved ones, appreciating the goodness around us, and paying attention to the deeper parts of our character and the character of others.

Make changes gradually, because simplifying our lives is much like dieting. We must think about it, then learn to make minor changes in order to make it stick. The great thing about it, however, is that the rewards become so delightful, continuing a simpler lifestyle becomes easier the longer we do it.

At first, simplifying may feel awkward, even terrible. Your kids will complain and you will feel restless, but hang in there. Resolve to make your change stick for at least two months. If, at the end of those two months, you feel miserable, allow yourself to incorporate the activity back into your life. But I'll bet that you won't. Having downtime with the family changes every relationship in the family. Best of all, it improves your attitude. I have never met a mother who has simplified her life only to later reintroduce activities and behaviors back into her life once she has given them up. The benefits of simplifying are far too rich.

HOW KRISTY FOUND MORE BY DOING LESS

Kristy came alone to my office several years ago. Whenever a parent comes alone, I know there's trouble. And trouble there was for Kristy. Her daughter, Sasha, was fifteen and making her life miserable, she said. Kristy couldn't understand, because she and her ex-husband worked hard to give their daughter everything they could. She attended a private school, danced ballet and jazz four times per week, and sang with an elite chorale group at her high school. Her grades were quite good and, as Kristy said, her daughter's life looked great "on paper." But at home, with her mother or her father, she was irritable, sullen, and rude. She avoided speaking to either one of them. Kristy asked whether Sasha's moods could be fallout from the divorce three years earlier and I told her that this needed investigation. And because Sasha was an only child, Kristy wondered if her daughter's behavior could simply be normal for a teen.

So I asked her some questions. Was Sasha sleeping well? Usually not, Kristy told me. The girl rarely fell asleep before 1 A.M. and she got up at 6 A.M. to catch the bus. How was she during dinner? Kristy didn't know; they never ate together since her daughter rarely came home before 8 P.M. because of one practice or another. And when she did get home earlier or on weekends, Kristy was frequently stuck at the office, trying to catch up.

How about fun? I wondered. Did the two ever do anything fun together? "Nope," came the reply. Sasha never seemed to want to be with her parents, only with friends. Even with friends, Kristy told me, she appeared temperamental and bossy.

After hearing the timeline of a typical week, I calculated that Sasha encountered her mother about three meaningful hours per week. By meaningful, I meant times when the two of them had an opportunity to catch up or talk. And the same held true with her father—he had about three hours as well. I decided to talk to Sasha and asked her to come into the office.

I noticed that the girl looked much older than fifteen. She dressed and acted like an eighteen- or nineteen-year-old. She was quiet and standoffish. After she warmed up, she divulged to me that she thought her parents were self-absorbed and uninterested in her (a much different picture than her mother depicted). Since I knew her mother and father, I silently gasped. Her parents adored her. They tried every way possible to give her a good life.

Sasha began crying and told me that her parents really didn't want to spend time with her; they wanted her to be good at dancing and they cared more about her grades than about her. And when it came to their work, both were more interested in their jobs than what was happening in her life.

At first I was dumbstruck by Sasha's anger. I wanted to tell her that she was simply wrong. But I knew that her parents needed to hear her feelings. She wasn't trying to be manipulative—her tears flowed from an honest hurt. Sasha, like almost every child I've ever cared for, simply wanted more time with her mother.

As I listened more intently, I realized a profound dichotomy that every mother grapples with: our intentions versus our children's beliefs. We often express love by scheduling, pushing, buying, and running kids around, but those don't often make our kids feel loved. And many times, as was the case with Sasha, our efforts backfire. What we intend as love gestures, they interpret as conditions to be met in order for them to be accepted and loved by us.

Kristy loved her daughter deeply. She realized that most of her efforts for her daughter arose from a deep sense that in order to be a great mother, she needed to push, provide, overschedule, and make a good income so that the two could go on nice vacations together. In fact, none of these is bad, but the mistake came when Kristy set up a certain lifestyle in order to prove to herself and her daughter that she was a good mom. What Sasha saw was quite the opposite.

Kristy took deliberate steps to simplify their lives. Specifically, she simplified her expectations of herself as a mother. She put less pressure on herself to perform well at work and took days off here and there. When she did this, she realized that she had to give up their nice vacations together, but she didn't mind, she later told me. The two learned to enjoy canoeing near their home or taking road trips. Sasha eased up on some of her after-school activities. Kristy wanted to buy her daughter a car when she graduated from high school, but she gave up this goal when her salary dropped because of the days she took off to be with Sasha.

Kristy told me several years later, "I never realized how much I was trying to compensate for my divorce by elevating the lifestyle I wanted to provide for Sasha. I pushed her and I pushed myself to do more and be more. I was scared to cut back on everything. But it gave me my daughter back."

By relieving herself of the internal pressure she felt because of her expectations, the enjoyment Kristy felt in her parenting skyrocketed.

Many times, as was the case with Kristy, simplifying life isn't all that hard. It may mean cutting one thing from our schedules or getting rid of a few things that are wearing us down. Believe it or not, I have heard mothers talk about the freedom they have gained from doing things as easy as getting rid of clothes or furniture. The freedom comes not only from having more space, but also from not having to fret about having too much stuff. For Kristy and Sasha, it took a bit of paring down on both of their parts, but led to a much larger portion of happiness for them both.

WHAT STEPHANIE LEARNED FROM HER MOTHER ABOUT LIVING SIMPLY

I was introduced to Stephanie about fifteen years ago while my husband and I were vacationing with our kids on a lovely lake in northern Michigan. Stephanie was vacationing on the same lake, and we spent many summer nights chatting about everything from cherry pie recipes to euthanasia. After that first summer vacation, we remained good friends, even though we lived in different states. Over the next few years she told me about her life and extraordinary family.

Stephanie grew up with a mother who insisted on a life of simplicity for herself and for her family. As the middle child of three, Stephanie grew up in a midsize town in Ohio. She lived in a large home on one acre of land and enjoyed being able to walk to school and ride her bike anywhere she pleased. Her mother never really worried about her whereabouts, she remembers, but then again, she told me that her perspective was skewed because her mother was very trusting and she wanted to be worthy of that trust.

When she was a teenager, her family vacationed in northern Michigan during the summer. She remembers the day her parents decided to buy a cottage on an inland lake. "I loved the smell of the place," she told me. "It was a bit musty, but it had a clean smell to it."

Stephanie recalled times she spent fishing with her dad in an old wooden boat on the lake and other days playing tennis with her mother. Because they owned a cottage, she and her siblings had to open the place and close it at the end of the summer. Those times, she said, were tiring. They involved scrubbing the floors, laundering sheets and blankets, and cleaning anything else her mother decided needed it.

"Opening the old place was so much fun because we knew that summer was ahead. That meant nights that didn't get dark until ten and mornings that began early. Mother always made us get summer jobs, and I worked at a day camp nearby. I would come home exhausted and complain to my mom that I never wanted kids. She just smiled whenever I said stuff like that.

"My favorite memories were nights when my sisters and I would make a fire by the beach and the neighbors would appear. We would sit around and tell stories and make s'mores until we felt sick to our stomachs. You'd think that we would have tried drinking or done things that most teenagers would do if they were out until the small hours of the morning with a bunch of friends. But we didn't. Our folks were always up at the cottage and we knew that our voices echoed back to the house because of the water. We were too scared to do anything stupid.

"I loved that old cottage. I learned to drive there on the gravel driveway. I had my first boyfriend there. Summer romance—it didn't seem then like life could get any better. I remember complaining to my mother about the size of the cottage. It had three bedrooms and my sisters and I always fought over who got their own room. We fought so hard one day that my mother found a solution. We all had to sleep in one room and the third was left for guests. She put bunk beds along one wall and a cot along the other. Can you believe it? Then we fought over who got the cot.

"When summer ended, we dragged our feet closing the old place up. It wasn't so much that we didn't want to clean, but that we didn't want to go home. We loved being north. Life seemed slower. Mom seemed happier and more rested. The trips home to Ohio in the car were usually quiet. Everyone—Mom, Dad, and my sisters—we all felt sad."

Stephanie continued to recall beautiful memories of her summers with her family in Michigan. But that wasn't the most remarkable part of her story. After she grew up and married, her parents sold their small cottage because taking care of a second home became too much of a burden for them. When she raised her own family, Stephanie and her husband chose to live near her folks so that they could help them as they aged. Her father died of a heart attack in his seventies and her mother passed away ten years after her father.

"Losing my mom was tough," Stephanie confided. "I adored my mother and thought that I could never live without her. We did everything together—we even grocery shopped together. I wish that I would have known more about her when she was alive. I think that if I knew then what I know about her now, my respect for her would have been so much greater. But she wanted it that way for a reason, I guess."

I was confused by her statement. I suddenly needed to know what she was referring to. So I took a chance that she would let me in on her secret. "What about your mother would you like to have known?" I asked.

"Well," she said, "after my mother's funeral, we cleaned out her belongings and put her house on the market. We knew that we would get a nice price for the house, but we wouldn't get rich after selling it. It was large, but not extraordinary. Several weeks after the funeral, my sisters and I went to see the family lawyer. We sat in his office without our husbands and listened while he read her will. When he came to the part where her estate was to be divided up, he stopped. He looked up from his desk and said to us, 'So the sum of my stocks, bonds, and CDs totaling approximately eight million dollars, shall be sold and divided equally between my daughters.'

"When the number eight million came out of his mouth, saying that we were shocked doesn't do justice to our feelings. We were beyond shocked. We were mad, exhilarated, sad, and anxious all at the same time. Why hadn't Mother told us about their wealth? We felt that she had lied to us somehow, but of course she hadn't. She just didn't tell us. Apparently, Mother inherited a large sum of money from her grandparents when she was young and stashed it away. We kind of felt betrayed and confused. But after the shock wore off, we began talking about Mom and the remarkable woman that she was. Actually—she was extraordinary. I don't think that I could have ever lived as simply as she did, having that much money," Stephanie said, still appearing surprised after five years.

There was one more question I just had to ask.

"So," I said, "if you could go back to being a kid, do you wish that your mother would have lived a life more in keeping with a multimillionaire?"

Without missing a beat, she said, "Absolutely not. I do believe that it might have wrecked my childhood. I'm not saying that being rich would have made me an unhappy kid, but I would have missed out on the great and simple things we all did together. And I wouldn't trade any of those times for any amount of money, especially now that my mother is gone."

Stephanie's mother embraced a lifestyle of simplicity because she knew that it gave her and her family something that money couldn't— freedom. It afforded them opportunities to learn how to suffer through long days as a camp counselor, to hang sheets on a clothesline, and to figure out how to have fun with just a yard and a lake but no friends. Could she have given these things to Stephanie and her sisters and lived in a bigger cottage and home and had more material things? Of course, but her unusual behavior tells me that for her, living out her conviction to keep life simple meant living as though she had far less in the bank. I think she just didn't want to jeopardize the rewards she gained from such a relatively simple lifestyle.

So the question for each of us mothers is, How can we abandon the habit of living frenetically and move toward living more simply? Here's how we start.

THREE WAYS TO MAKE THE HABIT STICK

#1: Identify and really live your priorities

Nothing is more exhilarating than spending time with someone who understands her purpose and lives with a sense of passion. As mothers, we must be able to clarify our purpose for our lives. Most of us would agree that our primary purpose as mothers is to raise emotionally, intellectually, and physically healthy kids. Now think about this. If we believe that this should be a goal for every day of our lives, then we need to ask ourselves if our daily lives reflect that purpose.

So often we lose focus because we get caught up in busyness. We wind up doing things that don't help us fulfill our purpose. And worse, we often willfully do things that work against our goal of raising healthy kids. That is precisely why we must periodically stop and reevaluate how we are living. We need to scrutinize our calendars and checkbooks to see whether they are consistent with our goals. Living simply means keeping our priorities front and center—on our calendars and in our checkbooks. Remember the list you made earlier in this chapter? Making a list of our top three priorities doesn't do us any good if all we do is write them down. They must be lived and embraced. Paring down activities helps us begin this process, and refusing to spend money on things that don't contribute to our goals is another way we begin to accomplish this simplicity.

Look at your list of your top three "real" priorities as a mother from the exercise you did earlier. Then take out your calendar and cross off whatever you see standing in the way of accomplishing these. Stop doing things for the wrong reasons and deliberately begin doing things for the right reasons. It will be amazing to watch the transition in the way you feel about life, yourself, and your kids. And then do the same with your checkbook. Pare down spending so that what you spend genuinely reflects your purposes.

You can even extend this exercise into the things you worry about. Remember, our worries reveal our deep concerns and we are concerned largely with things we feel are very important in some way or another. So, we can even simplify our worries if they are inconsistent with our goals. For instance, many mothers worry about what gifts to buy their kids for birthdays or Christmas. We feel guilty not getting our kids the same types of games or clothes that their classmates have. But so many times we know that buying certain things like violent video games flies right in the face of our primary purpose as a mom (to raise emotionally, intellectually, and physically sound kids). We know that the more time our kids spend on the couch playing video games, the less time they are doing something physically healthy. And we know that these games don't challenge them intellectually and the violence will probably dull their sensibilities. So why do we muddy the waters and keep life complicated by buying the stuff? We do so because we waffle when it comes to living like we mean it. So list your priorities, and then work to really make them important in your everyday life.

#2: Change the way you talk

There is a wonderful psychological phenomenon regarding the way we talk. What we say affects the way we think, and the way we think affects the way we behave. Therefore, if we train the way we talk, we can actually change the way we feel and act. This sounds too simple, but it works.

If you decide to make living a certain way a priority, talk about it. Make it stay in the forefront of your thoughts throughout the day and you will find that you no longer have to make the same effort to keep it as a priority. It will become one.

And the converse is also true. If we deliberately refuse to discuss things that we find insulting or ridiculous, pretty soon we will fail to notice those things. For instance, one of my pet peeves is women commenting on a friend's weight during a greeting. For instance, we frequently say, "Oh, hi! You look so good. Have you lost weight?" While we think we're being complimentary, in fact we are being derogatory because it feeds the notion that we highly value their appearance. (Otherwise, why would we have commented on it?)

We have become obsessed with superficial things like weight and appearance to the detriment of encouraging one another regarding more important things in life. So I decided to conduct a personal experiment. I refused to remark on another woman's weight for one year. This was quite a challenge because many times we mothers discuss issues we have with our own weight and how we feel about another woman's weight.

After a few months, an extraordinary thing began to happen. I stopped noticing people's weight. After even more months, I literally had difficulty seeing if someone had gained or lost a substantial amount of weight because weight became a nonissue in my mind. I felt free from thinking about it.

Living more simply means paring down what we talk about and taking real control over it. The truth is, we talk about things that are front and center in our minds. If we are determined to align our priorities, then we must keep our speech in line with those priorities as well. If you want your daughter to stop worrying about her weight, stop commenting on it. If you want to feel better about yourself, make a list of your strengths and compliment yourself every day on at least one of them. In time, this will change your perceptions of yourself.

While we must craft our own dialogue in order to align our speech with our priorities, there is a common change we can all make, and it's important for us mothers. We must let *yes* mean "yes" and *no* mean "no." So often our answer *yes* means "maybe" and our *no* means "well, let me think about it and I might change my mind." We make ourselves crazy by breaking these two simple rules and most women do it universally. I have read studies that show that women more often than men feel compelled to defend their position after they say no. For some reason (and this is particularly true when dealing with kids) we feel that we need to justify why we said no and convince the one we said it to that we mean it. Most fathers don't do this. They say no and then move on. We say no and then worry about the psychological harm we just caused our child. We must stop this and say yes only once and no only once. Getting to this point may take some practice and retraining of kids used to hearing it repeated, but they'll learn. This is a very straightforward way we can begin to simplify our speech and ultimately simplify our lives. How freeing it is to say yes or no, accept it, and then move on. Give it a go. You won't regret it.

#3: Loosen your grip

Life becomes unmanageable when we wrap our fingers around something or someone and we refuse to let go. The truth is, letting go can be one of the hardest tasks we could ever accomplish. That is why I wrote about seeing our lives, our possessions, and our children as gifts. If we do this, we can understand that we don't have ultimate control over them or even over our own lives. Then the letting go becomes a bit easier.

My suggestion is to loosen your grip on one thing at a time. Uncurl those fingers and start to release the easy stuff first. I chatted with a woman who had a terrific idea. Every time she received a new sweater, she gave one away. She made it sound easy. I'm sure it wasn't easy at first, because if she is anything like I am, every article of clothing in her closet has a story. Usually the story is ridiculously sentimental but nonetheless meaningful. I remember who I shopped with the day I bought the thing and feel that if I give it away, I will be cruel to that relationship. Or if a family member gave something to me and I haven't worn it in ten years, I feel like I am betraying that person if I give it away. This sounds ridiculous, but many of you probably do the same thing.

Hanging on to stuff doesn't keep us more connected to people, places, or past moments. Our memories do that, so we can let go. We can clean away the clutter that prevents us from spending time doing things more important for the present.

Freeing ourselves from too much stuff or too many activities opens new avenues, such as charity. I learned this lesson once in a very humbling manner. My college-age daughter signed up for a trip to work at an orphanage in Bolivia over her spring break. Before she left, she decided to take as many warm clothes with her as she could pack so that she could give them out to the children at the orphanage. She received word that nights get cold in Bolivia and both children and adults need warmer clothes. Being an industrious firstborn, she decided to raid our closets at home—without us knowing. She went into her sisters' closets, her brother's closet, and my husband's and mine and pulled a few items from each. She carefully chose sweaters, shirts, and pants that she thought the people at the orphanage would enjoy the most.

She failed to ask permission from us, with very good reason. Even though she took things we hardly missed, we would have probably balked and told her to go to Wal-Mart. We wouldn't have wanted to part with our clothes. Fortunately for the people in Bolivia, she simply took the articles, stuffed them into her duffle bag, and left. After I got over the shock of her stealing, I was quite proud of her.

Giving feels good. It is very often the right thing to do. And we can't give if we hold on too tightly to the things we have. I don't care who you are, what your income is, or how hard you fought to get what you have: Every one of us mothers has many things we can give to those in need. We have stuff, time, energy, and resources to offer. The wonderful part of giving things away is that the more we give, the more we want to give. It can become contagious.

Simplicity is the disciplined art of letting go. It means willfully determining that your inner self needs some focus, some paring down and reorganization of priorities. And once we have given attention to that inner self, it needs help. We must attach a pair of feet to it in order that it can stay alive and work out its intentions. Giving is the best way to help that process begin.

HABIT #9

||||||||||||||||||||||||||||||||||||||||||||||||||||||||||||||||||||||||||||||||||||||||||||||||||||||||||||||||||||||||||

Let Go of Fear

WHY MOTHERS WORRY, AND HOW TO STOP

I'll be the first to admit it: I am a recovering, albeit slowly recovering, obsessive worrier. Before my first daughter was two, I had mentally diagnosed her with leukemia, tuberous sclerosis, cystic fibrosis, and a few cases of meningitis. Not surprisingly, I was wrong every time. When my second was born, I rushed her to the hospital one Saturday morning to get an abdominal ultrasound. While changing her diaper, I poked around on her abdomen (out of habit) and discovered a mass extending to her pelvic bone. I was convinced that she had a rare tumor called a neuroblastoma. And of course, she didn't. When my pediatrician, a wonderful sixty-something Marcus Welby type, threatened to dismiss me from his practice after he learned about the multitude of X rays, blood work, and CAT scans I had ordered on my kids, I decided to stop examining them so closely. I learned to control the amount of tests I ordered and I even learned to keep my examining fingers out of their ears and throats, but it has been the passage of time (years, really) that has taught me how to relax and worry less about my kids.

Let's face it. We mothers not only feel that it is our right to worry about our kids; we feel that we are not good mothers unless we do so.

When we have nothing to worry about, we sometimes even make stuff up. I have had mothers bring kids to my office and point out rashes on their delicate skin that I couldn't see. They insisted the rash was there and I simply couldn't see it. This is how crazy we mothers can become. Of course, I don't get angry with these moms, because I am one of them. At least they have brought their rashy kids to me. I, on the other hand, have jumped over my pediatrician's head and ordered thousands of dollars' worth of tests on my own kids for a whole lot less than an invisible rash.

But here's what concerns me most: We are worrying more as time goes by. Sure, we have always worried about our kids' health, but these days we have amped up the list of things we worry about (technology and social media are just some of the many new things that concern us). We worry more frequently than we have in the past, and most importantly, worry is crushing us. We hear the horror stories on the evening news. We worry about our kids getting bullied on the Internet or happening upon a porn site. Around every corner are more influences on our kids to worry about.

And there is more—many neuroses are genuine and based on fact. We fret over our kids, our jobs, our financial stability. We are living in a volatile economic climate. Terrorism does threaten our security. But some of our fears are not well-founded. Many mothers I see fret over their kids' success when their kids are already successful. They worry about being thinner when they are already thin. Or they worry about being accepted by their peers when they have a lot of women friends.

Some of us have become out of control with our fears. Physicians prescribe far more anxiolytics than they have in the past. Research shows that the use of antidepressants (which have anxiety-reducing properties) rose 7 percent from 1997 to 2002.[*] And it continues to rise. If we haven't personally suffered from anxiety or panic attacks, we have talked a girlfriend through hers. Anxiety is also closely associated with depression.

Anxiety levels among mothers are rising in part because we feel that

---

[*] "Trends in Antidepressant Use," *AHRQ News and Numbers,* Agency for Healthcare and Quality, May 16, 2005, http://www.ahrq.gov/news/nn/nn051605.htm.

we have more to worry about. In many cases, this is true. Single mothers have to perform the job of two parents and many middle-aged mothers worry about their adult children and also care for their aging parents. One recent study found that "healthy, educated, middle-class women in stable relationships . . . who give birth to healthy, full-term babies experience disturbing rates of postpartum depression." The study went on to say that "the rate of anxiety of the women was 12.2%." And when we get depressed or anxious, guess what? Our kids pick up on our anxiety and their health is affected. Other studies show that stress during a mother's pregnancy may have an impact on fetal growth and a child's temperament.*

So let's get a grip on this. Life is too short. To whatever degree we can alleviate depression and anxiety, we've got to start. We have too much life to live, in spite of all of the bad stuff around us. There is far more good than there is evil and far less to worry about than we think. Let's take a look at the roots of our worry and knock them out of the park. We can. And we need to because when we worry, we get stuck in our own dark cage and life becomes miserable. In this chapter, I'll show you how you can conquer your fear by clarifying it, confronting it with brutal honesty, and, finally, desensitizing.

WHERE DO ANXIETY AND WORRY COME FROM?

Worry arises from fear. And fear erupts when we feel that we will be physically harmed (experience pain) or emotionally harmed (feel hurt, sadness, or grief). Fear originates from a part of our brain that acts to

---

*R. Feldman et al., "Maternal Depression and Anxiety Across the Postpartum Year and Infant Social Engagement, Fear Regulation and Stress Reactivity," *Journal of the American Academy of Child and Adolescent Psychiatry* 48:9 (September 2009), pp. 919–27; J. Henrichs et al., "Maternal Psychological Distress and Fetal Growth Trajectories: The Generation R Study," *Psychological Medicine* (August 2009), pp. 1–11; E. P. Davis et al., "Prenatal Exposure to Maternal Depression and Cortisol Influences Infant Temperament," *Journal of the American Academy of Child and Adolescent Psychiatry* 46:6 (June 2007), pp. 737–46.

protect us so that we can run away from danger. This means that when-ever we feel fear (worry), we put our body into "running mode." Our blood pressure rises, our heart rate goes up, and all parts of our body go on the offensive. We prepare ourselves to attack or flee so that we can get rid of whatever is threatening us. But here's the problem for us moms: The threats aren't going away. Fear comes and stays and we never let it go. Then another worry comes along and builds on the first. Many of us are continually in flight mode. Over time this takes a tremendous toll on our physical and emotional health. And it gets very, very tiring. As a mat-ter of fact, I see mothers who complain of exhaustion but have no med-ical reason for it. But when I dig, I find out quite quickly that many are chronic worriers. And then they actually wonder why they are exhausted all the time! Fear, especially chronic fear, is truly physically exhausting.

To compound things just a bit more, fear often overlaps with anger and sadness. Fear acts as a mask to many other emotions and once it is peeled away, we find either anger or sadness resting right beneath it. Fear acts as a self-protective mechanism because it diverts our attention away from feeling the emotions below it. This is a peculiar game that our hearts and minds play on us. It's almost as if our psyches know what we can handle and what we can't on any given day. Or at least our psyches think they know. For many of us, feeling anxious is simply a ruse, because we *can* handle the emotions underlying fear. We just don't realize it.

We run away from it because we don't want to feel intense anger or intense sadness. Kids often feel that if they face their hurt or anger to-ward a certain individual (many times a parent who has abandoned them), they will explode. They feel that if they really allow their hearts to hurt as intensely as they might, then something will trigger a volcanic eruption inside and they will not be able to survive the emotional episode.

We are no different from kids when it comes to facing deep feelings. Subconsciously, many of us feel (or believe) that if we see, if we feel, if we relive a certain event, we won't survive. This is precisely what women who suffer phobias experience. Those with claustrophobia are convinced on some irrational level that if they are locked inside an elevator, they will endure the terrible discomfort of gasping for air, suffocate, and die. Those who don't have that phobia might laugh at others for being irrational. But we shouldn't do this, because every one of us has been paralyzed by one fear or another. And almost every fear we harbor is irrational on some level. It isn't the event we fear so much as it is the emotional and physical pain associated with the event.

Think of fear as two different kinds: brazen or obvious fears, and those that are far more subtle—even hidden. Most of us can identify our obvious fears, such as the phobias I mentioned above. Personally, I am afraid of snakes and elevators. I know this about myself because I love to garden and my perennial garden is home to a family of snakes. And since I have worked in multilevel hospitals, I have contended with claustrophobia for a number of years. When I step into the elevator, I brace myself for the feelings of suffocation and increased heart rate, and hope that no one can see my flushed cheeks. But as much as these two phobias bother me, there are much more dangerous fears. The second type of fears, the hidden ones, are perhaps more dangerous, because we can't see them. They live like a gas that we can neither taste, see, smell, nor hear. But they are there, in full operation, directing the way we think, respond, love, behave, and talk. They are so pervasive that they affect almost every aspect of our behavior and feelings. If we fail to recognize them, they can break up marriages, cause us to do unbearable things to our kids, and keep us trapped in cages of self-loathing. They are dangerous precisely because they operate as though they have become part of our character. We mistake them for "personality quirks" or even blame others for them. These are fears that have arisen over time and imbedded themselves in our minds because of painful experiences or as a result of coping mechanisms gone haywire.

These hidden fears are ingrained in us and we can tease them out only when we take a hard look at our behavior patterns. For example, mothers who experienced the loss of a loved one during their childhood may subconsciously overprotect their own children for fear of losing them. They may hover over their kids or become too controlling. Other mothers who had painful relationships with their fathers may find themselves having constant negative thoughts about their sons. They simply can't understand why they can't get along with their son or feel compassion toward him. Other mothers who fear rejection may become work maniacs because they are afraid of feeling weak or unsuccessful and are driven to perform well enough to "feel good" about themselves.

But whether it is obvious or hidden, we can do something about fear. It's great news—we can handle it. In fact, we mothers can handle just about anything that is thrown our way if we trust ourselves. What we need to learn is that fear plays tricks on us, and once we recognize those tricks, we can confront almost any fear we face, because many are simply not rooted in reality. And for the fears that are rooted in reality, we can face those also. We may need to reorganize how we think, we may need to recruit a friend or two to help us along the way, or we may need medication or counseling for a while. But we can do this—we can overcome any and all of our anxieties. The first half of the battle begins with recognizing our fears and their origins. Second, the battle is won when we stare our fears down and also face the accompanying emotions. This second process can be more involved but any of us can accomplish it. So let's start by taking a look at some of our most common fears as mothers.

FEAR FOR OUR KIDS—FEAR OF LOSING CONTROL

I have never met a mother who doesn't worry about her kids' health (and of course you know I'm no exception!). Our worries go something like this: "I need to protect my daughter so that she doesn't get swine flu. If she gets swine flu, she may die, and if she dies, then I will be extremely lonely. I don't know if I could live without her." Or, "I know that my son is having trouble in school and this might cause his headaches, but he may have a brain tumor so I'd better get on the Internet and research brain tumor symptoms so that I can catch it early. Because if he has a brain tumor then he may die, and the thought terrifies me." I have even gotten to the point that I voluntarily tell mothers with children with headaches that the kid doesn't have a brain tumor, even if the parent didn't ask. Certainly, our kids' health tops the list of our worries.

Let's suppose, for the sake of illustration, that we worry about our child getting leukemia. From the moment our daughter had her first fever and episode of pallor, it dawned on us that we couldn't control everything that happened to her. We realized that something bad could come into her life and we would not, we feel, be able to do anything about it. Our imagination stirs and tells us that she might need chemotherapy or radiation, and we would have to watch her endure terrible suffering. Then what? Would we be able to handle it? Anxiety begins erupting and we feel our heart rate rise.

What is happening here? First, we are feeling a new level of fear of being out of control. Before we had kids, we knew there were a multitude of things in our lives that we could not control, but nothing was as scary as protecting our kids' lives. When it comes to our kids, control matters more than ever and we suddenly realize that we don't have it. We are smaller in our power than we ever thought. Women who are professionally successful and used to being able to control multimillion-dollar matters suddenly realize that the most important thing—their child's health—is out of their control. Mothers who have given up their careers, sacrificed their physical health, and surrendered their own comforts for their children learn in an instant that they cannot guarantee a good outcome. And this terrifies them. Furthermore, it doesn't seem fair.

In addition to facing the reality that we aren't in control as much as we think we are, we face more important, existential questions. Why would this happen? If God is real, why would He allow such a horrible situation? Our worry forces us to ponder the deep questions of life, and when we are unable to come up with answers, that frightens us, too. This is precisely why I feel that it is important to grapple with those deep questions sooner rather than later, as I discussed in the faith chapter. The best time to sort through them is not when we are feeling anxious.

Finally, we fear for ourselves and what our lives would be like without our kids. Would we want to go on living if one of our children died? We fear our sadness and pain. We don't want to be without them and so we worry endlessly. We worry that after having them in our lives, nothing would feel worthwhile. All of life might lose meaning. Sadness would consume us.

Now let's revisit this line of worry in a manner that is rooted in truth rather than fret. First of all, the overwhelming majority of kids never get leukemia. And second, for many who do get one form or another, there are excellent treatments available and new ones are on the horizon. Science has made great strides in decreasing the mortality rate for childhood cancers.

And if you are the type who recognizes this but quickly substitutes a car accident or some other tragedy for leukemia, remember that still, the overwhelming majority of kids make it to adulthood. Regardless of the malady we choose, the truth is that statistics are on our side. Almost all of our kids will outlive us. But why do we still feel so afraid? We fear something horrible happening to them because we can't control what will or won't happen. Furthermore, we are afraid that we might not be able to handle the pain, that joy will never return, or that we may never find meaning to live if we don't have our kids. But none of this is necessarily true, and even if it was, what could we possibly do to stop it? We can give up control because the truth is, we have a lot less than we think we do anyway. And if the worst happens, we can handle the pain—with the help of family, faith, and friends. Finally, we can find meaning after such a terrible loss because our value comes from many places, not simply from being mothers. Accept it. That's what life teaches us, if nothing else. That we are out of control almost all the time, but life will go on and very little, if anything, of what we fear will come to pass. And if it does, your life will somehow continue, I promise. We can live without feeling like we need to control everything all the time. But it's a lot easier to accept if we operate with a faith in God, as we discussed in the faith chapter.

FEAR OF REJECTION

Whether we are trying to make new friends, parent our kids better, or perform at a higher level at work, every one of us mothers has worried about not being accepted. Inadequacy is the bane of conscientious women worldwide. We are performers, women who meet all sorts of other people's needs, and we want to be Capable with a capital *C*. We want to be recognized for what we do, and we want to be appreciated. Neither of these can occur if we are rejected by those we long to please. Rejection means that we have failed, but it means so much more, or so we tell ourselves. It means that we are disliked because we are inadequate. And because we feel the constant need to fulfill others' needs (specifically our children's), inadequacy has an intense, painful bite.

Interestingly, we mothers often make a leap in our thinking that I have found uncommon in men. When we feel inadequate in one area of our lives, we immediately generalize it. We can't allow the feeling of inadequacy to stay role-specific. When we feel we have failed in one area, suddenly we feel inadequate in almost everything. I remember feeling like a failure after a patient died on my watch when I was working in the emergency room many years ago. I reviewed my decisions, the medications I administered, the timing of the medications and interventions, and while many of my colleagues argued that I had made no errors and that my patient had simply died because he had a terminal disease, I couldn't help feeling that I had failed him miserably. But my self-flagellation didn't end when I left the ER to drive home that night. I felt like a horrible physician, and that feeling prompted me to review my other responsibilities. So I also called into question my worth as a mother. After all, I spent so much time at the hospital, how on earth could I be a good mother? And then there were my parents and siblings, whom I rarely saw because I was either working or spending time with my husband and kids. Within a few minutes I had decided that I was a bad physician (and should quit), a bad mother, a subpar wife, and a worse sister and daughter. My failures piled up high in my mind and felt overwhelming.

When we feel that we have failed another person, we feel that we are therefore worthy of their rejection. The feeling that we have let someone important in our lives down hurts, but what hurts more is the belief that we should now be cast aside because of that failure. And if we should be cast aside, we feel worthless. The pain spirals downward and in short order we feel that we are not worth being loved, liked, or accepted. And when these beliefs settle in, we feel completely alone.

HOW ANNA LET GO OF CONTROL

Anna's situation was particularly tough because it had elements of both fears I've been discussing—her child's health, and rejection, in this case from both her daughter and friends who were appalled by her daughter's illness, which was anorexia. This is one of the most painful illnesses a mother can endure.

I have a theory about mothers and food. The most stressed mothers I see in my practice are mothers whose kids aren't eating well. Whether their infant has chronic diarrhea, recurrent vomiting, or any other illness that causes him to fail to gain weight (or worse, constantly lose weight), nothing pushes a mother's buttons like a child's failure to grow well. We believe that as mothers, the most fundamental work that we must do is to make sure that our kids grow well. If we can't succeed at that, we wonder, what can we succeed at? We are to be the ones who provide nutrition— from breast milk to spaghetti and meatballs. We feel good when our kids eat well and we feel proud when they want only our cooking. Mothers feed kids. That's how we first love them. Good nutrition is not only a primal need for our kids; it is one for us as mothers. (How many dads stress about their children not taking enough breast milk?)

When Anna called me about her seventeen-year-old daughter Helene's weight loss, I heard something in her voice that I had never heard before: terror. I had been Helene's pediatrician since early childhood, and Anna and I had developed a cordial, but not strong, friendship. Now she was crying and had some difficulty getting her words out.

"She just looks horrible. I have begged her to eat, threatened that she can't run track if she doesn't eat, but nothing works. She just keeps losing weight," she said.

When Anna brought Helene in to see me, I was stunned by her appearance. I barely recognized her as the same child I had seen two years ago.

Even with clothes on she looked haggard, pale, and skeletal. She had one of the worst cases of anorexia nervosa I had seen. Five feet six inches tall, she weighed ninety-one pounds—ready for hospitalization.

When I began talking with Helene, she looked like a frail baby bird ready to take flight. She was angry, anxious, and scared. She wouldn't sit still in the exam room while we talked. She paced. At one point she was so agitated that I literally parked myself on my stool and sat in front of the exam room door so that she couldn't leave. She was desperate to leave. Well, her disease was desperate for her to leave.

"Do you know why your mom brought you here today?" I asked Helene.

"She's crazy. She's mean! I need to get out of here. She says I'm too skinny but she just doesn't get it. I need to run and my times are better than ever. She just doesn't understand!" she yelled, on the verge of tears.

Anna cried while Helene wailed at both of us. I stayed in front of the door and refused to budge.

When both settled down, I addressed Helene. "I know that you don't want to be here. And I also know that you're not going to like anything that I have to say. But I need to because you are very sick. As a matter of fact, you are a whole lot sicker than even your parents realize. You need to go to the hospital and stay there awhile. Your life is totally out of control."

Helene let out a bloodcurdling scream, as though she were being stabbed in the chest with a knife. I hoped that the little ones in the adjacent exam rooms (waiting for their baby shots) didn't hear too much. I felt terrible for both mother and daughter. Anorexia nervosa is a nasty disorder and can tear families apart. The same is true with bulimia nervosa. These are not simply childhood illnesses, they are family illnesses because mothers (and fathers, but to a lesser extent) also suffer terribly but rarely get adequate support.

Even though it didn't feel that way at the time, Helene was on her way to recovery. But it wasn't easy. When Helene left, Anna said that her heart was breaking. She felt that she had failed her daughter on many levels. Her mind reeled with anguish over her parenting. Certainly she had been overbearing, overcontrolling, she believed. But I reassured her that she hadn't. Why hadn't she seen signs earlier? she wondered. Why had she dieted in front of her daughter for years and why had she made so many remarks about Helene's gorgeous figure when she was younger? The list of her worries went on and on.

The greatest pain, she said, was watching her daughter die before her very eyes and not being able to do anything about it. Anna had known in her heart for a long time that something was wrong, but she couldn't bring herself to face the seriousness of Helene's illness. At first, she thought that she could fix Helene's problems herself. She tried cooking different meals and bribed her daughter to eat. She also thought that others would judge her if she sent Helene to a treatment center or a hospital.

Once Helene got to the treatment center, things finally got better for both mother and daughter. Helene had the help she needed, and Anna felt that she could finally begin to breathe. Someone else was in charge. A team of experts fixed Helene's food and watched her eat. Counselors teased apart her twisted thought patterns daily and psychiatrists helped sever the grip that obsessive thoughts and feelings had over her. In the eight weeks that Helene was there, her mind was restored to clearer thinking and her depression began to lift. And Anna, too, began to grieve the deeper sadness of her daughter's illness in order that she could emerge on the other side of her grief. Both mother and daughter healed in different ways when the anorexia was brought under control by specialists.

When Helene came home the challenges weren't over. Anna had to learn to watch what she said to her daughter. She had to give up being a food policeman, watching everything her daughter ate. She had to prepare meals, set them in front of Helene, and then not pay attention to whether Helene ate. She had to refuse to talk about her daughter's weight, but when Helene wanted to go for a run and she wasn't medically approved yet, Anna had to put her foot down and not let her go.

After three years, I am happy to report that Helene is doing very well and, equally important, Anna is doing well. She would tell you that she is a changed person because of the fear and anxiety that she experienced with Helene's illness.

"I was beginning to really get it," she told me later. "I really wasn't in charge and I faced it and accepted it. Once I did, I began sleeping at night." Acceptance that she was not in charge—of her daughter's life, her death, her illness, or the amount of food she put in her mouth—made Anna sleep better.

But it was more than just acceptance that helped Anna. She needed to place the daughter whom she adored into the hands of others—like me. She had to trust me, the counselors, the dieticians, the psychiatrists, the entire team of people helping Helene.

Trusting others to help her daughter took a lot more discipline than she ever knew, Anna told me. Her heart felt raw, she said, and once she learned to trust others, she cared little about what people thought about her, her daughter, or her parenting. "That," she said, "provided enormous relief and personal growth."

Anna feared that Helene would recover from her illness only to dislike her mother intensely. Surely, she thought, Helene would uncover some horrific trauma that she or her father had imposed on her, and that would be the end of their relationship. Did that happen?

"Nope," she told me later. "As a matter of fact, we're closer than ever. I've learned to parent her better and she's learned to deal with her illness much better."

In dealing with her fear, Anna learned an extremely important operative dynamic: the illness was her daughter's, not hers. When she approached anorexia like appendicitis, she was able to let go of some of her guilt. The truth is, we mothers aren't responsible for everything that happens to our kids. As a matter of fact, we have a lot less influence than we think. Helene learned to be responsible for her illness and Anna learned not to "wear it" as her own.

For Anna, overcoming her fear involved opening herself to others. First she trusted me, then she trusted others in the medical field. This was extremely tough, she said, but once she began to see her daughter heal, she trusted more. She learned to trust herself more and to lean on her own instincts. "If I could rewind, I would have gotten her into treatment months earlier," she said.

When she came to the realization that she couldn't force-feed her daughter or make her deal with her obsessive-compulsiveness regarding food and thinness, Anna's anxiety heightened more. But, she would say now, that was a turning point for her as a mother.

But here's the most important point of all: Anna did it. She faced the illness, she faced her pain, she aided her daughter when she was in pain, and she not only survived, she thrived. She now has a fabulous relationship with her daughter—one that she could never have imagined when Helene was ninety-one pounds and starving. Both mother and daughter faced their fears and in doing so, completely shrank them.

MARION AND JOSH—LEARNING TO TRUST A SON'S LOVE

Fear is often so deeply imbedded that it affects how we think and act, and yet we don't have a clue that it is there. Marion, like Anna, harbored a deep fear that she was oblivious to until it caught up with her. When Josh was seven, his father left him and his mother, Marion. Shortly after the divorce, Marion brought Josh to my practice. Even during those early years of his childhood, Marion was terrified that Josh would reject her but didn't know it. She boasted to her friends and me about how "close" she and her son were. Marion's ex wandered in and out of Josh's life and Marion, because she was such a conscientious mother, tried hard not to criticize Josh's dad too fiercely in front of her son. She feared that this would only cause Josh to verbally shut down and not share his honest feelings about his father with Marion.

Life went relatively smoothly for the duo until the mid-teen years hit. Marion said that she woke up one morning, offered her son an omelet, and when he responded, heard another boy's voice. Overnight, Josh seemed like a different kid. He snarled at her. He grunted and refused to use words. When she asked how soccer practice was, he refused to answer and then simply ran to his room.

Marion immediately searched the Internet for books on the mind-set of fifteen-year-old boys. She had to get her son back. She came to my office in tears one day.

"I just don't understand," she said. "He's such a good kid. Last year, before his behavior really changed, his grades were good. He was polite. He even volunteered in a nursing home! We'd go to the movies together. He'd have friends over. We had so much fun together. Now he won't even look at me. He won't let me hug him. Nothing I say is right."

"So," I said, "what do you do? How do you handle him? His behavior must make it hard for you to know what to say or whether or not to say anything."

"I really don't know what to do. A few months ago I decided to take him on a vacation. I planned a trip for the two of us. I tried to figure out what would really make him happy. He's always wanted to go camping in the Rockies, so I took him and surprised him. It was miserable. The harder I tried to please him, the worse it got. We ended up coming home early because we got into a huge fight. He yelled and I cried.

"Things only got worse when we got home. He found new friends. He got a few tattoos and I told him I liked them to try and make him happy. It seemed that the more I supported him, the worse things got. The last thing that I wanted to do was criticize him. I was afraid of driving him away.

"One night at two A.M., the phone rang. It was the police. I thought they had the wrong number. They told me that they had Josh at the station with a few other kids and they had been caught drinking and driving. I knew they must be wrong because Josh was home asleep in his bed. I ran to his room and sure enough, I was wrong.

"I ran down to the station and saw him in a jail cell and burst into tears. I know I should have been mad, but I wasn't. I was terribly sad. To tell you the truth, I fear for his life right now. He's completely out of control."

We spent time reviewing Josh's behavior and life before his change and then after it. Clearly Josh was struggling with some depression and feelings of rejection from his father. At fifteen, he needed a man and no one was available to him. To make matters worse, Marion assumed responsibility for his problems and responded by trying to smooth things over for him. Rather than confronting his issues one at a time, Marion did what a lot of conscientious and loving mothers do: She worked to please her son. By doing this she hoped to draw him closer to her. She bought him things she knew he liked. She camped with him, said that she liked his tattoos, but each time she ventured to please him more, it backfired.

Not only did Marion feel that Josh's behavior was her responsibility;

she also felt guilty because his father had left. She knew how painful that was for Josh, but rather than addressing the issue, she tried to make life nicer. She wanted no conflict, no boundaries, no rules. That way she'd never be the bad guy, Josh would never be angry, and she'd never feel rejected. But guess what? He was already distant. He had withdrawn from her emotionally, and the harder she tried to woo him back, the more he withdrew.

In her clearest-thinking moments, Marion admitted that the reason she indulged her son was indeed fear of rejection. She needed him to love her. She was desperate for him to stay close to her, and when he pulled away, she sank her well-polished nails into him deeper. But she felt that it was okay, because she did it nicely. She indulged him.

Marion thought that the pain of being rejected by Josh (or of doing things that would cause him to back away more) would be unbearable. He was all she had. They were a team. Everyone else had left them and they needed to stick together. Marion realized, when probing more deeply, that she was afraid of feeling rejected by the only person in her life whom she ever really "connected with," and also realized she wouldn't feel valued as a mother: If Josh didn't like who she was, then she was a failure as a mom. If she believed that, then what was her life worth? Her marriage had failed and she had had a tough relationship with her parents (which wasn't her fault). So she couldn't risk feeling like a failure in this very important venture, too. She frantically did everything she could to prevent this from happening. So she indulged her son.

We can see how one fear can twist our thinking. It prompts other fears to arise and it causes us to act confused. I encouraged Marion to separate herself from her son and not fear rejection by him. The best thing she could do for their relationship was to toughen up and take control, because he was clearly out of control. She needed to set down rules (most fifteen-year-old boys act like crazy people without them) and she needed to stop wanting to please him. Her fear of his withdrawing his love for her paralyzed her thinking and manipulated her. This grown, bright woman had become like a marionette, dancing to accommodate every wish and pleasant feeling that she thought her son had. Her fear of rejection blinded her to what he needed—a strong, clear-thinking, adult mom.

When Marion realized her fear and faced it, she began to take charge of her own and her son's lives again. She refused to let the fear that he would hate her, reject her, and never want anything to do with her again control her relationship with him, and guess what began to happen? Josh began to come around. He continued to act out typical, silly fifteen-year-old-boy antics, but nothing as potentially harmful as what he'd done before. And he never landed in a jail cell again.

The power of our hidden fears can be enormous. An initially small fear can morph into a larger, broader one over time. When fear slides its ugly tentacles into our relationships, nothing good results from it. So we moms need to square off with our fears and learn to take charge over them so that they lose their power over us. The great news is that we can. We most certainly can. And once we're honest and expose our fears, we free ourselves.

Exposure is usually a whole lot less painful than we presume, but more importantly, fears kept secret grow larger. They get more powerful. And the tough part is, we don't even see it. But once we acknowledge the fear and externalize or express it, the fear shrinks. And we defeat it at last.

THREE WAYS TO MAKE THE HABIT STICK

#1: Clarify the fear

We can't fight what we don't see. Enemies must be identified and set apart. Fears are feelings, and as such, each fear must be teased apart from other feelings. This is particularly important because there is tremendous overlap in our feelings. We are angry because we are afraid. We become sad because we are afraid. There isn't always overlap, but we must be able to separate fear from the other feelings when there is.

One of the easiest ways to accomplish this and flesh fear out is to ask a series of "why" questions. We need to be bold enough with ourselves (and any close friends helping our efforts to overcome fear) to press ourselves regarding why we do what we do. This is extraordinarily eye-opening. For instance, every mother who works must ask herself why she works as many hours as she does. Is it really for the income? Is it because she doesn't want to face life without the success and identity that comes with working so hard? I have often pressed myself on this last issue. In other words, I need to know that I work because I truly love my work, not just for the money or because I am afraid of losing my physician identity. I need to know that I am still valuable as a woman and mother without those two letters after my name.

That is just the beginning. Any of our fears can be uncovered if we press ourselves regarding our motives for our behaviors—particularly the behaviors that cause us grief. It takes work and you may need the help of a skilled professional, but the work is worth it.

#2: Employ brutal honesty

Once we get what we're dealing with, the really hard part begins. We must face the demons down. We must tell someone what we are confronting and ask for help. There is to be no running, no avoidance. We must have the courage to admit specifically what we are afraid of and then repeatedly (see step 3) tell ourselves that we are in the process of smashing it. We must talk about it. We must imagine what life would be like if our worst fear came to pass. Thinking and talking about our fear diffuses its power and allows us to grapple with it more clearly. By facing the fear repeatedly, we invite it to reenter our lives, if you will, but this time in a fashion where we are in charge of it. We are the embracers of the fear and we are in control.

#3: Desensitize, step-by-step

When patients have anxiety or full-blown panic attacks, physicians often put them through a program of cognitive behavioral therapy. This is a desensitization plan that forces the anxious person to face her fear over and over. A good therapist re-creates a situation where the patient can envision herself frightened, so that her anxiety escalates. She is forced to live through a series of "what-ifs" regarding her anxiety.

For instance, a woman who struggles with claustrophobia, as I do, would be coaxed into a confined space for longer and longer periods of time. She can learn to face the what-ifs by allowing the worst-case scenarios to come to life.

The mother of one of my patients struggled with serious obsessive-compulsive disorder. She cleaned incessantly and her fear of disorder and dirt took an enormous toll on her relationships with her kids. She drove them crazy. But she told me that she had been able to control her phobia, and I wanted to know how.

"Tell me how you got over it," I asked one afternoon.

To my surprise, she laughed and said, "You're not going to believe me because looking back on it, although it felt horrific at the time, it was actually kind of funny.

"At first my therapist made me talk about things that grossed me out. He made me envision my hands covered in dirt. Then I imagined them covered in stuff I can't discuss with you. Over the weeks, he made me actually cover my hands in dirt. Then he made me sit and talk to him with dirt still on my hands. It got pretty gross. And I know this sounds crazy to you, but it was painful. I started crying at times. I jumped out of my chair and yelled at him once. But I knew it was working, and here's the best part—my final session with him.

"He brought popcorn into his office because he knew I liked it. We talked for a while and then he told me to use the ladies' room. But he said that I couldn't wash my hands afterward. I had to come back to his office and eat the popcorn with my dirty hands. As if this weren't bad enough, he walked me into the hallway in his office, stood outside the bathroom, and threw a few handfuls of popcorn on the floor. It was filthy. Then— you guessed it, he made me eat it. But then he pulled the worst stunt I can imagine. He took some of the popcorn into the men's room and touched a few pieces to the toilet seat—at least he told me he did. If I could eat it, he said, I would graduate his therapy program. Did I eat it? I sure did. I can't believe I did. It was horrible but one of the most important things I've ever done in my life."

I have to admit that I am friends with her psychiatrist and I can't believe that he went so far. I have never let him forget how he seemingly tormented this poor mother, but he knew better than I. Overcoming fears that keep us locked inside their cages requires war. And that's exactly what this mother did for herself—she declared war against her fear. As you can imagine, her relationships with her kids and husband are improved. But more importantly, she is a woman who is free. She no longer awakens at night sweating. She hasn't had a panic attack in several years. Now she can go out to dinner with friends and enjoy herself because she no longer obsesses about the server's hand-washing techniques or the cleanliness of the kitchen. She can simply enjoy herself and her company.

Of course, many fears are hidden and not as easy to identify and thus conquer. Personally, I do a lot of public speaking and I love it. I have spoken in front of thousands of kids, parents, physicians, you name it, and, oddly enough, I feel quite relaxed while lecturing, unless one particular person is in the audience—my husband. As peculiar as it sounds, the one person who encourages me the most is the one person who completely intimidates me when I speak. Why? I'm afraid that he will hear something that I say and think I'm stupid. Has he ever done this? No. He has neither criticized my speaking nor rejected any part of me as his wife, and yet when I see him in the audience, my palms go sweaty. I would rather speak in front of the pope than my husband.

My fear is irrational. And that is my first point. The overwhelming majority of our fears of criticism or rejection are irrational, and we must keep that fact at the front of our minds when we move forward to overcome them. What do I do to overcome my fear of rejection by my husband when I speak? I take a deep breath and invite him to as many of my lectures as possible. This makes me crazy inside. It ignites even more trepidation, but I need to address him more frequently in order to overcome this irrational fear.

My friend Sandy did the same with her girlfriends. As an at-home mother with four kids, she felt intimidated to join a business group for women. She was a psychology major in college "a hundred years ago," as she always said, and felt that she would have nothing intelligent to say to her peers. Would she have good contributions to make to the group? Of course. But that reality didn't help squelch her fear of feeling like a fool and being rejected by her friends. So what did she do? She joined (with a lot of coaxing) a women's investment group and a book club. But she didn't stop there. She made herself speak up in the groups. She wouldn't simply go and listen; she was determined to get over the gnawing in her gut that other women would think she was stupid, and so she made herself engage in discussions.

After many years of lecturing in front of my husband, I'm still not completely at ease, but my palms don't sweat and after the first few minutes into the lecture, I even forget he's there. And as silly and small as that may sound, that is an enormous victory for me. What also helped me get over worrying about his criticism is that I told him what I was worried about. When he rolled his eyes and said, "Are you kidding me? You're a great lecturer," I forced myself to believe him. And I forced myself to face my fear. Sandy has done the same (I guess that's why we're such good friends—two chickens commiserating and winning side by side). After two years of meetings with her financial group and her book club, she's getting ready to spearhead the startup of similar women's groups in her city. And her fear of feeling rejected? It's gone. Completely.

Desensitization of our fears is not for the weak of heart. Many are afraid of facing their fears and beating them. Some fears are easier to overcome than others, but with the help of good friends and professionals if needed, any of us can face them down.

Some of us have anxiety and haven't a clue why. If you are one of these women, commit to yourself that you will find the root of the anxiety, and if you can't commit to that yourself, get help. Others know their fear but feel that overcoming it requires too much energy. The truth is, living with fear consumes more energy than overcoming it. Fear saps precious energy from us over time, so this should not be an adequate excuse. No mother deserves to live with crippling fear. Each one of us deserves to live the freest life she can. Often the cure for our fear is far simpler than we think, because one of the tricks that fear plays on us is that it twists our thinking. It prods us into believing that fear can't be overcome, that doing so requires too much work. But we shouldn't be fooled. Most fears are real and all should be driven out, if not for us (though this is certainly reason enough), then for our kids. What we carry, they carry, too. Life is too short, and we all deserve to live it free of fear.

||||||||||||||||||||||||||||||||||||||||||||||||||||||||||||||||||||||||||||||||||||||||||||||||

Hope Is a Decision—So Make It!

WHY MOTHERS NEED HOPE

My daughter lived in India several years ago, and I will never forget the energy that radiated from her when she stepped off the plane. She announced in the baggage claim area that her life had been changed. Never before had she experienced such an intellectual and spiritual transformation. She had to tell me about it.

At once she recounted stories of women she met in shops, in homes, and in temples who endured indescribable poverty. She listened to mothers whose children begged in the streets and who died of illnesses that she knew were easily treated here in the United States. Her nostrils sucked in the stench of burning human flesh when the dead were incinerated in piles, one body heaped upon another. She saw mothers bathe their children in the Ganges River next to human waste and remains of the dead that had been left to float in the river. When she went to temples she witnessed mothers who abandoned their shoes at the door before stepping inside to beg the gods for better health for themselves and their children. And sometimes the same women would exit the temples only to find that their shoes had been stolen by kids who sold them on the streets.

What changed my daughter's life wasn't the smells, the visions of poverty, or listening to grieving mothers. She saw children who had been purposely maimed and put on the streets to beg. My daughter wondered how their mothers must feel. She saw a mother sitting along a street, holding a child on her lap. The child was crying, thin, and clearly starving. She spoke with other mothers who told her stories of their hardships— of poverty and the inability to find work or provide basic necessities (food and clothes) for their children. As she listened, she said, she often focused on the tone of voice they used or their facial expressions. And what struck her the most was that not all the mothers were as despondent as she expected them to be. In fact, many expressed hope in their voices.

What changed my daughter (and at times stunned her) was witnessing their faith and hope. The mothers of India were spiritually alive with energy and hope. In the midst of some pretty horrific living conditions, they exuded not happiness in the present, but hope for the future— whether for the next day or years ahead. Hope was alive inside them.

Life cannot be sustained without hope. That is what is so remarkable and intriguing about this tiny word. It has a mysterious and generous quality. We know hope when we have it and feel miserable when we don't. Sometimes we feel as though we can't control it, but the truth is that we can. The greatest secret to having a happy life is sustaining a vibrant hope.

Our hearts can pump blood through our bodies, thoughts can enter and exit our minds, and our stomachs can begin the digestion of the food we eat. But if these things happened and we had no hope in our hearts, we would be existing, not living. Therein is another power in hope. It transforms existence into living.

Hope demands that we believe in two things: a future—even if it is very brief—and the possibility of good occurring. When we have hope, we feel a conviction that some fraction of our lives will get better than it currently is. Improvement, joy, healing, or something greater than our current state of being (or someone else's being) will happen soon. Hope makes us look forward, not backward. And every one of us mothers needs to look forward because the mistakes we make and discouragement we feel many days yank us steadily into the past. We need to focus forward if we are to enjoy life, change, improve, or simply be jolted from our current state of unrest.

After having listened to thousands of mothers over the past twenty years, I am convinced of one thing: None of us lives with enough hope. Whether we have a positive, upbeat personality or suffer chronic depression, every one of us needs more hope because we need more from our lives than just existence. Having a positive attitude about life is very important. Some of us have it because of our nature, while others have to work hard to get a positive attitude. But having such a good attitude is not the same as having hope. It may be part of it, but the two are separate. A positive attitude helps us look more brightly at situations, but hope allows us to grab on to something that will help us believe that life in the future will be better, that good will come.

I have had the privilege of watching mothers cope with some really tough situations. Some have had terminally ill children; some have had children with birth defects or cancer. So I have watched how many mothers handle their pain, and I can tell you that without a doubt, the mothers who thrive and get through their difficulties with the most resilience are those who have hope. They may not know what lies around the next corner for them or for their child, but they have hope that someone other than themselves (God) has plans for them and is in control.

The good news for all of us mothers is that having more hope is easier than we think, because deep inside each of us is a cistern filled with hope. It leaks from its sides occasionally, but we need more of that water. We need to crack the tank wide open.

After my daughter returned from India, we had many great talks about life there, especially for mothers and children. And usually when she described life in India, my daughter became visibly upset. She wondered about mothers here in America. She struggled with our lackluster attitudes toward life, our distant or buried spirituality and consistent negative fretting in the midst of enormous excess. What is wrong with mothers in the United States? she wondered. We have so much more materially, educationally, and medically. Why should she want to be a mother someday, given that when she looked around here she saw such tense, worried, and anxious moms? What she wanted was to be like the women in India, because they enjoyed something deep and mysterious. She wasn't angry, but she was sad and pensive. She needed answers. Was it the Indian women's faith that gave them hope? Was it the gods they prayed to instead of our Judeo-Christian God? Or was it simply a personality difference expressed by different genetic compositions?

We talked and dug through her deep questions. I believe that we found some answers.

WHERE HOPE STARTS

When we are children, we fall asleep at night knowing that in the morning the light will come again. Darkness will pass and the sun will peek through the morning sky. We know that there will be food to eat and school to go to. Life will progress around us regardless of anything we do. Good will happen in some way or form. We believe this whether we are happy kids or sad ones. Leaves turn brilliant colors in the fall and apple trees plump with blossoms every spring. We can be mean, upset, or pouty all day long but we know that good things will happen around the next corner, regardless of what we think or do. We know this because hope lives within us. We don't pull it in or wish it to be. It is there. We are born with hope. We embody hope during our childhood.

As we grow older, we get beaten up by life. External circumstances bear down on us and people we love get sick. Death becomes a reality and we begin to see darkness that many of us didn't know about when we were children. As we age, something in us pushes hope away. It begins to go underground, if you will; it doesn't leave us, because it is part of our nature, our being. Coworkers make us cynical, friends make us angry, and families hurt us. Children disappoint us and our work leaves us feeling empty. We search for something we cannot grab hold of, something that will satisfy our deep longing. But since we usually look in the wrong places, we experience feelings of hopelessness. We have lost or failed and those feelings lead us to shove hope far away. We will accept hopelessness because it makes more sense than feeling hopeful. Hopelessness is safe. It allows us to know that we have nothing to lose by embracing it. Hopelessness leads to nothing. Hope leads to something good but that frightens us because we can't bear one more disappointment. We decide on hopelessness because it is safe.

At age fifty-two, I feel hopeless about ever being able to get back into shape. I used to love to run. For thirty years I ran because it altered my mood and lightened the dysthymia that snaked its way into my mind. I ran off frustrations and anger and sweated out "the stink," as my dad used to call it. Now my legs are weaker and I sit a lot because of my work, and running is harder. Every part of my body is migrating south and none of it wants to cooperate in moving back up north. Accepting our shifting bodies comes with age and that acceptance is good. But I have seen some friends become hopeless (if that is not too strong a word) about ever feeling healthy and strong again. Sure, my muscles are shrinking, but since I used to love running, I decided to start up again. I won't ever have my past strength, but who cares? Hope tells me to move ahead and have fun with what I have.

My friends have expressed hopeless feelings about their marriages, their jobs, or their finances. Are these really hopeless? I don't know, but I doubt it. In most situations, we can grab on to hope and change our situations. We can lean on our own abilities and corral a bit of chutzpah so that we can do what is necessary to change our circumstances. We can be the ones to change things, or we can rely on life, God, or the laws of nature to take hold and implement changes. After all, one thing that age has taught us is that things never stay as they are. Change in the near and distant future is part of life, regardless of what we do.

Realizing this fact should give us more hope, but it doesn't. For me and for my friends, this knowledge of constant change only serves to drive us deeper into a downward spiral once we have become discouraged. If we look back at the lives of the lovely women whom my daughter met in India, certainly they endured the same dynamics of change that we do. But for some reason, they were able to hang on to hope better than many of us do, and we need to understand why this is.

We are born with hope. We learn that good things happen that are out of our control, are detached from our own wishes or actions. The sun rises because something causes it to rise, and this is good. But later, cynicism sets in and we become frustrated as we see pain around us. We particularly become angry when hurt happens to ourselves or our loved ones, and we feel that there is nothing we can do about it. We get mad at our own limitations. We begin to recruit whatever rests inside us in order to make situations better. For instance, if we are frustrated in a bad marriage we will try to get our husband to change, or perhaps we will change ourselves to accommodate the marriage. If this fails, we may find another way out of our misery—exercise, shop, eat, or have an affair. When this fails, we become cynical and dig an interior grave for the hope that we once enjoyed. We feel hopeless because we have come to realize that we cannot fix a problem or even make ourselves feel better.

We bat hope away once, and then we do it again and again. That is problem number one. Problem number two happens when we try alternate paths to making our bad situations better, and the new paths fail. In short, we find wrong answers to our problems because we use the wrong methods to fix them. If we are depressed, we drink. If we are mad, we scream at our kids. And if we are sad, we eat Häagen-Dazs. We compound our problems by trying the wrong solutions, and thus hope disappears.

Think about the Indian mothers. When they were hopeless, they refused the illusion that they could fix many of their problems. They realized that many of their circumstances were out of their control, so they didn't attempt to fix them. They surrendered. They had little legal recourse, sparse medical help, and no counseling for much of their psychological pain. They had no gyms to go to or ice cream in the freezer. They went to the temples and pleaded and prayed.

Could it be, then, that we lose hope because we try to trump it? We see it as unnecessary because we believe that we *can* do something, even if that something is the wrong thing. Our efforts supplant hope. If the sun doesn't rise, we will figure out how to make it come up. We will make our frustration go away by doing something that will divert our attention and so make us feel better. Maybe we'll work harder at the office, take on more projects, etc., to avoid seeing that we can't do a darn thing about the sun's behavior. Something or someone else is in charge of it.

Hope fades because we suppress it and because we refuse to acknowledge that inherent in the hoping is a realization that other forces, bigger and more powerful than us, are at work. If we refuse to acknowledge this external work, we will constantly try to correct what is wrong. But that isn't within our power.

To be a mother who has hope is to make two important leaps. First, we must train ourselves to be optimistic and think positively. This takes work and many of us are afraid to do this. Second, *we must let hope release our control*. Neither being optimistic nor being positive forces us to do that. Yes, hope says to us that we must believe positively, but we must also put our hope in something or someone. These are the two areas where we make mistakes when it comes to maintaining hope in our lives. We either lose hope because all optimism has been beaten out of us by painful circumstances, or because we refuse to accept that we have no control over many situations. Until we fully face the latter, we cannot live a life of genuine hope. But it is possible, and I'll help you see how. In this chapter, you'll learn how to cultivate an attitude of appreciation, how to trust, how to work on expecting good things in the future, and finally, how to challenge negative thinking.

HOPE GIVES US MEANING AND PURPOSE (AND EACH OF US NEEDS MORE)

Stop and think about the last time you felt really excited. I don't mean simply the last time you were in a good mood, but the most recent time in your life that you felt that deep, guttural joy of anticipation. Maybe you were waiting to go into labor with a child. Perhaps you were gearing up to start a new job or even preparing wedding arrangements. You were excited because something good was about to occur—something that was going to change your life in a substantial way. You were filled with hope because in your mind's eye, you saw great things stirring in the days ahead.

But something else was going on as well. You were hopeful because that change involved a shift in how you saw yourself. You were getting ready to feel a greater sense of purpose or passion. Mothers preparing for labor understand that they are needed in order to keep their tiny child alive. With a new job on the horizon, your hope includes a sense that you can contribute something meaningful. And a new wedding gives you a sense of direction, a change in the role you will play on a daily basis.

When we look forward to future events, we are filled with excitement because we believe that life will make more sense. Things will come together as they never have before and our lives will take on new meaning and deeper dimensions. Having hope gives purpose and meaning.

This is no small matter. We need to know this because there will be many days as mothers when we wonder whether life is worth the trouble. Some mothers doubt their ability to influence their kids; other mothers become discouraged because their lives feel meaningless and empty. Dark is dark and it blinds those who live in its midst. We need to keep hope alive in our hearts and dig deep inside to find it so that we can live with an inner awareness that we matter. Every one of our lives matters. Every one. Hope keeps us aware of this truth.

As we age, we can become dull and cynical to those who are young and passionate around us. We harbor these feelings because we have been in their shoes and been banged around a bit. The passion has died because we gave up hope that anything we tried made any difference at all. It might have, but we lost sight of that because we tired of pushing our ideas ahead and campaigning for our dreams. We dreamed, worked, and saw some failures. And because we are human, we allowed our failures to take us under. In short, when we gave up holding our beliefs and passions dear, we gave up hope and life became confusing and dull.

So we need to take our passions back. We need to relearn what our lives are about. How in the world do we do that? Look inside. What makes your heart skip a beat? Can you even remember? Of course you can. We all can. We have had dreams, both outrageous and small, and thinking about these dreams launched us into another world. We saw ourselves there.

When I was in medical school, I dreamed of being a surgeon. I love to cut and sew, and I love to concentrate intently on things. But while pursuing that dream, I learned that I loved helping kids even more, so my dream took an unexpected turn and I became a pediatrician. To this day, when I walk into an exam room and see a sassy toddler, my heart leaps. I was born to love and care for kids. Their illnesses, their health, their needs, the way they change their mothers—these are all my passions.

We all have unique gifts. Some women are gifted with the ability to soothe others. Even the inflections in their voices are calming. Others motivate. Some mothers lead others to challenge themselves and in so doing, these leaders become energized by using their own talents. Our gifts are as diverse as our hair color and fingerprints. But these gifts are the results of our passions. Find yours. Seek it out—even if you can't allow its full expression just yet. Find it anyway. Build your dreams around that gift and when the time is right, let it rip. Life is too short to live without passion.

We need to communicate the importance of passion to our kids, but also the importance of hope. We are mothers who are put into our children's lives to change who those kids become. We exist to give them life, but also to make them better than who they would be without us here. The best of our influence in their lives isn't the clothes we help them choose, the schools we pick out, or even how we encourage them. The great influences we have in our kids' lives involve the values we instill and the beliefs we teach them.

Look at your kids. Study them. You are there. Your daughter tells the truth because you do. Your son laughs easily because he feels safe with you. Your life and sweat run in their bloodstreams. Don't kid yourself. Genetics gave them their brown eyes and maybe even a charismatic personality. But *you* brought them to life. Your son comes home after school and wants you. No one else can make him feel better about life than you can. He has hope because you give him reasons to be hopeful. You talk to him about his future. You anticipate his happiness and coach him when he hurts. When his girlfriend breaks his heart, you listen and love him. And you drill hope back into him. No one can do this the way you can.

EDNA'S HOPE FOR ELLA

Edna was a mother filled with extraordinary hope. I first met her when I was caring for her four-year-old daughter Ella, who had fallen into a swimming pool and nearly drowned. Edna found Ella floating in the family pool, and after yanking her from the water, she tried furiously to resuscitate her. She was unsure how many minutes Ella had been underwater, but when Ella came to the hospital, she barely had a heartbeat.

After hard work by the ER physicians, Ella improved somewhat. Her heart rate picked up but she still didn't breathe on her own. She was transferred to the intensive care unit, where she stayed for many weeks. Neurologists told Edna and her husband to take Ella off life support because they said that the outlook for her was grim. She would never be able to walk, speak, or feed herself, and she would always have serious cognitive impairment. In fact, most children in Ella's situation have very little chance of recovery to any state other than this. I understood exactly why the specialists told the parents this. Edna thanked the specialists for their opinions but said that she wanted every aggressive treatment given to her daughter. No pulling the plug, at least not then. Ella continued to live and a few weeks later, began breathing on her own. She was transferred from the ICU to a regular pediatric floor in the hospital and it was there that I received my introduction to Ella.

I can still see her tiny body clad in the ugly gray hospital gown, lying deathly still on her bed. Ella had two or three folks by her bed and Edna was one of them. When Edna first greeted me, she acted like I was the first person that she'd seen in the hospital. She was fresh and polite rather than exhausted and cynical, the latter being what I had expected. She spoke to me as though the two of us were going to be friends, which is certainly what we became. But somehow her kindness bothered me. It made me sadder. Angry parents of sick children are easier to work with because I can be more guarded, more emotionally distant.

Edna wouldn't let me be. She pulled me toward the family with an irresistible energy. At first I couldn't understand it. After several weeks, I got it. She was positive; she believed that her daughter was going to be well one day. And she didn't seem like a kook. Whenever we talked about Ella, she spoke bluntly and directly. She was clearly well educated regarding her daughter's illness and she spoke with a clear realism. But overriding her understanding, her realism, and her affection for her daughter was hope. She let everyone with whom she came in contact know that she had very strong hopes for Ella. She hoped that Ella would open her eyes. She hoped that Ella would stand up and walk. She hoped that Ella would speak the word *Mommy* one day. Never did I see Edna's hope waiver in the three months that I cared for her daughter.

I am embarrassed to admit that I frowned upon her positive attitude and her hope when I first began taking care of Ella. I was concerned that she was falsely encouraging family and friends and that when she verbalized her hope, she was leading them on. Heartbreak was around the next corner, I believed, and she was setting loved ones up to fall hard when Ella failed to recover. But after several weeks of listening to Edna and watching her, I began to believe that she knew something that I didn't. Though perhaps she didn't. Perhaps what she really had was the bold audacity to hope for the impossible and to risk believing the impossible. I never knew what was on in her mind during those months. I simply saw a mother who refused to give up. But what if Ella died, I wondered. Wouldn't Edna fall that much harder?

At night when other physicians had gone home and the nursing staff was skeletal, I would make rounds. Cardiorespiratory monitors would gently chirp and an occasional child would cry out for his mother. I would see other mothers asleep in rocking chairs with their babies curled into their chests. And one vision I could always count on was Edna or her husband seated next to their comatose little girl holding her hand, mumbling soft words into the bedsheets or up to the ceiling on Ella's behalf.

After three months, I was transferred to work in a different part of the hospital and other physicians took over Ella's care. Every once in a while I stopped in to see the little girl and the lovely sight of her mother holding on to her. One afternoon I got a phone call. It was Edna. She was choking on her tears. Ella had opened her eyes and recognized her mother. Hope had won.

After Ella's initial recovery began, her little body went gangbusters. Ella soon stood up and one day walked across her hospital room. She grunted words and even smiled on occasion. The more she returned to life, the more hope Edna mustered. She was delirious with excitement. And what did she expect for her daughter, I asked one day. "Nothing. I expect nothing," she told me. "But I hope for everything."

Shortly after the one-year anniversary of her accident, Ella walked out of the hospital. She was speaking words that made sense and she called Edna "Mommy." Later Edna told me that if that word was all she ever got out of their yearlong ordeal and the hope that sustained her, all the work was still worth it.

I was so overwhelmed by Ella's recovery that I pressed Edna for answers. She beat the odds that the medical professionals had wagered and what had transpired in her life over the past year was miraculous, supernatural. How did Ella come back to life? I needed Edna to tell me what she knew.

"I guess we just leaned real hard on two things," she told me. "We refused to give up hope and we believed in God's goodness." Those two things sounded pretty hefty to me. I needed time to let them percolate.

Edna first *chose* to be hopeful. While everyone around her warned her to be cautious and stay prepared for the worst to come, she mentally leaped over their advice. She commanded her heart to believe that healing was possible. If it didn't happen and Ella died, then she believed that God would help her handle that. She told me once that, for her, hope was a deliberate choice and it was a frightening one. Then I wondered to myself, Is choosing hope simply a way for a mother to take control? Or is it a way to give up control? If we are superstitious, we might think it is a way to take control. For believing may cause healing to come—as if the believing itself were a rabbit's foot. Hope, to a superstitious mother, may be a way to make magic appear. But superstition wasn't in Edna's idiom.

Then I realized that having hope was Edna's way of surrendering control. She wasn't frantically researching cures or asking the doctors to do unreasonable things. She was just quietly waiting, praying, and loving. In her mind's eye, she took her daughter's ill body and placed it into God's arms. He would be in charge where she couldn't be. I believe that after Edna did this, she experienced a lightness. I could see that in her face over the days I cared for Ella.

So the second part of having hope is giving up control (and this is really tough for us mothers). Edna gave full control of Ella's healing over to a good and kind God. In some ways, she was forced to. Like many mothers who face grave situations, Edna stared God in the face. There was nothing that she could do except trust Him with her child. She later told me that that position was "the safest place to be." I never learned about Edna's religion or her theology or what kind of church she attended. She never quoted me Bible verses. She showed me what she believed and told me how much she needed God. From her voice, I saw that she trusted Him. She liked Him. No, she loved Him. When she talked about her thankfulness, her eyes sparkled. His character was extraordinary. That's how she was able to put her hope in God. She knew that He was good and that He loved her little girl.

Trusting only works if we know the person whom we trust. She believed that she knew God and His personality, if you will. I was intrigued. Her logic made sense because when we hope, we hope in someone, and she knew the person in whom she hoped. She wasn't about settling for pie-in-the-sky hope. She demanded the real thing and she got it. As she put her hope in God, she felt that her whole life was at stake. "I felt as though my heart was cut right from my chest and that I handed it to God. It was terrifying. I couldn't sleep. But the more I hoped, the more I hoped. I guess that you could say that God never let me down," she concluded.

Those long months in Children's Hospital with Edna and Ella reminded me of G. K. Chesterton's famous words: "To love means loving the unlovable. To forgive means pardoning the unpardonable. Faith means believing the unbelievable. Hope means hoping when everything seems hopeless."

HOW ROSABELLA KEPT HOPE ALIVE

Some mothers are optimistic by nature. Others are bubbly, upbeat—always looking on the positive side of all equations. I am none of these. I am a skeptic by nature, prone to see gray, not white. Maybe it's genetics, maybe my upbringing; maybe it's my parents' fault. No matter, the problem is mine, and many mothers I know see the world with a bit of smudge on their glasses as well. We are thinkers, worriers, ready for the next shoe to drop. Life feels fragile and untrustworthy. We must be prepared and diligent in our preparation so that we are not disappointed too much when the next blow comes. Life just seems to hurt a lot.

Mothers are by nature very cautious in all things—particularly when it comes to our kids. We want to be savvy in our judgment and realistic about our expectations. We will be cautiously positive, cautiously optimistic because we know that the world is a terribly harsh place for us and for our kids. None of us wants to feel any more hurt than we need to.

But the problem for most of us mothers is that we avoid hope. We refuse to be hopeful in the name of realism. We don't want to believe false things; we want to confront life as it is. Since we see it as largely negative, we choose to see only negative. Life feels safer that way. The problem is, we lose hope because being hopeful feels frightening. And it can feel foolish.

Having hope is an act of the will. Although each of us harbors some hope deep within, we must force it to the surface. It must become real and alive.

Choosing to hope is a two-part process. First, we make a willful decision to see a situation in a positive light. This can be very difficult for women who have learned to be chronically negative or sad. Negativity and sadness can become a way of life for many women who grow up with criticism or abuse. In order to let go of the chronic negativity, we must recognize it. This can be difficult at first, but once we begin the process, it gets easier.

Sadness is the emotional counterpart to negative thinking. When this settles in, feeling positive or optimistic can be very difficult. The truth is, much of the sadness mothers feel on a continual basis isn't simple grieving—it is a habit. Sadness can be a trained response to many situations. Again, many women are trained from early childhood to feel chronic sadness, anger, and even despair. If they do, we can see how the whole notion of feeling hopeful can seem to be quite an enigma. Experiencing positive emotions seems almost impossible to mothers who endure constant ridicule or other forms of hardship.

The second part of learning to be hopeful, then, is to confront negative thoughts and feelings and replace them with positive ones. Then we are to actively think hopefully and feel hopeful. Again, for women who have lived with constant negativity, the idea of deliberately allowing ourselves to feel hopeful is frightening. We feel vulnerable and prepare ourselves to be disappointed. But we need not feel this way. We can feel hopeful and optimistic and refuse to wait for the next shoe to drop.

Rosabella, a longtime friend who is twenty-eight years my senior, did. We have known each other for eighteen years now, and over those years she has become a mentor to me and one of my heroes.

Rosabella changed her life by choosing to be hopeful. She is the mother of three grown children. For the first twenty years of her marriage, she lived in Papua New Guinea, where she worked as an artist and missionary. Each of her children was born in her tiny home nestled in the mountains, with her husband attending to her deliveries. Although she was American, she chose to stay in Papua New Guinea when they were born rather than travel back home, where she could have had good medical care. When her children were teenagers, she and her husband came back to the United States for a few months' furlough. After a few weeks, her husband went for a jog but never made it past his garage. At age forty-six, he died of a heart attack.

Rosabella didn't know which way to turn. She had no money and no job. She and her husband owned their small home in Papua New Guinea, but she knew that she didn't want to go back without him. Rosabella became despondent. She suffered depression and loneliness. She had disconnected from friends in the United States because she had lived so long overseas. All of her support was thousands of miles away and she couldn't get to any of it. Additionally, she had to parent three grieving teenagers all by herself.

Rosabella told me that the day she found her husband lying cold on the cement floor of the garage, her life turned upside down. She looked beyond the yard of their rental home and saw emptiness. She felt as though her insides had been ripped out.

"I realized shortly after my husband died that my life could go in one of two directions. I couldn't think about details—like money, schools for the kids, or friends—at first because that seemed too overwhelming. I knew that life was completely out of my control. I could either choose to live and be positive, or die and give up. I chose the first. I had seen so much poverty and illness and I knew what giving up hope would do to my life and my kids' lives. I had to choose hope. After all, I had nothing to lose."

Rosabella did anything but lose. She looked up rather than down. She found employment as an illustrator. She made friends and asked for help. "If I collapsed, my kids would collapse and that simply wasn't an option," she told me. "Life was extremely hard. The kids struggled. They felt like foreigners in their own home and missed our old life. They missed their dad and I couldn't be enough for them. That's when I really began leaning on God."

Interestingly, Rosabella recounted that when she was a formal missionary, her faith in God was not as strong as it is today. I was surprised. I imagined that her faith would have been just the opposite—strong when she was overseas working with her husband and weaker when she came home and he was dead. Didn't she feel betrayed by God? I wondered. Here she had served so many years in an environment that wasn't very safe for her family and what she ended up with was a dead husband and three kids to finish raising all on her own. Since I was terribly curious about her faith, I asked about it.

"In fact," she told me, "I never felt closer to God than after my husband died. I decided that He either was real or He wasn't, and I really needed to know. So I told Him that He needed to come through for me.

He would be my only hope and He would either help provide me with what I needed or He would let me down. I can say now, after thirty years, that He never let me down. Not once."

The marvelous part of Rosabella's story is that the more she hoped, the easier it became. She determined that she would not become negative and she told God that she was putting every hope she had on His shoulders. She asked again and again for help and it worked. Did she become rich? No. Did she go on to have an easy life? Certainly not. But as she charmed me with stories of her life since that time, she spoke with a lilt in her voice. She asked me to see her artwork. As she showed it off, she seemed to want to boast about her God—who helped her and her children more than thirty years before.

Hope is not for the weak at heart. It is for women who need help. And whether we need help parenting, getting over the death of a husband, or living a happy life, we need hope.

So here's my final question for us mothers: What holds us back from hoping right now? I know that there are many excuses. Hoping requires emotional and mental energy. We are busy. We frenetically chase more to do, to buy, or to accomplish because that's what we know how to do. We think that one day we will stop and ponder the bigger things. We will have time later, when we are older and need to contemplate death and the meaning of our lives. Why do we do this? Why do we wait, conscious of the fact that we only rub salve on our deep needs? Would our lives be different if we lived hoping for that which is unseen, rather than chasing material dreams or trying to get ahead?

I know our lives would be different, and they would be so much better.

FOUR WAYS TO MAKE THE HABIT STICK

#1: Cultivate an attitude of appreciation

Oprah Winfrey has told her viewers over the years that if you are a woman born in America, you are one of the luckiest women alive. She is absolutely right. We who birth our children and raise them in the United States don't worry about our kids dying from worm infestations, polio, or whooping cough, to name just a few illnesses. The vast majority of us know that our kids can be well fed and have a school to go to. If we need work, most of us can find it. It might not be what we want, but it will be a job sufficient to get food on the table and a roof over our kids' heads. If our spouses are abusive we can divorce them (divorce was legalized in Chile just seven years ago). We have a say in political arenas and in our professions. Other women have paved the way for us to get equal (or at least approaching equal) pay for the work we do. If we choose to work outside the home, most towns and cities have good child care.

You get my point. While many of us would look at the list above and take many of these things for granted, we can't afford to do this. Many of these freedoms are freshly won and someone along the way did a lot of work to make them happen. They are no small deal. We live with the attitude that of course we should enjoy these things, because having them is a right, but until relatively recently that wasn't the case. Furthermore, many of them can be taken away. We may lose our job; a child may die. New infections may erupt and vaccines might be unable to prevent them. One just never knows.

Focusing on what we have is important. First, it keeps us grateful for what we have so that we will pay attention and care for it all—our children, our own health, our jobs. These are the big things we should care about. We should quit wasting energy complaining about the small stuff because if we lose the big stuff, we will quickly realize how small the small stuff really is. Good things are here. And since we have those good things, we can stay hopeful and look forward to a brighter future with our healthy kids, our solid jobs, and our good medicines. An attitude of appreciation helps keep us hopeful. Being hopeful doesn't mean that we hope for more and more. Quite the contrary: It reminds us that we can have hope because we have received blessings and that we can be very content with what we have.

Second, staying appreciative keeps us from complaining. Think about the act of complaining. Does it make us feel better? Does it change a bad situation? Does it diffuse anger and put hurt feelings to rest? The answer is no to all of these. Complaining accomplishes nothing of value. When our kids, do it, we nag them to stop because it drives us crazy. We see where it takes them and what it does to those who are forced to listen. It pulls everyone within earshot down. Furthermore, complaining begets complaining. One of the powerful ways to cultivate a hopeful and positive attitude is to refuse to complain. This is hard. We are surrounded by friends, kids, and spouses who complain. News anchormen and anchorwomen complain. Songwriters complain. We have become a culture of complainers because we have so much available to us. The irony of having a lot is that it makes us want more. If you don't believe me, watch a family divide up the family home and furniture after a loved one's death. Those who have the most, want the most. If a sister has a larger home, she wants the grand piano for her living room. Forget that her little brother doesn't even own a home—he will take the Corelle plates and bowls. The older brother who has a boat will take the larger car so that he can tow his boat.

This is peculiar but understandable human behavior. When we have a lot, we take a lot. When we have less, we take less. One would think that those who have the most would feel appreciative and content, and perhaps they do. But the sadness comes when having things causes us to focus on what we are missing rather than on what we have.

Living with a sense of hope demands that we recognize and appreciate what we have. Otherwise we will always yearn for a little more, and this makes us anything but hopeful. It makes us anxious.

#2: Learn to trust

Trust has become a frightening word for many mothers. We can't trust our kids. We can't trust our spouses. We can't trust our bosses, and sometimes we can't trust ourselves. Or so we think. Nothing raises a mother's hackles like telling her that she must trust another person to get a job done or to meet a need she has. Trusting is not only frightening, it seems heretical to a conscientious mother. We are the providers; we are the ones whom people can lean on. Furthermore, we are trained to learn to be independent and self-sufficient. Many of us have had to be. Often we have to get the job done for our kids alone and we rely on our own strength. Many of us have found that if we trust another, we only find disappointment, and so we fall back on ourselves and retreat from leaning on others.

While independence is good in many instances, the truth is that we are very dependent people. We are relational; we need communion and connection. If others are to provide that for us, then we must trust them to some extent.

When it comes to staying hopeful, we need to trust others. We must hope *in* someone. Since hope is a forward-moving action, we are believing that someone will help us in the future. They will be there; they will come through. We can hope in ourselves, and this is fine, but it is insufficient. We need others to be there for us for life to be good.

Many mothers put hope in their kids. Others put hope in God. Personally, I think that God is a better bet. If God is real, then believing that He is good helps us put trust in Him for future events. Hope keeps us moving forward and by putting hope in God, we are choosing to believe that ultimately He will bring about good for us.

Hope is a tricky thing. It demands something from us, and specifically, it forces us to make a decision about trust. We either choose to trust God so that we can put our hope in Him or we don't. If we choose not to trust Him, then we can't hope that He will be there for us. Hope and trust are interwoven.

Here's where trusting takes a bit of faith and again, I don't think that it's wise to go blindly into it. We would be fools to trust God if we believed He was cruel. And just as we would never trust a three-year-old to babysit an eight-month-old sister—the three-year-old simply doesn't have the wherewithal—we would be foolish to trust a person or god who has repeatedly failed us.

So we must trust carefully. In order to do this, we need to know the person we put trust in very, very well. Even then, some friends and spouses can be trusted for only certain things and not for others. That's okay. We just need to know their limitations. But when it comes to God, we don't have to worry about those limitations because we can trust Him for anything.

Trust is hard, and since hope requires that we trust the one in whom we place our hope, it too is hard. But that's what we mothers are really good at—doing the hard things in life.

#3: Expect good things to come

Much has been written about the power of positive thinking and energy in bringing about positive results in a person's life. I'm not well versed regarding these theories because as a physician, I am a scientist at heart. I want proof of things. If I can't have reproducible results from good science, then I at least want to be able to see things with my own eyes. So I am quick to say that simply having positive expectations doesn't mean that good karma will necessarily follow. Maybe it will and maybe it won't. To me, hope is more substantial than karma. Hope is something that we can control and identify. We can change it, refuse it, or run with it. Being hopeful means believing that God or another loved one will act to bring about good things in the future. Therefore, we must wait for those things to happen and be ready to acknowledge them when they do. Hope allows us to wait expectantly. What exactly do we wait for? one might ask. We wait to feel better. We wait for life to go better for our kids. We wait for healing, for recovery, and for better health. We wait for a job to come, for the sadness of the empty nest to fade. We wait believing that better will come, and we make that belief palpable in our hearts. We feel it, and we stake our hope on it.

It is natural to ask, then, if this is a reasonable thing to do. Or if it is silly, blind, happy thinking. I don't think that it is and here's why. Happy thinking is not rooted in anything substantial. Believing that good things will happen is just a collection of feelings. But expectantly waiting for good puts something at stake. First, it puts our relationship with the person we hope to bring about good at stake. Second, expectant waiting is founded on a belief system that has been around for hundreds of years. The Jews expected good things to come from God. Christians waited for God to bring them help during their lifetimes or at least bring them into heaven at the end of them. When we choose to wait expectantly, we choose to join millions of others who have done the same thing. We join them in believing in some sense of eternal truth that hope in God is a good thing, is substantial, and is not crazy. (Maybe all the millions of others who did so before us were crazy, but that's another discussion.)

As with other aspects of adopting a hopeful attitude, waiting for good things is frightening. It feels very risky. And it is. We look for good things and worry: What if they don't come? Does that mean that we will always feel let down? No, it just means that we wait longer, because if we don't, then we may be forced to scrap hope altogether. And that, for all of us mothers, would feel disastrous.

#4: Challenge negative thinking

If a visitor could come and sit inside our minds for forty-eight hours, what would she see? Would she hear mostly negative thoughts or would she be awash in the excitement we feel about life? True, none of us would ever want anyone to see what whirls inside our minds. But what goes around in there is important, so let's take a look at it.

Many mothers are constantly surrounded by negativity. If you weren't feeling bad at the beginning of the day, one temper tantrum by a tired two-year-old at the mall will do it. We make in our minds a steady groan. When will things get better? Why won't our seven-year-old behave? Why won't our husband help out more at bedtime? Why won't the football coach let our son play? After all, he is a senior. At the end of a mother's day, negative thoughts can feel so overwhelming that we just want to go to sleep in order to escape. We just want to turn off our mind for a few hours. We can then refuel and face the next day.

For mothers who have suffered serious loss, such as divorce or the death of a loved one, negative thoughts can be overwhelming. Depression is a serious issue for many mothers, and when this level of negativity strikes the mind and heart, all a mother feels is darkness everywhere. Inescapable darkness. And where such darkness resides, hope has little chance of erupting.

Here's the first bit of hope. Depression is treatable with two primary tools: the challenging and restructuring of negative thought processes, and medication. It's a very difficult but successful process. What we learn from treating depression is that even extremely dark thinking can be changed. If that can be changed, how much more can mothers shift less negative thoughts into more positive ones.

When this process begins, hope has a chance of weaving its way in and taking over. A fragment can be driven through rock-hard negativity, and when the initial cracks emerge, it is only a matter of time before the entire lode of negative thinking falls apart. We can't begin the infusion of hope if we don't recognize that we are forbidding its entrance. Yes, many mothers refuse to allow hope into their minds and hearts because it is frightening. Many are so trained to wait for "the next shoe to drop" that believing otherwise would be dangerous. Waiting in a constant state of readiness for the next bad thing to happen requires that they keep hope outside their minds.

This is no way to live. If you are a mother who holds on to negative thoughts, perhaps it has become a habit that you don't even realize you have. Or perhaps you know that you are in the habit of habitual negative thinking but are too afraid to let go of it.

There is a good way to find out if you are one of these mothers. As we discussed in the solitude chapter, find some time when you can be alone. Sit quietly in a chair and think about doing something that makes you really happy. If you have to think back to something you did many years ago, do that. Now hold on to that thought. Feel that feeling. What is it like to feel so light, so happy? Remember being there. Remember the warmth that you felt.

Once you feel that you have adequately allowed that good feeling to percolate from within, stand up from your chair and tell yourself to hold on to that feeling. Go make dinner and stir your spaghetti sauce believing that life can be that good again. No, the same things won't reoccur, but you can feel that good anytime you want to during the day. Tell yourself that it is emotionally safe to hold on to those good feelings.

If a voice inside you says no, that doing so will never work, or you have a gnawing sense inside that feeling so good is dangerous, you have been trapped. Negative thinking has built a barrier to hope deep inside you and you must knock it down. The only way to do this is to admit that you have a habit of negative thinking. You have formed a thick crust over your heart against hope and even pleasure, and this is no way to live.

Truthfully, almost every one of us has had this happen. We have become cynical in our fatigue. Thinking negatively requires less energy than being positive. But what I am talking about here is challenging negative thoughts and going to battle with them. They will occupy space in your mind—valuable space. Think of the space in your brain this way: There are only x number of spots for thoughts to rest. So, will you allow them to all be taken up with ugly thoughts? You have a choice—we all have a choice.

If mothers who are in the throes of postpartum depression can bat ugly thoughts away, so can you. Any of us can choose to think in the way we desire, and when we do, lovely, wonderful hope has a place to fit into our lives. And the best news is, it has a place to grow.

Acknowledgements

||||||||||||||||||||||||||||||||||||||||||||||||||||||||||||||||||||||||||||||||||||||||||||||||||||||||||

I would like to thank my terrific agent, Dan Conaway at Writer's House, for his wisdom, support, and counsel with this entire manuscript. I am grateful to Jill Schwartzman, who guided me and encouraged me not only with this book but with *Strong Fathers, Strong Daughters*. Jill, you have been a delightful boss. To Susanna Porter, my editor at Ballantine—thank you for your insights and guidance. I would also like to extend warm thanks to the fabulous team at Ballantine: Libby McGuire, Kim Hovey, Theresa Zoro, Susan Corcoran Waters, Jane von Mehren, Melissa Possick, Kristin Fassler, Quinne Rogers, and Sharon Propson, for their input, advice, and hard work. They are a great team to have on your side.

I would also like to thank my confidante, advisor, and "right arm," Anne Mann, for her tireless work, patience, and commitment to me. I certainly don't deserve all that she gives me. To my (not really crazy) sister, Beth, thank you for believing in me every moment of every day. Your humor and fortitude inspire me. Thank you, Peg, my awesome mother-in-law and number one fan, for your endless enthusiasm for all of my work.

I owe a huge debt of gratitude to my family for their long-suffering.

Thank you, Mary, for your love, and thank you, Alden, for reading my words. Charlotte and Laura, I thank you for your love, encouragement, and prayers, and Walter, I thank you for the joy that you bring me every day. Finally to my husband, Walt, thank you for sticking with me and loving me as a mother and wife when I haven't always deserved it.

ABOUT THE TYPE

This book was set in Caledonia, a typeface designed in 1939 by William Addison Dwiggins for the Merganthaler Linotype Company. Its name is the ancient Roman term for Scotland, because the face was intended to have a Scotch-Roman flavor. Caledonia is considered to be a well-proportioned, businesslike face with little contrast between its thick and thin lines.